MY YEAR 2009:
FACING THE HEAT

SELECTED BOOKS BY THE AUTHOR

POETRY

Dinner on the Lawn (College Park, Maryland: Sun & Moon Press, 1979, 1982)

Some Distance (New York: Segue, 1982)

River to Rivet: A Manifesto (College Park: Maryland: Sun & Moon Press, 1984)

Maxims from My Mother's Milk/Hymns to Him: A Dialogue (Los Angeles; Sun & Moon Press, 1985)

Along Without: A Fiction for Film in Poetry (Los Angeles: Littoral Books, 1993)

After (Los Angeles: Sun & Moon Press, 1998)

Bow Down (Piacenza, Italy: ML&NLF, 2002)

First Words (Los Angeles: Green Integer, 2004)

Dark (Los Angeles: Green Integer, 2012)

PROSE

Letters from Hanusse (Los Angeles: Green Integer, 2000)

My Year 2001: Keeping History a Secret (Los Angeles: Green Integer, 2016)

My Year 2002: Love, Death, and Transfiguration (Los Angeles: Green Integer, 2015)

My Year 2003: Voice Without a Voice (Los Angeles: Green Integer, 2013)

My Year 2004: Under Our Skin (Los Angeles: Green Integer, 2008)

My Year 2005: Terrifying Times (Los Angeles: Green Integer, 2006)

My Year 2006: Serving (Los Angeles: Green Integer, 2009)

My Year 2007: To the Dogs (Los Angeles: Green Integer, 2015)

My Year 2008: In the Gap (Los Angeles: Green Integer, 2015)

My Year 2009: Facing the Heat (Los Angeles: Green Integer, 2016)

Reading Films: My International Cinema (Los Angeles: Green Integer, 2012)

My Year 2009:

Facing the Heat

READINGS

EVENTS

MEMORIES

by
Douglas Messerli

GREEN INTEGER
KØBENHAVN & LOS ANGELES
2016

GREEN INTEGER
Edited by Per Bregne
København / Los Angeles
www.greeninteger.com / (323) 857-1115

Distributed in the U.S. by Consortium Book Sales & Distribution
/ Perseus Books, www.cbsd.com / (800) 283-3572
Distributed in England & throughout Europe by Turnaround Publisher
Services, Unit 3, Olympia Trading Estate, Coburg Road, Wood Green,
London N22 6TZ, www.turnaround-uk.com / 44 (0)20 88293009

First Green Integer Edition 2016
Copyright ©2016 by Douglas Messerli
Essays in this volume have previously appeared in *Art Là-bas*,
Green Integer Blog, *Green Integer Review*, *EXPORING* fictions,
New Review of Literature, *PIP (Project for Innovative Poetry)*, *N^th
Position*, *Or*, *Rain Taxi*, *Shearsman* [England], *Reading Films: My
International Cinema* (Los Angeles: Green Integer, 2012), *Sibila*
[Brazil], *USTheater, Opera and Performance*, *World Cinema Review*

Design: Per Bregne
Typography: Pablo Capra
Cover photographs: (clockwise, from top left):
Inger Christensen, Flannery O'Connor, Yvonne Rainer, and Harry Partch

LIBRARY OF CONGRESS IN PUBLICATION DATA
Douglas Messerli [1947]
My Year 2009: Facing the Heat
ISBN: 978-1-55713-429-5
p. cm – Green Integer 264
I. Title II. Series

Green Integer books are published for Douglas Messerli
Printed in Canada on acid-free paper

Table of Contents

Too Darn Hot: An Introduction

According to the Kinsey report
Every average man you know
Much prefers his lovey dovey to court
When the temperature is low

But when the thermometer goes way up
And the weather is sizzling hot
Mr Pants, for romance, is not

'Cause it's too, too, too darn hot
It's too darn hot
It's too darn hot

—Cole Porter

FROM THE VERY beginning of 2009, I realized that things seemed to be heating up—and not just as a result of global warming. After the "gap" of 2008, in which opposing sides attempted to read each other from a nuanced distance, it became clear that President Barack Obama now had to face the heated wrath of the losing party. Moreover, people and events seemed to be coming together in sometimes exciting but equally often fractious ways. One might say that the underlying theme of the year was one of "friction," the frottage of two opposing forces that sometimes led to thrilling consequences, but just as often resulted in explosions and dangerous conflagrations. Even when looking back on history, as in the revivals of two great plays and a musical of the late 1950s and early 1960s (*Exit the King*, *Waiting for Godot*, and *West Side Story*), the action was bathed in a series of sweaty struggles between warring gangs, life and death, and despair and salvation that was simply "too darn hot"—to borrow the title of Cole Porter's song from *Kiss Me Kate*. Wendy Walker's deconstruction of the famed child murder of Savill Kent in the 19th century burned with an intense blue flame that was reiterated in the myths of Bluebeard in films that I encountered during the same year. I pondered the consequences of seemingly perverse sexual practices of figures Woody Allen and Roman Polanski.

Even a religiously-inclined lady author of the South such as Flannery O'Connor was revealed through her biography, published this year, as a prickly figure battling for a Christianity of the early martyrs as opposed to a warmed-up, "Kumbaya"-sing-along theology practiced by some modern-day Roman Catholics. My friend Betty Freeman, a long-time supporter of the avant-garde, who died during the year, expressed, in her last months, her impatient anger with many contemporary American musical tunings. Fortunately, I was able to enjoy a concert by one of the artists she had supported, the outsider composer Harry Partch.

I, myself, spent some of the year in Southern Italy, suffering, but also enjoying, the African-borne sirocco I first encountered on the island of Ischia as well as touring the volcanic ruins of Pompeii and elsewhere.

Hedda Gabbler threatened to burn manuscripts and shoot her lovers. Yvonne Rainer recreated Stravinsky's ritualistically feverish ballet *The Rite of Spring*. Upon the death of American-Canadian poet Robert Blaser, I revisited his essays collected in *The Fire*. Even the cold rooms of the Bohemian quarters of Paris were heated with love in a production I saw of *La Bohème*. In short it was a steamy year that fired-up my imagination

I anthologized three movies devoted to the heated confrontations between management, police, and leaders of American unions: and I reconsidered, in various contexts, "How to Save the World," perhaps the most hot-button issue one might imagine, given the endangerment we now face of our own planet.

Fortunately, I had a large number of cool and collected friends and admirers who fanned me with brisk encouragement and sometimes even heated doubts—both sorely needed—throughout the year. Among these are Bruce Andrews, David and Eleanor Antin, Mark Axelrod, Thérèse Bachand, Susan Bee, Charles Bernstein, Régis Bonvicino, Lee Breuer, Robert Dean, Raymond Federman, Betty Freeman, Tony Frazer, Homeira and Arnold Goldstein, Brad Gooch, Rebecca Goodman, J. Hoberman, Tom La Farge, Eric Lorberer, Vibecke Madsen, David and Gail Matlin, Deborah Meadows, Suzanne Muchnic, Martin Nakell, Paul Nelson, Marjorie Perloff, Jeffrey C. Robinson, Peter Rosei, Jerome and Diane Rothenberg, Ronald Tavel, Paul Vangelisti, and Wendy Walker. My companion-husband Howard Fox read and commented on many of these essays and accompanied me to several of these events. The endlessly patient and supportive Pablo Capra took out months to typeset, edit, and correct these essays, on top of inviting early discussions about some of their topics; perhaps no one now knows me so well.

Warm Up

BOB MARTIN (BOOK), CHARLES STROUSE (MUSIC), AND SUSAN BIRKENHEAD (LYRICS) **MINSKY'S** [BASED ON THE FILM *THE NIGHT THEY RAIDED MINSKY'S*, WRITTEN BY ARNOLD SHULMAN, SIDNEY MICHAEL AND NORMAN LEAR, DIRECTED BY WILLIAM FRIEDKIN, FROM THE BOOK BY ROWLAND BARBER] / AHMANSON THEATRE, LOS ANGELES / THE PERFORMANCE I SAW WAS ON FEBRUARY 10, 2009

WITH A SCORE by the noted Broadway composer Charles Strouse (*Bye Bye Birdie, Annie, Applause* and other musicals), a book by Bob Martin (of *The Drowsy Chaperone* fame), and directed by Michael Ritchie (*The Drowsy Chaperone* and *Curtains*), the production of *Minsky's*, over 10 years in the making, represented the possibility of good old-fashioned musical fare, and, if nothing else, promised a highly enjoyable evening. And in that sense, this Los Angeles production did not disappoint. Certainly it tried hard to please.

The problem is just that. Martin writes out of a nostalgia for Broadway musicals and older forms of theater. And as most of such nostalgia-based assemblages do, he readily posits the old saw that when times get tough (as they were for the Depression-era New York Lower East Side National Winter Garden Theatre, the home of Minsky's burlesque—and, with a wink and nod, we all know might be equally for us today) it's important to return to the old values of theatrical entertainment: God damn it, kids, we're going to put on one hell of a show!

Indeed the leading actors, ensemble, set designer, costume designer, and light director do just that. Unfortunately for Martin and the musical's producers, today is not 1930, and even then, we are reminded, burlesque, the subject of this love letter to past entertainments, was already near death. Perhaps had Martin simply reproduced some of the burlesque scenes and sketches, we might have been titillated—as we were in the original movie—at the very least. But his book has emptied the plot of almost everything that could give heart to his work, replacing it with a shell of sugary sweetness that even the most gushing sentimentalist (I have admitted to crying for joy during many musicals in my life) might have found cloying.

Billy Minsky's theater is having hard times; not only are the audiences for his burlesque performances dwindling, but Randolph Sumner, a self-appointed destroyer of all that defines the joys of life—he warns his daughter Mary not to smile too much—has begun to direct his energies to closing down The National Winter Garden.

A driven man, clearly in love with theater and those performing on the stage they describe as "home," Billy is nonetheless dissatisfied with life and seeks out the help of a psychiatrist. Meanwhile, the straight-lipped Mary Sumner finds herself in a similar position, and, in one of the best scenes in the musical, she undergoes a psychological evaluation next door to Billy (the matching pair of "shrinks" later fall in love), after which—through the machinations of a blind man more out of a Buster Keaton movie than a burlesque sketch—they meet up and immediately fall in love.

Both the lead actors, Christopher Fitzgerald and

Katharine Leonard, are superb performers, but it is hard to draw the audience into their characters when they have already been treated as such cardboard types. Yes, of course we know the truth will have to come out, that Billy is not a fellow reformer, but, in fact, is the devil Minsky himself. And the lies he has told Mary will obviously separate them for a while from the natural course of love, but....

That's just the trouble, we know the entire story before it has even begun. The rest of this musical, accordingly, has little to do but to strut its beauties around the stage in numbers like "Cleopatra," "Bananas," "You Got to Get Up When You're Down," "Workin' Hot," and "God Bless the USA" and, in one predictable if excellently performed piece, get "Tap Happy." It is as if the entire musical *Gypsy* were centered upon the performances of Tessie Tura, Mazeppa, and Electra, the three Minsky strippers of that work. But then, those three *were* actually strippers and their gutsy performances were far more interesting and downright shabby than the cleaned-up dances of this musical as presented in "Keep It Clean." Who'd a' thought that Disney's *The Lion King* could be sexier than a musical about burlesque?

Despite my cyni-
cal remarks, however,
I must admit that
the wonderful *Min-
sky's* cast danced their
hearts out, flashed
winning smiles, and did everything in their not so diminished powers to keep it all going. At moments, true
theater poked out its puny head, particularly in the musical's wittiest song, "I Want a Life," sung with deadpan
humorlessness by Minsky's nerdy bookkeeper (John
Cariani) and the daughter of Minsky's backer, a dour
little woman whom he is desperately trying to get off
his hands (*Saturday Night Live's* Rachel Dratch). Together they harmonize about a life where "a button is
something to sew on" (an earlier song explained that in
burlesque parlance a "button" is what ends an act) and
"...where pies are [just] dessert." As they briefly minuet
about one another, it almost appears that, despite their
preferences for humdrum living, they might break into
dance; yet the two stubbornly stand in place, adding
the possibility "where no one will dance."

Yet all of this seemingly endless energy depressed
me even more. Like Mary Sumner, early in the work,
I just couldn't get a smile onto my face in reaction
to their spectacular engagement with life. A kind of

gloom had set in.

Because of the vacuous story and characterizations, the dances and songs of *Minsky's* seemed always to be a warm up that generated no spark. There was, alas, no fire in this work's idolizing heart.

LOS ANGELES, FEBRUARY 11, 2009
Reprinted from *US Theater, Opera, and Performance* (February 2009).

Sparks

SALVADOR COMMARANO (LIBRETTO), GIUSEPPE
VERDI (MUSIC) **IL TROVATORE** / THE METROPOLITAN
OPERA, MAY 8, 2009

MY SEEING VERDI'S operatic warhorse *Il Trovatore* at
the Metropolitan Opera had more to do with contin-
gency than with choice (it was the only production I
could see during the few days of my stay in the city).
But as with many of my activities it now seems, in the
context of the concerns of *My Year 2009*, appropriate. Like so many of the essays of this year, the plot of
Verdi's opera is also about "facing the heat," the characters having to endure the punishments for their own
present errors and judgment, as well as the sins of their
ancestors of the past.

In this case, the gypsy woman Azucena's mother
has been burned at the stake for "bewitching" an infant
in her care, the current Count di Luna's infant brother.
To avenge her mother's death, Azucena apparently kid-

napped the young boy and threw him into the flames that burned her mother to death. Only the charred remains of a baby were discovered on the pyre, and since that day the Count has sought out the murderer for fear of further revenge.

Meanwhile, the Count has fallen desperately in love with a young woman, Leonora, serving his wife in the court. The woman, meanwhile, is smitten with wandering troubadour Manrico, who also happens to be the leader of the partisan rebel forces threatening the Count's rule—and who is, incidentally, Azucena's son. Discovered in Leonora's presence, Manrico is challenged by the Count to a duel, a fight unto death. Manrico quickly overpowers the Count, but strangely resists

murdering him. He releases the Count. The war between the two forces continues, with the Royalist forces winning, resulting in Manrico's near-death. He lives only because he has been dragged from the battlefield by his mother and nursed by her back to health.

In the camp the gypsies sing of their tireless work, their spirits raised only by the site of a pretty woman, the famed anvil chorus performed in this production as an almost sexual assertion of masculinity. Indeed, the strikes of the hammers upon the anvil almost sent real sparks into the audience, and certainly Verdi's joyous chestnut does remind us of the fire of the past.

For, as almost anyone can foretell from the brief and somewhat absurd plot spelled out above, Manrico is doomed in his love for Leonora. Azucena is captured near the camp and is held captive in di Luna's castle, and when Manrico's army is defeated, he joins his mother within the cells of the castle.

Leonora escapes, returning to the castle and promising herself up to di Luna if he will release his prisoners. Di Luna agrees to release Manrico, and Leonora rushes to tell him. Manrico, however, is outraged at what he believes to be her betrayal of their love. Leonora, having planned all along to cheat di Luna of her love, has taken a poison which acts faster than expected, and she dies in Manrico's arms. Di Luna, witnessing the death, sends Manrico to his execution, while Azucena reveals the truth: mistakenly she had thrown her own son onto the pyre and, accordingly, Manrico is di Luna's long-lost brother.

Yet, despite these facts, *Il Trovatore* is not really a revenge tragedy but a story of four failed human beings who all come together in the "Moon Count's" castle, creating a kind of lunatic world. Three commit unspeakable acts and the fourth is apparently incompetent. Azucena has been so caught up in revenge that she has, "accidentally"—a nearly unthinkable word in the context—murdered her own son, and although she has been a loving mother to Manrico, we nonetheless must recognize her as a reprehensible being. The Count, for his part, is also caught up in the past, becoming so determined to find his brother's killer that he destroys the sibling in the act. The Count is courting, moreover, a woman who is an intimate of his wife. Manrico, the troubadour, is a terrible warrior, unwilling even to kill a brutal enemy in a duel; more importantly, he is a soldier who loses all battles in which he participates. He is not even a good "troubadour"—a devotee of courtly love—attacking Leonora at the very moment that she has sacrificed her own life for him. Leonora, in turn, enacts a suicide that saves neither her lover nor his gypsy mother. The fires within each of them, fueled by love, envy, anger, and hate, spark each other's inevitable destruction.

The production I saw at the Met, with Hasmik Papian as Leonora, Želijo Lucic as the Count, Marco Berti as Manrico, and Mzia Nioradze as Azucena, was a superb rendition of this opera, with Papian (better known for her other opera character Norma) and Nioradze as standouts for their performances.

NEW YORK, MAY 9, 2009
Reprinted from *Green Integer Blog* (June 2009).

Sweating It: Three Mid-20th Century Tragicomedies

SAMUEL BECKETT **WAITING FOR GODOT** / STUDIO 54, NEW YORK CITY; THE PRODUCTION I SAW WAS A MATINEE ON SATURDAY, MAY 9, 2009

ARTHUR LAURENTS (BOOK), STEPHEN SONDHEIM (LYRICS), LEONARD BERNSTEIN (MUSIC) **WEST SIDE STORY** / PALACE THEATRE, NEW YORK; THE PRODUCTION I SAW WAS ON THURSDAY, MAY 7, 2009

EUGÈNE IONESCO **EXIT THE KING** / ETHEL BARRYMORE THEATER, NEW YORK; THE PRODUCTION I SAW WAS A MATINEE ON SUNDAY, MAY 10, 2009

THROUGH ACCIDENTAL INTENT I saw three plays on my recent trip to New York City, all works from the 1950s through the early 1960s that revealed not only Auden's description of that period as "The Age of Anxiety," but reiterated for me the dramatic tensions at play in 1950s society. All three works might be described by the subtitle of *Waiting for Godot* (1953), a "tragi-

comedy," although one does not necessarily think of that phrase in relationship with *West Side Story*. Yet its appropriateness became clearer than ever upon seeing Arthur Laurent's new production.

The terrified participants of Beckett's landscape—in this production presented as an inhospitable plain surrounded by rocks—have seemingly nowhere else to go, although they incessantly speak of "going." Although Vladimir (stunningly played by Bill Irwin) and Estragon (Nathan Lane) spend each night separately (sleep is probably the most isolated activity that man endures), they gather each morning to discuss, in the absurd language of Laurel and Hardy, their possible alternatives and attempt to entertain themselves until the arrival, promised each day to Didi (Vladimir), of Godot.

Numerous readers and critics of Beckett's work have speculated that Godot is God. He is, after all, seen as the agent of their salvation when, at the end of the play, they discuss possible suicide:

VLADIMIR: We'll hang ourselves to-morrow. *(Pause.)* Unless Godot comes.

ESTRAGON: And if he comes?
VLADIMIR: We'll be saved.

Even the child who reports each day that Godot (pronounced in this production as *God*ot) will not arrive describes his master in the standard Christian manner: a man with a white beard. Yet if this elusive Godot is God, perhaps we would be better without him, or, at least, better off not spending our entire lives in wait.

The conditions of their lives—both are tramps who apparently recall a previous life in which they were better off—are abhorrent. Gogo, in particular, is plagued by swelling feet, and is often unable to remove his shoes. Each night, so he tells Didi, he is beaten while he sleeps. So too is the child's brother beaten by Godot.

The appearance of a passing landowner (he claims to own all the land about), Pozzo (grandly performed by John Goodman), and his slave, Lucky (John Glover), demonstrates the scandalous condition of others. Carrying Pozzo's dinner, table, and folding chair, Lucky stumbles about on a chain, whipped from behind by Pozzo. Both Vladimir and Estragon are horrified to discover someone worse off than themselves, but gradually perceive that Pozzo is completely dependent on Lucky; and when Lucky is commanded to dance and to think, we discover he is such a clumsy oaf and academic bore that he is perhaps more useful to the world in his sub-

jugation than in freedom.

Even more disconcerting is the Alzheimer's-like condition of all Beckett's figures save Didi. When Pozzo meets up with the two on the second day, he is even more dependent on others than previously, but has no memory of meeting the two tramps a day earlier. Estragon must be reminded each day of the previous day's events and is often incredulous of Didi's recountings. Even the child who reports for Godot cannot recall seeing Didi each day. For Didi it is as if what he perceives is eternally in question, and he spends much of the play trying to uncover evidence that his vision of reality is correct.

But that is just what makes this work a tragedy: there is no reality. And it is also that which makes it a comedy, which induces us to laugh: because there is no reality, these beings have nowhere else to go. Their entreaty to "go," "Yes, let's go," results only in stasis. They have no choice but to return day after day to their rocky lives to wait for someone who may beckon, but will probably never come. In Beckett's final stage instruction, *They do not move*, even the most determinist of us realizes that we are all "frozen" into our own ridiculous lives. Like figures of the *commedia dell'arte*, we can only pull up our trousers and wait for the inevitable end of existence.

Ionesco's less performed *Exit the King* (1962) explores just that end. King Berenger's (Tony winner Geoffrey Rush) empire has, over his long rule, shrunken extensively. The sun has frighteningly diminished and a large sinkhole threatens to suck up the entire kingdom. As Queen Marguerite (Susan Sarandon) recognizes: "The party's over," reporting to her husband that by the end of the play he will die.

Terrified by that fact, Berenger fights his approaching death with the tenacity of a spoiled child let loose at a table of doting adults. The palace maid (Andrea Martin)—although complaining of the endless burdens of her job (she is only one of three who continue to serve the court)—servilely straightens his winding robe, picks up the crumpled carpet, cooks, and performs thousands of other chores. The King's younger consort, Queen Marie (Lauren Ambrose), coos her love, insisting that he continue to fight his inevitable death.

Fight he does, but with the attacks coming every few moments, Berenger's absurd pleadings and rush of memories become more and more ridiculous. What may seem to be a topic that would send most audiences fleeing from the theater is here transformed into a long-standing joke (almost overplayed in this production),

as the King dies and dies and dies, Marguerite cheering him on as Marie tenderly dotes on his numerous last gasps.

One of the difficulties in this play (as in Beckett's) is to keep those laughs coming while, at the same moment, the audience grows uneasy in its recognition that it, like the characters, simply must wait and die. And although Ionesco could be as wickedly ironic as Beckett at times, Beckett's crisper diction—which at nearly every moment seems to combine the tragic with the comic—allows his play to better function than Ionesco's broader farcical conceits. Still, in all, *Exit the King* is a brilliant play that tenderly takes the King (and we, his consorts) from life into death.

Both of these plays, accordingly, offer us a world in which its characters are literally forced to face the void, nearly swooning in its heat.

Based as it is on Shakespeare's great tragedy, *Romeo and Juliet*, *West Side Story* at first appears to be without the comic redemption of the Beckett and Ionesco plays. Yes, there are comic moments in Laurent's script: the self mockery of the Jet's psychologically frenzied lives expressed in "Gee, Officer Krupke" and the equal-

ly playful putdown of the Shark women against a girl who wants to return to Puerto Rico in "America" (note: unlike the great dance scene in the motion picture version of the musical, in which both Shark males and females dance "America," the stage version includes only women). And there are those tender and light moments "Something Coming," "One Hand, One Heart," and "I Feel Pretty"(sung in this production in Spanish). But for most viewers, I suggest, *West Side Story* would not seem to be properly described as a *tragicomedy*. Where's the comedy? many might ask.

If we recognize, however, that *West Side Story* presents us with a society with no adult moral examples (Doc is so passive he is completely ineffectual, the police are nearly as disgusting in their prejudices against

the Puerto Ricans as the Jets), it becomes clear that the world of this musical is as absurd as that presented in both the Beckett and Ionesco works. Living is being part of a gang, and being part of a gang is to be willing to fight, kill, or be killed. Although both Maria and Tony attempt to live outside that reality, they have no other choice, and are inevitably pulled through the vortex of love and hate into the absurd world surrounding them.

On the streets of the Upper West Side, New York, Tony has no choice but to fight for his own kind, even if it means destroying, in the process, the woman he loves. Only Maria seems intellectually able to create a different reality, a reality not based on territorial and familial domains, but on love; despite the fact that Tony has killed her own brother, she insists that her love for Tony takes precedence.

Obviously Tony's inevitable death produces no laughter. But in terms of the play's inverted realities, his death returns that world to normality.

The singing and dancing of this production was excellent, and the leads, Matt Cavenaugh and Josefina Scaglione, were far better than Richard Beymer and

Natalie Wood. But I still prefer the movie version, simply because its characters are better delineated than in the stage production, and Jerome Robbins' filmic dances, particularly "America" and "Cool" (which on the stage is performed in the drugstore early in the play), are simply masterpieces which are nearly impossible to match. Although Laurent's new direction brought two of the songs into Spanish, it had no great effect on the timbre of the piece, and the cute dancing chorus members detracted from the anxiety of the world the script expressed.

As the film's Baby John made clear through his tears, and the gang's pent up fears released in "Cool" evidenced, the young men and women of Bernstein's West Side New York were also forced to live in a sweat. And unlike the film, where there is at least a hope of change as the gang members come momentarily together to carry off the body of the slain Tony, in the stage version his corpse remains bound to earth, Maria mourning him alone as she declares that she too has now learned "how to hate." As in *Exit the King* she has now come face to face with death; and as the curtain falls, just as the characters in *Waiting for Godot*, she is frozen in space.

LOS ANGELES, MAY 30, 2009
Reprinted from *US Theater, Opera, and Performance* (May 2009).

The Fire Behind Myself

ROBIN BLASER **THE FIRE: COLLECTED ESSAYS OF ROBIN BLASER** (BERKELEY: UNIVERSITY OF CALIFORNIA PRESS, 2006)

THE DEATH ON May 7, 2009 of American-Canadian poet Robin Blaser sent me to my office shelf where I keep books waiting to be read. For three years Blaser's collected essays had burned its presence into my eyes, but only now, six months after his death, have I actually found the time to read this important book.

Beginning with his famous manifesto-like essay, "The Fire," Blaser argues that the business of poetry and poetics is creating a cosmology. He means that, as he explained in a 2009 interview with Paul Nelson, not so much in a "religious" sense—although he himself admits to the influence of his Catholic childhood—but in a larger system of a world view. When asked for the specific components of the cosmology that he and his friends Robert Duncan and Jack Spicer attempted to create, Blaser answers in that 2009 interview (published in *Golden Handcuffs Review*):

The main components are, first, that there isn't one. That was what you felt and this was what the 20th century tried to do to us. It took us away and Marxism didn't help at all unfortunately with that problem. Marxism is quite a different thing, but that's when we're already social and know how to move and then Marxism can speak to you. Otherwise, you're fucked. You've not got a cosmos with which: Where's God? Well you're sure not going to...even an old Catholic like me isn't going to turn into THAT. And Spicer, I mean, Spicer's view of the Catholic Church [laughing heartily] IS ONE KICK IN THE ASS AFTER ANOTHER! HA! and I just loved it. And Duncan, ooooh Duncan. He was an occultist in some part and the occult tradition was a fascinating one. We all came to know of it. But the occult was a counter Christian, counter religious tradition that was also a religious tradition, whatever a religion means, essentially to be tied to a world at large. So all of us were busy working around it, sometimes at quite a loss. ...It was simply a matter of finding language as the way with which you could walk on a piece of earth....

In short, as Nelson suggests, for Blaser the search for a cosmology, an entire system of being, was a process rather than an end. As opposed to a lyrical self-expression, Blaser approached poetry as a serial-like search—what in other essays he describes as a revelation of the "real"—that in its intensity metaphorically "burns up" the poet, leaving a fire behind him.

This "process," he argues, moreover, can only occur in a community, and most particularly in a community of poets. Attacks against "coterie" ignore the reality that poets band together because:

Such communities tend to build a structure for men who wish to keep, hold and record the passionate relation with the outside that the world, the nation, needs. This is the only place where such talk goes on.

Discourse, accordingly, is at the center of Blaser's poetics, even in this early essay, and most of the works in this volume resound with voices, often contrary voices that express a kind of explosion of ideas surrounding the subject at hand.

This kind of dialectical commentary can often seem an onerous task for the uninitiated reader; Blaser's essays are filled with references not only to his poet friends, Duncan, Spicer, Olson and others, but to philosophers and contemporary thinkers, from Hannah Arendt, Walter Benjamin, Jacques Lacan, Alfred North Whitehead, Giorgio Agamben, Maurice Merleau-Ponty, to all of Greek and Roman mythology, along with writers such as Homer, Hesiod, Ovid, and Dante. Fortunately, Blaser's commentary is accompanied by an Introduction and highly informative Afterword by Miriam Nichols who expertly takes the reader by the hand through the dense thickets of Blaser's poetics.

If nothing else, what any reader comes to realize early on in Blaser's work is that his writing, both the poetry itself and the criticism, is not a historical recounting of the "other," but an immersion in both the thinking process and in the lives of the writers on whom he focuses, all creating a kind of Memory Theater, "a box with tiers, where the initiate would take the place of the stage and look out on the tiers, which in an ordinary theater would hold the audience—here there are images upon images, so that a man could hold the whole world in view."

Such an impossible undertaking, made even more difficult by the impact of differing demands upon the poet's attention, particularly the call for social and political involvement that claims little role in the poetic imagination, itself might truly "burn up" the poet. One by one, Blaser takes up some of those issues, in "The Particles"—the role of the political, for example, in which he dismisses various views of what political poetry might be before going on to argue that it is the passionate *particularity* of poetry, its never-ending search for truth or "reality" and the commitment of the poet to this search that demonstrates most clearly poetry's relationship with the polis as opposed to statements *about* political positions which merely reiterate frozen thoughts, dead images of the society at large.

Blaser cites the wonderful example of the Spanish writer, Miguel de Unamuno, Rector of the University of Salamanca. After a rabid speech by General Millan Astray, "thin, emaciated, one eye and one arm," in which he called for the extermination of all who stood against Franco, Unamuno rose and gave a speech beginning:

> All of you are hanging on my words. You all know me, and are aware that I am unable to remain silent. I have not learnt to do so in seventy-three years of my life. and I do not wish to learn it any more. At times, to be silent is to lie. For silence can be interpreted as acquiescence. I could not survive a

divorce between my conscience and my world, always well-mated partners.

Describing the General as a "symbol of death," Unamuno closes:

> Unfortunately there are all too many cripples in Spain now. And soon, there will be even more of them, if God does not come to our aid. It pains me to think that General Millan Astray should dictate the patter of mass-psychology. ...You will win, but you will not convince. You will win, because you possess more than enough brute force, but you will not convince, because to convince means to persuade. And in order to persuade you need what you lack—reason and right in the struggle."

The crowd might have killed the Rector right there had not a Professor of Law taken Unamuno by one arm and Madame Franco by the other and quietly left the dais. Unamuno remained a prisoner in his house, Blaser tells us, until his death at the end of that year.

For Blaser it is the persuasion, through particularities, the "particles" of reality, that matters and is at the heart of any truthful political act.

That argument continues in "The Stadium of the Mirror," in which Blaser explores the relationship of poetry to the public in terms of aesthetics and psychology

rather than the political. Here Blaser argues against the imaginary stage of poetry which the child mistakes as an "image of psychic wholeness," and argues instead for another version of the Memory Theater in which the mirrored stadium incorporates "as much of otherness as the poet can see and hear," internalizing, in short, a great part of the world inside of the poet's self.

Blaser's vision of the poet and his roles, accordingly, demands enormous undertakings, a knowledge of history, literature, language, politics, and much else, that transform the poet's role into a near Herculean act. It is, obviously, something that might indeed burn the poet up, actually destroy the living man. And in his beautiful testament to his beloved poet-friend Jack Spicer, we see precisely this self-immolation. Although the story has been told many times, it is worth repeating.

One of two Spicer essays in this book, "The Practice of Outside," describes some of Spicer's methods, the creation of the serial poem beginning with not having any idea where one is going. Spicer, as Blaser claims, used a simple language that resembled his own way of speaking so to be able to live in that language and, as he wrote in his book *Language*, to "have the ground cut from under us." Blaser argues:

> Just here, poetry may become a necessary function of the real, not something added to it.

This living through poetry came, however, at a "remarkable cost." As Spicer once declared: "Neither baseball nor poetry are for amusement." Spicer's life, filled with contrariness and complexity, along with a deep dependence on alcohol, demanded a price.

At the end of this long essay, Blaser returns to a scene in which he had previously left us, at Spicer's bedside in the San Francisco General Hospital, where he is soon to die.

> I have already said his speech was a garble. He could manage a name once in a while. Otherwise there were long runs of nonsense sounds. No words, no sentences. That afternoon, there was something like a dozen friends around his bed, when it became clear that he wished to say something to me. By some magic I can't explain, everyone left to let it be between us. It was odd because I didn't ask them to leave and Jack couldn't be understood. Their affection simply accounted for something inexplicable. Jack struggled to tie his speech to words. I leaned

over and asked him to repeat a word at a time. I would, I said, discover the pattern. Suddenly, he wrenched his body up from the pillow and said,

> *My vocabulary did this to me. Your love will let you go on.*

The strain was so great that he shat into the plastic bag they'd wrapped him in. He blushed and I saw the shock on his face. That funny apology he always made for his body.

Along with Blaser's observations in short and long essays on Olson, Louis Dudek, George Bowering, Mary Butts, the artist Jess and others, *The Fire* encapsulates the immense demands he puts upon the role of poet, a figure, like Joan of Arc, destined to be burned up in the glory of his or her faith.

LOS ANGELES, NOVEMBER 1, 2009
Reprinted from *Sibila* [Brazil] (December 2009).

I never met Robin Blaser, although I have had fairly frequent correspondence with him, at least since 1993 when I included several of his poems in my anthology From the Other Side of the Century: A New American Poetry 1960-1990.

In 1996 I invited him to send a poem for my *Poets'
Calendar for the Millennium*, which, because of financial difficulties, never came to be. But we corresponded
about the poem he had sent, "Pentimento." Later, I intended, so reveals my correspondence with him, to publish
that poem in my "celebration of Sun & Moon classics,"
50. The galley I sent him contained a couple of typos, one
of them, we both agreed, a charming one—"moonbum"
instead of "moonburn," to which he responded, "That's a
good one! even on Sunday!" Oddly, the poem never appeared in the final book; I have no idea what happened
except to explain it as a work I simply forgot to include.

With the closing of Coach House Press, which had
published his great collection of poetry, *The Holy Forest*,
I offered to take over the distribution or reprint it in *Sun
& Moon Press*. He reported that he would get back to me
after his return from England in November of 1996, but
I believe he never did. The University of California Press
published a revised and expanded edition of that book in
2006.

More recently, I had been in touch with him in 2006
for the newest *Gertrude Stein Awards* volume, but this
time our communications were through his friend Meredith Quatermain, since his condition was described as
frail.

LOS ANGELES, NOVEMBER 2, 2009

Burned Up

HENRIK IBSEN **HEDDA GABLER**, ADAPTED BY
CHRISTOPHER SHINN / ROUNDABOUT THEATRE COMPA-
NY, AMERICAN AIRLINES THEATRE / THE PRODUCTION I
SAW WAS A PREVIEW ON JANUARY 17, 2009
    HENRIK IBSEN **HEDDA GABLER**, IN *IBSEN: FOUR
MAJOR PLAYS, VOLUME I*, TRANSLATED BY ROLF FJELDE
(NEW YORK: SIGNET CLASSIC, 1965, 1992)

AS *NEW YORK TIMES* critic Charles Isherwood suggested in his piece (January 18, 2009) on the upcoming production of Henrik Ibsen's *Hedda Gabler*, Hedda
is an "antiheroine" who inevitably draws actresses to
her. She is, to put it mildly, one of the nastiest people of
1890s Norway, and one of the "meanest" (as Isherwood
describes her) women in theater history.

To start, she has just married the innocent scholar
Jørgen Tesman without any love for the man (she cannot even abide his scholarly interests in domestic crafts
of the Middle Ages) but for the reason, as she puts it, "I
had danced myself out.... My time was up"—in short,

43

within the confining society of the time, as a woman in her late 20s she is in danger of being described as an old maid.

Equally without purpose, she has demanded they move into a large city house, replete with expensive furniture, this despite the fact that Jørgen has not yet been offered the teaching position he hopes will help with the expenses. Rather than accommodating Jørgen and his beloved aunt, Hedda demeans both by pretending to believe the aunt's new hat—purchased especially to please Hedda—belongs to the servant, who has tossed it upon the chair. The flowers sent to honor her return from her honeymoon are trashed.

Later it becomes clear that Hedda has had close relationships both with Jørgen's intellectual foe, the romantic and dissipated Eilert Løvberg, and with the family's friend, Judge Brack, who has helped attain and fund their new house and belongings.

These relationships, however, are not exactly sexual, for Hedda is what we might describe today as a sexual tease, drawing the men toward her only so that she might have control over them. The minute they cross the line, she pulls out her father's (the General's) pistols and shoots. Indeed Hedda might be said to represent the military way of life. Uninterested in cultural history, she uses the past only as a method of strategy, of determining how to control the men under her "command," demanding of Løvberg, as she hands him one of her pistols, death. When Judge Brack, a far more clever opponent, wilily finds a way to put her under his control, she reacts with the only response she knows, committing suicide with the remaining gun.

Hedda is, quite clearly, an intense woman burning up with desire, but so afraid of losing her self-control, so determined to rule each situation, that she must destroy everything around her, including the brilliant manuscript Løvberg has just written and lost on his way home. Like the uncontrollable behavior fuelling her actions, she burns his book in the stove, destroying his metaphorical "child," the only force of life and possibility in the play, and, in that act, seals her own doom.

Yet, as Isherwood and others have pointed out, this "queen of mean" must reveal some other qualities just to make her believable. We need to comprehend her beauty, her wit, her positive qualities—whatever they are—just enough to understand why the intelligent Løvberg, the slimy Brack, and the doddering academic husband all find her so necessary in their lives.

For, in the end, all she has touched, all she has thought she controlled, turns to naught. Løvberg does, indeed, die, but as the result of an accidental shooting in the groin, not a bullet through the head. Brack has no real need of Hedda; for him she is simply another tool for manipulation. And "poor" Jørgen ends up happily with Mrs. Elvsted, an attractive woman who has just left her husband to help Løvberg with his writing, who now will surely find a soulmate in Tesman. Accordingly, if Hedda is only presented as a mean, hateful being, the play ends in a black hole as the energetic center of the work (represented by Hedda and Løvberg) collapses, leaving us with only good, empty-headed, bourgeois folk. Despite her aberrations, the audience needs to have been in love with Hedda!

Unfortunately, the preview of the production I saw in New York on January 17, 2009, offered no solution to the problem. Although Mary-Louise Parker may have been perfect as a sort of sexual gamin in previous plays such as *Reckless, Prelude to a Kiss,* and *How I Learned to Drive,* here she has little sexual warmth, mouthing Hedda's evil wit with a not so subtle wink and nod, slowing down the action so that, by the end of the play, we feel superior to all the characters in the work. Her intense queries directed at Mrs. Elvsted, for example, seem more like an interrogation than the somewhat desperate questions of a jealous woman.

Similarly, Michael Serveris' Jørgen Tesman is played as such a fool that even if Hedda feels his offer of marriage was her last chance, we, like Løvberg, cannot comprehend her decision. Rather than creating an innocent alternative to Hedda, Ana Reeder's Thea Elvsted seems an even greater simpleton than Jørgen, unable to understand the comic manipulations of Hedda concerning their shared years in school.

Christopher Shinn's adaptation of this play, as far as I could tell upon rereading the Fjelde translation of the play a day later, eliminates any possibility that Hedda may have good qualities, such as her determination to remain faithful to her husband. Anything that might have softened Hedda, to help us see her as the great lady we are told she is, seems to have been obliterated. In the end, when Judge Brack reacts to Hedda's suicide, "People don't *do* such things!" we might almost respond: "But then Hedda isn't really a person, is she?"

LOS ANGELES, JANUARY 24, 2009
Reprinted from *USTheater, Opera, and Performance* (January 2009).

Burning Blue

WENDY WALKER **BLUE FIRE** (BROOKLYN: PROTEO-
TYPES [PROTEUS GOWANUS], 2009)

Sometimes the revenant is discovered because his
grave is visible, usually by either a blue fire or blue
glow.... The blue glow, in European tradition, is
frequently interpreted as the soul, and it is seen as
an indicator of buried treasure through much of
Europe, apparently because it shows where a body
is buried, and bodies were frequently buried with
valuable grave goods.

—Paul Barber, *Vampires, Burial, and Death: Folk-
lore and Reality,* as quoted in *Blue Fire*

WENDY WALKER DESCRIBES her new book, *Blue Fire*,
as "a poetic nonfiction." This book concerns the notorious 19th century child murder of Savill Kent, which
was thought by many at the time to have been com-

 mitted by his nursemaid, Elizabeth Gough, and Savill's father, Samuel, on account of the boy's having awakened during the night and witnessed them in a sexual embrace. The Road Murder, as it was named, was one of the most sensational events in England of the late 19th century, resulting in an explosion of media coverage and inspiring at least two fictions of the day, Wilkie Collins' *The Moonstone* and, created out of events revealed at the inquest, Charles Dickens' *The Mystery of Edwin Drood*; there were also two prose recountings, John Rhode's 1928 book *The Case of Constance Kent* and Joseph Stapleton's 1861 book *The Great Crime of 1860*, the latter book attempting to remove any blame from Stapleton's friend, Samuel Kent. Indeed, Walker found the "rhetoric, marked by the easy confidence of an educated man," so repellent that she had difficulty in reading it.

The inquest, which also focused on the possible guilt of Savill's sister, Constance Kent, ended, because of lack of evidence in an investigation that was badly bungled, in the conclusion that Savill had been "murdered by persons unknown."

After the trial, Constance was sent away to France,

to the Convent de la Sagesse. In 1863 she returned to England to enter St. Mary's Convent in Brighton as a nurse trainee. There she met and came under the influence of Rev. Arthur D. Wagner, a member of the Oxford Movement, who wanted to return the practices of Anglicanism closer to the Roman Church, and who was a particular enthusiast of confession.

What occurred between the young woman and her confessor is unknown, but two years later Constance traveled to London in his company to confess to the Road Murder. Her detailed description of how she had committed this crime was, as Walker describes it, "A tissue of fiction, contradicting forensic evidence and important testimony." Yet Constance was tried by a judge who sentenced her to death. For the next 20 years Constance Kent was remanded to penal service in five national prisons: Millbank Prison in London, Parkhurst on the Isle of Wight, Brixton, Woking, and Fulham. Her sentence of death having been commuted, in 1885 she was released, moving to Australia under the name Ruth Emilie Kay to live with her brother William. At the age of 46 Constance began nursing studies with a woman who had trained under Florence Nightingale, and over the rest of her life she served in several hospitals, becoming matron of the Paramatta Industrial School for Girls before serving at a tuberculosis sanatorium in Mittagong and, at the age of 66, opening

an old age home for nurses. Constance Kent lived to 100 years of age.

As anyone who has read the circumstances around this murder has wondered, why did Constance Kent admit to a crime—refusing to deny her testimony for the rest of her life—that she most probably did not commit? How can one come to any understanding of a figure seeking and achieving so much good after, at least in her own mind, committing such an atrocious act? The child, after all, was not just smothered, but cut with a knife before its body was thrown into the privy!

The problem here, as Walker recognizes it, is how to "tell" this story without making further assumptions about the young woman's life or simply throwing a web of one's own imaginative desires across the almost obliterated truth of the circumstances.

To "trick" herself into reading the biased Stapleton book, Walker employed a method used by John Cage, the mesostic, in which she selected "one word from each line of Stapleton's book, proceeding line by line but never choosing two words that followed consecutively." This she poses as a "poetic" revelation of the now-liberated text on the left-hand side of each page, while on the right she selected extant passages from texts about the murder, including Constance's own "Sydney Document," written in response to Stapleton's book, and selections from other works in the Kent library. Walker also traveled to the houses and graveyards of the Kent family and to churches known to contain mosaic works done by Constance during her imprisonment, representing those visits with photographs.

The result is an amazing work of erudition that not only asks important questions about Constance and her family, but reveals the cultural context surrounding a young, somewhat bored and occasionally rebellious girl, haunted, perhaps, by the familial relationships between her own mother, who lived in one part of the house, and her father, who lived with the nanny, Mary Pratt (who later became the second Mrs. Kent) in the other. Constance's mother, perhaps always a frail woman—several of her children died in childbirth—was also rumored, mostly by the father, to be mentally unstable.

As Walker demonstrates, the role of a young English girl of this period was to live a life of such overwhelming sacrifice that it might lead even to invisibility. What women represented was more important than their reality: they were emblems of perfection, even saintliness.

Constance was none of these. She was an intelligent and highly curious child who was punished, time and again, for the smallest of infractions or inability to learn her school lessons by Pratt. She had seen her mother, moreover, ousted from her own life in a manner not unlike the wife of Edward Rochester in *Jane Eyre*. So unhappy was she that, at one point, she convinced her younger brother to escape with her to sea, with the hope of joining their elder brother, Edward, who had enlisted in the Merchant Marines. She cut her hair, dressing as a young boy, and the two escaped to Bath where they were uncovered by a hotelier and returned to their father.

By quoting from various reports of the murder (including newspaper clippings of the time, Rhode's and Stapleton's books, and Constance's own writing) and Victorian writings as varied as Dickens, Collins, Elizabeth Gaskell, Charles Kingsley, John Ruskin, Florence Nightingale, Sir Walter Scott, Charles Darwin, and numerous others, the author recreates the tenor of the period, with the reader beginning to comprehend the psychological aura of this young, rather plain-faced, slightly obstinate child. Walker does not "explain" or answer anything, but through her choices of texts conjectures, convincingly it seems to me, that if Constance did not commit the crime, she felt, in her sense of failure and out of her confused emotional responses to family life, that she was nonetheless *guilty*—guilty of something. Her own disposition was to give of herself, to sacrifice, and the only way she knew how to accomplish that for her own family, whether or not she realized the truth of the situation, was to take on what was perhaps her father's guilt, to become the scapegoat that might salvage the others' beings. Given her outsider role within family life, perhaps she had no other possibility.

My only quibble with Walker's work—and even that word is perhaps too strong since it is apparent that Walker is purposely bringing up these issues—is the book's subtitle: "a poetic non-fiction." *Blue Fire* is indeed "poetic," but not simply because of Walker's application of the mesostic method. As Walker and I have discussed previously, all great fiction writers are also excellent poets. Walker herself has proven that in all of her fictions, and major fiction writer-poets such as Herman Melville, James Joyce, Djuna Barnes, and William Faulkner have often done their best poetry writing in their fiction rather than in their books described as poetry. Walker's word choices in the mesostic construction, lines such as "strides of blood among questions / those consequences of narrative," "insinuation of screen in truth / to conduct criticism," "any English simplicity of negligence can say / reading this after usual murder son feelings / will question truthfulness of women" (I

Blue Fire
Wendy Walker

could quote from almost any page), are more emphatically prose-oriented, in that they reveal possible "truths," rather than attending primarily to language. I am not suggesting that these passages are not poetically compelling or linguistically challenging, but positing the idea that, perhaps because of the source material, the mesostic work syntactically suggests a prose coherency.

Her "non-fiction" passages, on the other hand, although all representing material from extant works, are more fictional in their careful arrangement than some so-called novels. Prose, it seems to me, pretends, at its heart, to a sense of "truthfulness," however slippery we know it to be. Whether the prose writing be autobiographical, historical, philosophical, sociological, political, reportorial, whatever, we expect the truth, even though we recognize that truth in all these fields is a nearly impossible thing. That is why, when we discover a work described as prose such as James Frey's *A Million Little Pieces* (touted as prose by Oprah Winfrey) is actually fiction, there is a public outcry.

But that is just the problem. It is our presumption that there can be an objective reality that separates prose writing from fiction, that misleads us time and again, the reason, in fact, that Walker had such difficulty reading Stapleton's prose. All prose is equally imbued with the writer's desires, imagination, miscomprehensions, and personal views, immediately transforming what is presented as "truth" into a kind of fiction. Perhaps only in a purposeful fiction can we really speak the truth.

In *Blue Fire* Walker is less interested in discerning any one "truth," than in questioning the multiple possibilities; and in that sense, her book is not directed in the same way as "nonfiction," but represents an extremely artful construction of texts not at all unlike fiction.

I read the book, accordingly, by using the mesostic passages as poetically-charged prose that stands alongside and against the reportage and writings of the period, the one overlaying the other, ricocheting into new realities. (Indeed, I attempted to do something similar in one of my own works, *Along Without*, in which I used short passages of other writers' fictions to create the "story" for a film, in which the characters spoke in a highly poeticized diction.)

To repeat, *Blue Fire* uses poetry and prose, but in a manner that is closer to fiction, I would argue, than most works describing themselves as such. For the soul beating at the heart of Walker's work is, like blue fire, a revelation of warmth and desire, a buried treasure hidden through the actions of a young girl who gave up her soul in order to enrich others' existences—a truth that was not to be comprehended in Constance's real life.

LOS ANGELES, DECEMBER 14, 2009
Reprinted from *Or* (No. 4, April 2010) and *EXPLORING* fictions (December 2009).

Two Bluebeards

Locked Out

CHARLES BRACKETT AND BILLY WILDER (BASED ON THE PLAY BY ALFRED SAVOIR, *LE HUMITIÈME FEMME DE BARBE-BLEUE*), ERNST LUBITSCH (DIRECTOR) **BLUEBEARD'S EIGHTH WIFE** / 1938

IN RETROSPECT, Ernst Lubitsch's *Bluebeard's Eighth Wife*—based on a 1921 play by Alfred Savoir and preceeded by a 1923 film directed by Sam Wood—seems like a slightly uncomfortable mix between Bartók's *Bluebeard's Castle* and Preston Sturges' *The Lady Eve*, the would-be tyrannical lady-killer being trumped by the loving but vengeful wife, successfully awarding her man his comeuppance so that a "real" marriage might finally be consummated.

This comedy alternately is absolutely charming and mean-spirited, the latter arising from a problem with its casting: as *The New York Times* reviewer Frank S. Nugent noted in 1938, it is simply impossible to imagine

the lanky, aw-shucks-likeable Gary Cooper as a multi-millionaire serial-spouse. That's not to say that the wonderful Lubitsch doesn't give it a serious try, adding even a few insightful perceptions about the Perreault-Bartók work to which the movie very vaguely makes reference.

From the very first scene, Lubitsch establishes that Bluebeard (Cooper) is definitely a dominating figure, portraying him as a "top"—a man attempting to purchase only a pair of pajama tops—as opposed to Nicole de Loiselle's (Claudette Colbert) bottom—a woman who is happy to purchase the bottoms as a gift to her down-on-the-heels, money-conniving-Marquis father (Edward Everett Horton). And, as in Bartók, he prefers dark, while she suggests light, but with the added dimension of "stripes," hinting, perhaps, at his soon-to-be "locked out" situation.

Colbert, as always, plays her character as a refined European to Cooper's straight-forwardly tenacious American who cannot comprehend why his immediately wanting to marry the mademoiselle meets with her utter disdain. The fact that she dismisses him hardly fazes him; he not only feels he should be awarded for his straight-forward honesty, but that he "deserves" her since he has, metaphorically, purchased her from her father by paying for the ridiculous trinket from Louis XIV's bathroom—an  elaborately embellished contraption so petite that he can perceive it only as a washbasin.

The Marquis, however, in his underhanded dealings has made his family deeply in debt, a problem which a marriage to such a rich man would quickly resolve. This interminably innocent American attempts to charm the object of his momentary affection, memorizing—just as he does the details of his business associates—the history of Louis XIV; and, despite herself, Nicole seems to actually fall in love with this ungainly courtier. Everything seems to be proceeding glowingly until he begins to reveal the existence of seven (the film, apparently, conflating the number of the Bartók opera's rooms with the wives) previous wives. Unlike the operatic Bluebeard, this innocent galumpher has allowed for a pre-nuptial agreement to pay each of them $50,000, saving them from murder, as in the Bartók versions of the mythical Bluebeard's paramours.

The Marquis' daughter, almost without missing a beat, decides to take him up on the offer, if only he will raise the ante to $100,000, while she determines to teach him an important lesson about love from a pre-feminist perspective. It's absolutely delightful that Lubitsch, once described by Mary Pickford as a "director of doors," regally uses his somewhat deserved moniker by reversing the situation of Bartók's work, representing Nicole as locking herself away from her new husband, refusing him any sexual access and permitting him conversational entrance only upon appointment. As in the operatic work, Lubitsch's film is a movie of seemingly endless doors locked and bolted—but this time from inside! It's enough to make any red-blooded *Americun* male go mad, and this Bluebeard does end up, predictably, in a straitjacket, with Nicole gloating over his shocked embarrassment.

Of course, there are a lot of other silly shenanigans along the way, some featuring the effete would-be lover Albert De Regnier (David Niven), who is forced to play secretary to Bluebeard and who, in an absurd series of misunderstandings, is beaten up by a hired wrestler and threatened with strangulation by Bluebeard—a perfect role, I might argue, for Niven, who always strikes me as a man about to puke over the impropriety of the roles Hollywood has forced upon him. Horton, as the Mar-  quis, gets several chances to puff-up and putter-down as only he can; and Elizabeth Patterson has the short-lived opportunity to shine as the mean-hearted, level-headed Aunt Hedwige. But everything and everyone is truly un-important in this tale, as we wait for the moment when Bluebeard, like a cartoon figure who has been bonked over the head one-too-many-times, pops out of his con-straints to give the heroine what she has been asking for behind all those closed doors: a good old-fashioned fuck—or shall we describe it for what it really is, a rape?

Maybe Nicole should have asked the questions on everyone else's mind: why did Bluebeard divorce all those other women? And what ever happened to them? Despite what seems to be the usual Lubitsch sexual so-phistication, the film is too prudish to let us know what goes on behind all those closed doors.

LOS ANGELES, FEBRUARY 20, 2009
Reprinted from *World Cinema Review* (February 2009).

A Mad Salome

CATHERINE BREILLAT (WRITER AND DIRECTOR)
BARBE BLEUE (BLUEBEARD) / 2009

IN THE 1950s, two young sisters sneak into an abandoned attic to check out the space, play games, and read their favorite stories, including the gruesome Charles Perreault fable, *Bluebeard.* Marie-Anne (Lola Giovannetti), the eldest, is a highly sensitive and frightened child, who, although having been charged to care for her sister, Catherine (Marilou Lopes-Benite), is very much controlled by the precocious younger girl, who reads the tale to the elder.

The girls' storytelling alternates with the tale of two other sisters, Marie-Catherine (Lola Créton) and Anne (Daphné Baiwir), living in 1697. The fairy-tale sisters are attending a private school run by nuns, when they are called to the office of the Mother Superior, who tells them their father has just been killed and, since the family no longer will be able to pay for their educations, sends them immediately home. On the voyage home, we gradually discover that the younger of these two, like the sister of the 1950s, is strongly independent of mind and acutely aware of the economic and social future with which the children will now be faced. It is an unjust world, where monsters like the infamous Bluebeard, rumored to have murdered his previous wives, live in enormous castles, while they, without dowries and now deeply in debt, must either submit to becoming nuns or join the court as ladies-in-waiting, neither of which they perceive as viable futures. Here too, the elder is obedient and religious, much like her mother, a pious girl, who, despite her great beauty, is conventional in her thoughts and emotions. The younger sister, Marie-Catherine, on the other hand, is determined to live in a castle just like Bluebeard's, and chides her mother for forcing them into black clothing and penitent behavior—particularly as many of the family's possessions are being taken away as payment.

It is only a matter of time before an emissary of Bluebeard shows up to the house to invite the financially strapped daughters to a party at the castle. From the invitees, the overweight and ugly Bluebeard (Dominique Thomas) will choose a new wife and give financial support to her family. With no dowries and a life of poverty ahead, the mother and her children have little choice but to attend the affair, while secretly hoping, perhaps, that they may be spared from being the subject of his attentions.

The forceful outsider, Marie-Catherine, however sees it as an opportunity to obtain all the things she has missed in life. Moving away from the other celebrants, she attracts Bluebeard's attention, and after conversations with him, in which she expresses no abhorrence for the man who recognizes that almost everyone sees him as an ogre, he determines to marry her. The young girl is simply delighted to have a new dress—her first—made for her alone. After a quick ceremony in the cathedral, she enters the castle of her dreams.

Although willful, the girl seems, as Bluebeard himself describes her, as innocent as a dove, but with the self-assuredness of a hawk. Having agreed not to sleep with her until she comes of age, Bluebeard has prepared a small bed for her in front of his own. But she refuses to serve as his connubial lap-dog, and demands her own room—a very small one, however—again something she has never had before. She forces the monster to agree to never enter her room without her permission (a condition, incidentally, made also by the Claudette Colbert character in *Bluebeard's Eighth Wife*, as described above); yet in the middle of the night she sneaks into his room to observe the rotund man in his sleep.

Indeed, it first appears that she has taken the upper hand in the relationship. The girl actually appears to be happy in the company of this elderly and educated being, who shares some of his immense knowledge with her, as he appears ready to share with her everything he owns. When he travels away on a long business voyage, he happily hands over the keys to every room in the house and encourages her to invite her family and friends to the castle in his absence. Marie-Catherine does so, but is seemingly caught in the arms of a young knight when Bluebeard unexpectedly returns. In fact, the girl has been telling the young man just how comfortable she is alone with Bluebeard in the castle; and soon after, she convinces the ogre that she is overjoyed at his return and pleased that they can retire once more into their own private world.

Soon after, however, Bluebeard again sets out for another business trip, once more handing over all the keys, yet this time adding another golden key to an attic room that he forbids her to enter. She promises to obey his orders, but obviously cannot resist attempting

to discover what lies behind that one door. No sooner has he left, than she enters the room to discover the bodies of Bluebeard's ex-wives hung, like carcasses of meat, upon the wall, with pools of their blood welling up on the room's floor. Shocked and terrified by what she has discovered, she drops the key into the blood; upon leaving the room she attempts to wash the blood away, but cannot rub out its stain. While she is still attempting the clean key, Bluebeard unexpectedly returns to find her face pale. As they sit down for dinner, he demands back the keys. She quickly gives up the large keys, but claims to have lost the small golden one. Forcing her to produce it, Bluebeard discovers blood upon it and condemns her to immediate death.

Marie-Catherine pleads, unsuccessfully, for mercy, but does get permission to spend a short time in the highest tower in order to pray. There she attempts to summon troops and family members to come to her aid; but Bluebeard soon appears, ready to cut off her head with a large saber. Once again, the girl coaxes from him one more concession, that he kill her instead by stabbing her with a jeweled dagger through the heart.

As Bluebeard goes to retrieve the knife, arriving musketeers take over the castle, evidently killing the monster before he can destroy his latest wife.

This beautifully filmed tale alternates with the storytelling by the two young 1950s siblings and the mythical story. Increasingly, as the younger girl tells the story—seeming to modulate it with her own embellishments—the elder grows more and more terrified, ultimately attempting to escape from hearing Catherine's words, and, in so doing, falls through the attic trapdoor to her death. At the same moment that Marie-Anne rises to see her sister lying below, their mother comes to call them home, apparently unable to see the cause of her daughter's tears: the other, now dead daughter, dressed in blue gingham, lying below on the concrete floor.

The film ends with Bluebeard's wife, Marie-Catherine, stroking the head of her former husband, laid out on a platter like the pate of John the Baptist over which Salome rejoiced. Suddenly these two stories seem to shift, almost as if we have discovered a new pattern in a kaleidoscope: Bluebeard's death, which will now allow his wife to live out her life in the manner of which she has dreamed, has required the death of her more timid and pious other, the sister whom she has admittedly used time and again as a scapegoat. The stronger, feminist woman of the future has won out over the meek and mild maiden of domesticity and despair. But at what cost, director Breillat seems to ask, has she achieved her victory? Might it even lead to the madness of Salome? The viewer alone must determine whether to celebrate or despair over the young girl's lack of moral vision—or wonder whether she ever had a choice.

LOS ANGELES, DECEMBER 22, 2009
Reprinted from *World Cinema Review* (December 2009).

A Vigorous Medley of Voices

READING IN CELEBRATION OF **POEMS FOR THE MILLENNIUM, VOLUME THREE: THE UNIVERSITY OF CALIFORNIA BOOK OF ROMANTIC & POSTROMANTIC POETRY**, EDITED BY JEROME ROTHENBERG AND JEFFREY C. ROBINSON (BERKELEY: UNIVERSITY OF CALIFORNIA PRESS, 2009) / LOS ANGELES, BEYOND BAROQUE FOUNDATION, FEBRUARY 13, 2009

ON FRIDAY, FEBRUARY 13, 2009, Beyond Baroque celebrated the publication of Jerome Rothenberg's and Jeffrey C. Robinson's new anthology, *Poems for the Millennium*, the third volume in Rothenberg's (the other two co-edited by Pierre Joris) encyclopedic presentation of international poetry, this volume devoted primarily to 19th century writing.

It was a cold, rainy night, and, accordingly, the audience was small, but despite the underheated room at Beyond Baroque, there was a warm feeling among those attending.

The evening began with Jerry and Jeffrey sharing

the stage to quote from a few individuals about the effect of Romanticism on 20th and 21st century writing, including remarks by Breton, Paz, Duncan, and Lyn Hejinian, the latter who wrote:

> If in the 19th century, as Gertrude Stein said, people saw parts and tried to assemble them into wholes, while in the 20th century people envisioned wholes and then sought parts appropriate to them, will the 21st century carry out a dissemination of wholes into all parts and thus finish what the 19th century began?

Los Angeles poet Will Alexander followed, read-

ing from Dostoevsky's *Notes from the Underground*, a work which he described, in what seemed surprising to me, as having been a sort of lodestar to his own writing. Jerry and Jeffrey again read short passages from Shelley, Keats and Wordsworth, including the last paragraph of Charles Darwin's *The Origin of Species*, relevant since that book's 150th anniversary was being celebrated this week, as well as Darwin's 200th birthday. The last paragraph of that book is itself revelatory:

> Thus, from the war of nature, from famine and death, the most exalted object which we are capable of conceiving, namely the production of higher animals, directly follows. There is grandeur in this view of life, with its several powers, having been originally breathed into a few forms or into one; and that into one; and that, whilst this planet has gone cycling on according to the fixed law of gravity, from so simple a beginning endless forms most beautiful and most wonderful have been, and are being, evolved.

San Diego fiction writer and essayist David Matlin

followed, presenting a powerful reading of Melville's "A Squeeze of the Hand," about the highly sexual immersion of hands in whale sperm from *Moby Dick*. He also sang, a cappella, from the anonymous Russian "Song of the Bald Mountain Witches & Magic Nymphs":

Kumara
Nich, nich, pasalam, bada.
Eschochomo, lawassa, schibboda.
Kurmara
A.a.o.—o.o.o.—i.i.i.—e.e.e.—u.u.u.—ye.ye.ye.

I had chosen to read the nearly impossible-to-perform ode to "The Wall Street Inferno" by Brazilian poet Sousândrade. I recounted how, when I visited Haraldo de Campos in Brazil in the late 1990s, he had immediately put this work into my hand, declaring that I must publish it! How delightful, I reacted, that we now have a section of this work available in English. Jerry read the stage-directions, while—in a vigorous medley of voices, if nothing else—I performed the various cries, lectures, sermons and other proclamations of the poem's cast of thousands:

(xeques appearing, laughing and disguised as Railroad-*managers*,
Stockjobbers, Pimpbrokers, etc., etc., ballyhooing:)

—Harlem! Erie: Central! Pennsylvania!
= Million! hundred million!! ten digits!!!
—Young is Grant! Jackson,
Atkinson
Vanderbilts, Jay Goulds are midgets!

As Jerry mentioned later, he felt that this was one of the craziest poems in the entire 930-page volume! I also read a much quieter prose-poem by one of my favorite philosophers, Søren Kierkegaard, a man who presented himself more as a poet than a religious thinker.

Jeffrey read a small selection of Romantic writers, followed by Jerry reading from several pieces, including his translation of the Polish writer Cyprian Norwid's "Chopin's Piano":

6

And—now—ended the song—And I
No longer can see you—only—can hear
Hearing what?—like when boys baffle boys—
—The keys still resisting
The source of their yearnings unsung
They softly push back on their own
By eighths—then by fifths—
And murmuring: "He—has started to play?
Or uncaring—cast us aside?"

Performance artist Simone Forti read another rendition of that last paragraph of Darwin's *The Origin*, "The Telegraph Harp," along with excerpts from the journal of Henry David Thoreau, and a couple of poems by the early 19th century Vietnamese woman poet Hô Xuân Huong:

> Screw the fate that makes you share a man.
> One cuddles under cotton blankets; the other's
>   cold.
> ...
> You try to stick to it like a fly on rice
> but the rice is rotten. You slave like the maid,

but without pay. If I had known how it would go
I think I would have lived alone.

Jerry closed this joyful series of readings with Edward Lear's charming satire of himself, "How Pleasant to Know Mr. Lear":

> He reads, but he cannot speak, Spanish;
>   He cannot abide ginger-beer.—
> Ere the days of his pilgrimage vanish,—
>   "how pleasant to know Mr. Lear!"

How pleasant to get to know this grand anthology. Similar readings have already taken place in San Francisco (with Michael McClure, Michael Palmer, Leslie Scalapino, and Jack and Adele Foley) and San Diego (with Matlin, David and Eleanor Antin, and Michael Davidson), and I know the Rothenberg-Robinson team will take this poetic circus, performed by other casts, on the road. Jerome mentions that he and Jeffrey will be reading soon in New York, at Harvard, and the University of Pennsylvania.

LOS ANGELES, FEBRUARY 15, 2009
Reprinted from *Green Integer Review* (February 2009).

From a Crawl into Flight

MARTHA CLARKE (DIRECTOR AND CHOREOGRA-PHER), RICHARD PEASLEE (MUSIC) **GARDEN OF EARTH-LY DELIGHTS** / MINETTA LANE THEATRE, NEW YORK CITY / THE PERFORMANCE I SAW WAS A MATINEE ON JANUARY 17, 2009

HIERONYMUS BOSCH'S 16th century triptych of paradise, earthly delights, and hell is the source of Martha Clarke's dance performance, first presented in New York in 1984 and revived in 1987 at the same theater in which I saw it this year, the high-ceilinged Minetta Lane Theatre.

Clarke's work however is only tangentially related to the Bosch painting, since its rich reds, greens, and blues are replaced in the performance with various shades of white and brown, only the sheer body stockings worn by the dancers lending the scene a pinkish glow.

And while Bosch presents us with three versions of

what delight might signify—the paradisiacal serenity before the fall, the lusty play and abuse of the earthly world, and the dark and sadistic tortures of Hell— Clarke's work is more clearly inspired by a Puritan-like vision of reality, as she explores, through body and motion, mankind's transformation from animal being to gluttony, greed, lust, torture, war, and murder.

One of the most lovely moments in an hour of many wondrous scenes occurs at the very beginning of the work, as the 11 dancers gracefully move forward on fingers and toes, a species not yet fully able or willing to stand erect. Yet soon, bearing branches in ritualistic gestures, they come together as humans, in pairs and in small groupings that predict the inevitable fall from grace, Eve biting the apple and Adam too, as the snake sensuously writhes between them.

From the beginning of this revelation of flesh, I wished that Clarke had allowed her dancers to perform naked instead of being ensconced in the sickly flesh-colored body stockings that wipe out all but the general shapes of their handsome bodies. I say this out of no prurient interests—dozens of Broadway musicals and plays these days feature nudity—but am simply suggesting that the appearance of dancers such as Sophie Bortolussi, Daniel Clifton, General McArthur Hambrick, and Whitney A. Hunter seems an occasion to truly witness the delights of human flesh.

In the second "triptych," the revelers have truly found "society," and are now dressed in Medieval peasant garb, one festooned in a codpiece. Accordingly it is the earthly garden itself where Clarke most clearly explores both the pleasures and abuses of human sexuality. Here too she represents the "potato eaters," as a man seemingly swallows dozens of potatoes before vomiting up his dinner.

Some figures gracefully dance while others imitate copulation. Priests (played by the musicians of Richard Peaslee's haunting score) attempt to control the various

disruptions, including a few individuals who have suddenly gone aerial, flying in and out of the stage frame through pulleys and ropes. However, their attempt at order ultimately results in even greater torture—represented as a metaphorical presentation of the Spanish Inquisition—of these free-spirited souls, chaos eventually breaking out.

In the final hellish spectacle almost all dancers—again sporting bodytights—take to the ropes, spinning almost out of control over the audience, tumbling head over heels high above us, who have become almost voyeurs of the human hell to which we are witness. It is terrifying—and liberating.

By the work's end, we realize what miserable beasts our species has turned out to be, how spirituality and ritual have been converted into warfare and other acts of hate. As the audience turned to go, a woman in front of me commented: "Not a very encouraging portrait of our kind, is it?"

Perhaps not. But what other earthly creatures could take their bodies from a virtual crawl into flight?

LOS ANGELES, FEBRUARY 5, 2009
Reprinted from *Green Integer Blog* (February 2009).

Ritualizing the Rite

VALERY GERGIEV (DIRECTOR), WITH THE CAST OF
THE MARINSKY THEATRE **STRAVINSKY AND THE BAL-
LETS RUSSES**
  YVONNE RAINER (CHOREOGRAPHER, AFTER MILLI-
CENT HODSON), WITH PAT CATTERSON, EMILY COATES,
PATRICIA HOFFBAUER, AND SALLY SILVERS **ROS INDEXI-
CAL** AND **SPIRALING DOWN** / REDCAT (ROY AND EDNA
DISNEY/CALARTS THEATER), AT THE DISNEY CENTER,
LOS ANGELES / THE PERFORMANCE I ATTENDED WAS
THE LOS ANGELES PREMIERE, THURSDAY, JUNE 25, 2009

BY INTENTIONAL COINCIDENCE, a few weeks before
attending Yvonne Rainer's *RoS Indexical* and *Spiraling
Down*, Howard and I attended a high-definition showing of Emerging Pictures' *Stravinsky and the Ballets
Russes* at the Music Hall Theater in Beverly Hills. That
film included performances of three Stravinsky ballets
by the Marinsky Ballet Company with the Marinsky
Theater Symphony Orchestra, restaged in 2003 from

the original choreography and danced in the original costumes. The three ballets included *The Firebird, The Rite of Spring,* and *The Wedding,* all of which were highly engaging reconstructions of the originals.

Of particular importance for me, however, was seeing *The Rite of Spring* just previous to Rainer's homage, dissection, and spoof of that great work. The day after seeing the Rainer piece, moreover, I watched the tape of the first reconstruction of Nijinsky's original, performed in 1987 by the Joffrey Ballet in Los Angeles.

From a *corps de ballet* of several dozens of dancers, Rainer slimmed down her company to four dancers, Emily Coates, Patricia Hoffbauer, Sally Silvers, and Pat Catterson, the last of whom was replaced in the production I saw by Rainer herself, now age 75.

The tone of Rainer's version was established almost immediately by the four sitting around a card table, listening to something on headphones. They begin by humming and thrumming the overture to *The Rite of Spring,* droned so out of tune it is barely recognizable.

As the First Act, "L'Adoration de la Terre," begins, three of the women (in the original, many of the group dances were split by Nijinsky into groups of three) gather, as the old men do in Nijinsky's version, to celebrate the spring with the heavy stamp of their booted feet. Here, in spritely colored work-out clothing, the women start by imitating the original but quickly move to other positions as, sometimes working in unison, but more often splitting apart into ones or twos, they reiterate some of the hand, arm, and head gestures of the Nijinsky choreography. To her "indexing" of the original, Rainer adds often hilarious and touching riffs, from Groucho Marx's daffy backward shuffles (remember his incredible dancing in the movies?) and Robin Williams (presumably from his Bob Fosse imitations in *The Birdcage*) to Sarah Bernhardt's melodramatic gestures. Every so often, the exhausted dancers—they are, after all, performing all the various chorus numbers—retire to a couch, where they temporarily rest, change from shoes to Kleenex boxes (suggesting, I gather, the various different tribal outfits of the original dancers), and appear to be deciding what to do with the dreadful audience response.

For Rainer has layered her performance to include the riots of the original. Early in their dances, various placards fall from the ceiling, dangling like posters in the sky, announcing possible responses to the work. From the soundtrack of the BBC rendition, *Riot at the Rite*, we hear various shouts and hateful remarks,

Nijinsky counting loudly to his performers so that they, unable any longer to hear the music, might continue the dance. At one point a mob of planted actors, a couple in the costumes of the original designer Nicholas Roerich, rush to the stage, demanding the company return to TriBeCa, where Rainer's New York home is located.

Certainly this historical intervention adds further dimension to the work. But the high British accents declaring their dismissal and outrage made the reactions seem arch and absurd; certainly French would have been more to the point, and, like others in the audience, I wished we might have had the "riot" performed in the original language.

The unflappable dancers, however, ultimately maintained their demeanors, bending down occasionally to return, in mime, some of the missiles presumably hurled their way. As the performers began the memorable "Dance of the Virgins," those terrifying figures who ultimately decide which of their members is to be sacrificed, Sally Silvers falls to the floor in a faint, referencing the original fall of the young woman selected to die. Throughout, Silvers humorously huffs and puffs her way through these dances, sometimes in Marx Brothers style, leaving everything out that the others do except for the final position (the other two dancers are younger by at least two decades),  lending her highly satiric dancing style (Silvers, like the others with whom she dances, is also a noted choreographer) to the whole. Not to be outdone, however, the other two later fall, and in lieu of the final end of the sacrificial victim—raised in her death above the heads of the original male chorus—each of Rainer's women take turns at demonstrating their dramatic skills in dying by falling upon the couch, with Silvers most riotously clumsy, and Rainer almost unable, it appears, to climb over its arms.

Yet, throughout this exhausting dance, these four women stomp, march, float through the air, twist, turn, and gesture with arms, hands, and fingers along with Stravinsky's raw, barbarously rhythmic, and often blaringly atonal chords, exhibiting an incredible energy and beauty that might almost be said to outdo any large *corps de ballets*. Rainer declared at the beginning of the work that her performance might be seen as "geriatric," but if her graceful movements represent the consequences of old age, bring it on! We should all be so beautifully lithe.

LOS ANGELES, JUNE 27, 2009
Reprinted from *US Theater, Opera, and Performance* (June 2009).

Before this performance, I joined my poet friend, Bruce Andrews— who has had a long-time relationship with dancer Sally Silvers and on this occasion accompanied her to Los Angeles—at Traxx restaurant at Union Station. At the performance itself, I conversed with Marjorie Perloff, her daughter Nancy, poet Deborah Meadows, and her husband Howard. In the audience were other acquaintances, Stanley and Elise Grinstein and Steve Levine and his wife Janet Sternberg, Levine being the President of CalArts.

Flying Over the Heart

NOT SINCE MY earliest days of flying has a flight been quite as pleasant. Most of the country was very cold, but the trip occurred over mostly clear skies and, while I usually sit on the aisle, this time a beautiful black woman—an actress, as it turned out, on her way to President Obama's inauguration—claimed the aisle seat, "confining" me, so I first thought, to the window.

For much of the trip, during the flight over the deserts of Nevada and Utah, I read. Despite the rather spectacular scenery of Colorado, I focused instead on Heimito von Doderer's "Divertimenti 4" and "Divertimenti 5." Nebraska in my estimation is a rather boring state from 39,000 feet. I felt much the same, I have to admit, when my family drove through that state when I was a child. But this time I became fascinated with its small towns, whose streets and houses I could just make out, despite our height and the few seconds it took to pass over them. Every now and then the flat perspective I was witnessing would flash into a row of lights as the sun suddenly played on the windows of houses and cars below.

Then came the Missouri River as we passed over into my home state of Iowa, with its square-shaped division of every country mile and an absolutely splendid vision of the state capital, Des Moines, with a sudden projection upwards of its downtown skyscrapers. I waved to my sister, who works in the city for the State Department of Education.

A few moments later I spotted, a bit higher on the horizon, my hometown of Cedar Rapids-Marion. I threw a kiss to the rest of my folk. Then came the great Mississippi with what I presumed was Dubuque upon its banks.

For a while I returned to reading; von Doderer is a very compelling writer. Just as suddenly I caught a glimpse below of what I knew to be the outskirts of Chicago, and soon after witnessed the vast layout of what used to be called "the Second City." At first I thought we were too far south to be able to see the Center City—but almost immediately after, as if I had donned 3-D glasses, the heart of the city sprang up into dimension directly below, with Lake Michigan follow-

ing after. I was awed by the beauty of the city.

After Chicago, the clouds hovering over the great lake stole my view and I returned to my Austrian master. Von Doderer was lamenting the failure in all of us to enjoy the sensuous pleasures of life. I stealthily glanced out the window at his command to notice a break in the cloud layer and note how cold the water of Lake Michigan appeared dressed in its tentacles of occasional ice, just as quickly conjuring up the possibility of crashing into those icy waters. A fearful thought, I said to myself, for no one could possibly survive those frigid waves.

I returned to reading, stimulated with a Bombay

Gin (probably the cause for my eating, later that evening, at the Indian restaurant The Earthen Pot on New York City's Columbus Avenue and 72nd Street), witnessing, soon after, the city of Cleveland, which I had previously seen only by bus on a trip back from New York City to Madison, Wisconsin as a young man.

And then, nothing more until we were barreling into Newark, with the sun glimmering, dark snow clouds catching the spectral colors of the rainbow outside my window. How do you explain these sights to a plane-load of individuals who have all, save me, closed their small window blinds to watch mediocre Hollywood films, television reruns, computer games, and to sleep?

Our destination reached, I awaited my limousine in the bitter cold for a half hour, and when I finally hailed the driver, an affable Haitian whose first day it was on the job, he reported that there had been a huge backup in the entry to the pickup spot, and that, a short while ago, a plane had gone down into the Hudson River! Fortunately, all the passengers, including an infant, had been plucked from the frozen waters to safety. "What a miracle!" he proclaimed, a statement reiterated in the media numerous times the next day.

Having missed the exit to the Lincoln Tunnel, we took the Holland, which to our surprise was free of its usual rush-hour traffic. As any good driver trying to reach the Upper West Side might, he opted for the West Side Highway, which also was amazingly quick until we reached 40th Street, whereupon we encountered dozens and dozens of police cars and, soon after, television and radio trucks. The myriad blinking of red, yellow, and blue lights created a strange and almost surreal aura about the place, as, for a few blocks, we were trapped in a traffic jam—which turned out to be caused not by the terrifying plane accident but a collision of an SUV and a large truck. Since the police were all gathered in that spot, however, we were quickly sped around the impediment and for a couple of blocks we raced forward before spying, just to our left, the airplane sinking into the freezing Hudson's waters.

We quickly turned off, moving over to the 8th Street and up into Central Park West were I was to stay on this visit at the apartment of Sherry Bernstein. Sherry, worried by my late arrival, had called Charles in alarm. "Had my plane also crashed?" she, like any worried mother, wondered.

I assured her it had not.

NEW YORK CITY, JANUARY 15, 2009
Reprinted from *Green Integer Blog* (February 2009).

Archetypal America

THORNTON WILDER **OUR TOWN** / PREMIERED
FEBRUARY 4, 1938 AT HENRY MILLER THEATRE / THE
PRODUCTION I SAW WAS AT BARROW STREET THEATRE,
NEW YORK, MAY 10, 2009

FEW AMERICAN PLAYS can lay claim to being almost
a dramatic "national anthem" other than Thornton
Wilder's *Our Town*. Susan Bee recently suggested that
everyone of a certain age who performed in high school
theater was, at one time or another, in *Our Town*. I performed as a minor character in just such a production.

Over the years, however, it has seemed to me that
this archetypal drama without sets or costumes has gotten a little stale. Howard and I attended a production at
Arena Stage in Washington, D.C. around 1973, when
they also performed that work, among others, in the
Soviet Union.

I remember that production primarily for the acting by Robert Prosky as the stage manager. Prosky per-

formed it in a manner that was so "folksy," I could hardly bear the sentimentality of the piece. A 2003 television production starring Paul Newman and directed by James Naughton seemed even more lifeless.

I also have the feeling that over the years, in some productions, more and more props have crept onto the stage despite Wilder's insistence that the play use only three props at most. But perhaps this is just an illusion brought about by the busy verisimilitude of the productions I've seen.

The 2009 production at the Barrow Street Theater in New York, accordingly, was a welcome change. Directed by David Cromer, this *Our Town* was a dusted-off rendition, where part of the audience, an important feature of the script, appeared onstage (I among them), and were asked to read the questions in response to the academically inclined lecture of Professor Willard, who describes the geological history of Grover's Corners and surrounding territory.

The stage manager of this version, Cromer himself, lost the New England accent usually lathered on in heavy doses, and spoke in a more appealing everyday language, sometimes injecting energy through his hur-

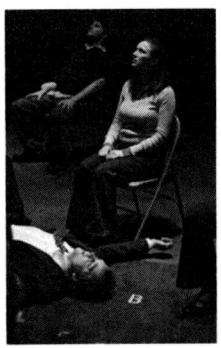

ried asides into a work that has a tendency, in its slow spin of storytelling, to fall into lethargy. With only two tables and four chairs, Cromer created a believable pair of houses in which live the Gibbs and the Webbs, whose children grow up, marry, and die in a few short hours. The abandonment of the New Hampshire-isms was a particular advantage, I felt, since the play is so universally "American"—however one defines that—that this work has always seemed to be more at home in the author's own state of Wisconsin. Wherever Grover's Corners is, it exists more in the mind than in reality, and to place it in any particular locale seems to me beside the point.

So casual were the actors, dressed in mostly contemporary clothing, that even the heartrending wedding scene and the nearly impossible-to-perform cemetery conversation among the dead lost a great deal of their sentimentality.

Interestingly, after paring down the characters' lives and actions to almost abstract imitations of life, Cromer pulled out the naturalistic stops, so to speak, for the famous final scene when Emily Webb (Jeniffer Grace in this production) asks to go back "home" for one day in her life. Suddenly a curtain behind the stage was opened to reveal an entire kitchen, with a table set with plates, silverware, napkins, a working water pump, and a stove where Emily's mother, costumed in turn-of-the-century dress, fries up bacon and pancakes. The startling comparison of the abstractness of the rest of the production with this highly realist scene brought home, with amazing results, one of Wilder's major themes: that we are too busy living life to really see it. Perhaps only the dead can truly smell the coffee, but on the Mother's Day Sunday I visited this play, the entire audience shared in the experience, as tears fell from nearly everyone's eyes. In a strange way, it was if Wilder had restated, within a narrow realist context, Ionesco's absurdly comic observations about life and death.

LOS ANGELES, MAY 29, 2009
Reprinted from *US Theater, Opera, and Performance* (May 2009).

The Miraculous Child

JEAN-PIERRE AND LUC DARDENNE (SCREENPLAY
AND DIRECTORS) **LE SILENCE DE LORNA (LORNA'S
SILENCE**) / 2008, RELEASED IN THE US IN 2009

AS I DESCRIBED their work in two films (*L'Enfant* and *La Promesse*) in *My Year 2004*, the Dardenne brothers combine Christian symbolism with current social issues in a manner that is somewhat similar to the work of Robert Bresson (see my essay on Bresson in *My Year 2000*). And through their focus on immigrants and petty criminals, their work also resonates with the outrageous moral fables of Flannery O'Connor.

In this newest film, *Lorna's Silence*, two young Albanians, seeking a better life, find their way into the criminal machinations of a petty mobster, Fabio. To obtain Belgian citizenship, Lorna (the photogenic Arta Dobroshi) has paid a young junkie, Claudy Moreau (played by the Dardenne regular Jérémie Renier), to marry her. She and others who have helped her have particularly chosen Claudy because of the probability that he will soon die, and Lorna will be free to marry a Russian, for a great deal of money, also desiring to become a citizen of the European Union.

The movie begins with Lorna depositing money into a savings account and inquiring about a loan. And throughout the movie, the camera focuses time and again on financial transactions, not only for daily purchases, but in Claudy's case—who asks that Lorna take his paltry life savings—to keep his money safe from his drug habit. Both the temporary husband and wife see money as the route to their dreams and needs and are clearly willing to do most anything to obtain it. Lorna and her boyfriend Sokol, the latter who works as an itinerant day laborer participating in shady activities related to Fabio and his group, plan to use their money to buy a small food stand, one of the dozens throughout the city of Liège, where the film's action takes place. Claudy, who has been paid to marry her, however, suddenly decides to come clean, with her help, putting all of Fabio's plans in jeopardy.

Early in the film, Lorna appears quite impenetrable, a woman without sentimentality, willing to do almost anything to achieve her goal. But as Claudy sickens from withdrawal, she is affected  by his passionate pleas for help, and gradually awards him some attention, ultimately delivering him over to the hospital for his cure. Now since he will not, apparently, die from his habit, she attempts to get a quick divorce by painfully bruising herself in almost comical runs against doorways and walls to prove that Claudy has beaten her. Her visit to the police station enrages Fabio, however, who now fears the police will suspect something and that it will further delay Lorna's marriage to the Russian.

Visiting Claudy, she demands that he strike her in the presence of a nurse. But the young man, despite his drug dependence, is a nonviolent being, insisting he would never strike a woman, and he is unable to do so when he tries to enact her plot. It is this basic goodness in him that gradually begins to chip away at Lorna's coldly calculated composure. And when Claudy returns home, she chases the local drug dealer from her house and refuses to give Claudy back his money for a purchase, fighting him to the floor, an encounter that

ends with the two engaged in intense sex.

The divorce decree has come through, but Fabio and the Russian cannot wait. As Lorna returns to her menial day job at a cleaners, Claudy rides away joyfully on his new bicycle, insisting Lorna keep his money in the envelope. In the very next scene we observe Lorna almost ritualistically folding and packing away his clothing. Claudy, so the police report says, has overdosed, which we know was not an act of his own volition.

Soon after, as Lorna excitedly inspects her and Sokol's new café, she finds herself unable to climb the stairs. It is evident that she is pregnant—with Claudy's child! Her first instinct is the obvious one: she must abort it. But in the Dardennes' films, nothing happens quite like one might expect. At the clinic she panics even before they inspect her body. She bolts from the place, reporting to Fabio that she will have a baby.

Fabio insists she will have an abortion the next day, but at the meeting with the Russian Lorna is to marry, she dares to ask, through a translator, what he might think if she had a baby. He is outraged, ready to renege on the deal, until Fabio intercedes, insisting that she is not pregnant and will be checked over by a doctor as evidence! Later that night, Lorna collapses in painful cramping, and is taken to the doctor's, where they declare that, indeed, she is *not* pregnant,  and suggest further tests. A chance encounter with the nurse to whom she had first reported Claudy's beating of her hints to Fabio that she is about to tell the truth. And he rushes her from the hospital, insisting, through an intervention with her boyfriend Sokol, that it would be better for her to return to Albania. In the end, both Lorna and Claudy have attempted, but been unable, to resist their own immoral values.

It is only at this point that Lorna truly becomes silent, as a knowing and maternal-like glow suddenly appears on her face. Forced to return all of her money, with Sokol taking back his portion of their savings, she is left, it appears, with only a few euros and the money she had hidden away from Claudy, which she now intends to use for the child whom she insists—despite the doctor's proclamation—will soon be born. As an associate of Fabio drives her away, it quickly becomes clear that he is not taking the route to Albania, but driving her to some out of the way spot to kill her.

Stopping in the woods to pee, she grabs a large

rock and, returning to the car, dashes it into the head of her would-be assassin, racing into the woods without a planned destination. Eventually she finds a small shed, which she forces open and in which, after gathering wood, she starts a fire, speaking to her child as she acts, something to the effect of, "Perhaps tomorrow we will find a friendly house, where they will feed us. Now we must sleep."

It is clear that, despite the desperation of her potential fate—she may be seriously ill and is without a single possession—Lorna is determined to live and bear her child. Is she deluded? Gone mad? Possibly. She has, however, clearly been morally redeemed, has seen the error of her life and regretted her actions. Like the mother of Christ, she has had, symbolically, to flee to Egypt. But Lorna must escape even *before* the child's birth, finding her own stable nonetheless. Miracles, so the Dardennes suggest, are known to happen.

LOS ANGELES, AUGUST 9, 2009
Reprinted from *Nth Position* [England] (August 2009).
Reprinted from *Reading Films: My International Cinema* (Los Angeles: Green Integer, 2012).

Strange Bird

BRAD GOOCH **FLANNERY: A LIFE OF FLANNERY O'CONNOR** (NEW YORK: LITTLE BROWN AND COMPANY, 2009)

FLANNERY O'CONNOR **COLLECTED WORKS**, CONTENTS SELECTED AND CHRONOLOGY BY SALLY FITZGERALD (NEW YORK: THE LIBRARY OF AMERICA, 1988)

BORN IN SAVANNAH, GEORGIA on March 25, 1925, Mary Flannery O'Connor was the only child of a devoted and extended Catholic family. Her mother, Regina Cline, was part of the wealthy and noted Cline family of Savannah, and Regina's second cousin, Mrs. Raphael (Katie) Seemes, rented them a small Georgian row house next to her own mansion and garden. Several of Regina's relatives had also established homes in the former state capital, Milledgeville, to the northwest, and during summers the O'Connors visted the town, staying in the home where Regina had grown up, once the interim governor's mansion. They also regularly vis-

ited the nearby farm, Andalusia, owned by her uncle.

In his new biography of Flannery O'Connor, Brad Gooch dutifully notes the family's comings and goings, based on brief mentions in the local newspapers. But, except for their scuttling between houses, little of interest occurs in O'Connor's youth except at age five, when she was filmed by Pathé with her pet chicken who was rumored to walk backward: at first, things did not go well, but

> Finally, as the afternoon wore on, the bird began to back up. O'Connor, a natural mimic, jumped next to her and began to walk backward as well. The [camera] operator stuck his head under his tent. A few seconds later, the hen hit a bush and abruptly sat down. Exasperated, "the Pathé man" gathered his equipment and made a quick exit....

The only major literary contribution of her youth was a satirical portrait of her extended family. And, although Gooch goes out of his way to normalize her Catholic-school girlhood, one cannot help but perceive her a bit like the red-faced child in O'Connor's story "A Circle in the Fire," her face buried in a book from which, from time to time, she would peer out at the world. At age 12, she was overly wise and determined to not grow any older. And, in some respects, Gooch and others hint that, at least sexually, she remained that age throughout her life.

One aspect of her childhood education, however, reveals a great deal about her later writing. Attending the local Catholic school, O'Connor, in third grade, began resenting certain of what she described as "nun-inspired doings." As Brad Gooch describes her "tussles" with authority:

> In a state of mind somewhere between a child's daydream and one of the scriptural visions she heard preached about the church, she imagined bouts with a guardian angel she pictures as half nun, half bird.

As O'Connor wrote to her friend, Betty Hester, years later, "From 8 to 12 years it was my habit to seclude myself in a locked room every so often and, with a fierce (and evil) face, whirl around in a circle with my fists knotted, socking the angel with which the Sisters assured us we were all equipped.... You couldn't hurt an angel but I would have been happy to know I had dirtied his feathers...."

Having lost his Dixie Realty Company (later expanded to include the Dixie Construction Company), in part due to the Great Depression, her beloved father soon after began to show signs of illness, lupus, which would eventually kill him—and, years later, O'Connor herself. In 1938, having been appointed a real estate appraiser for the Federal Housing Administration, he and the family moved to Atlanta, an experience hated by Flannery and, evidently, by her mother, for the two returned in the fall to live in Milledgeville—appropriately named, given O'Connor's love of chickens, peacocks, geese, and swans, a "Bird Sanctuary"—with the father remaining weekdays in Atlanta, a city much vilified in her story "The Artificial Nigger," where grandfather and son agree: "I'm glad I've went once, but I'll never go back again!"

Over the next two years, O'Connor became active in her high school newspaper, the *Peabody Palladium*, drawing cartoons and contributing writing. On February 1, 1941, however, tragedy struck her life with the death of her father, a man, she felt, who would have written had he had the "time or money or training or any of the opportunities I have had." Her second novel, *The Violent Bear It Away*, was dedicated to him.

O'Connor came alive, so it appears, during her college days at Georgia State College for Women, lo-

cated, as she later joked, across the street from her Milledgeville home. There she quickly became active as a cartoonist, regularly contributing to the college literary magazine, the *Corinthian*. Soon after she began to publish short prose pieces and stories in that magazine and the *Colonnade*, where she became art editor and also published weekly cartoons. Indeed, O'Connor took her cartoons seriously enough that she sent some for possible publication in *The New Yorker*. It is fascinating to think what might have happened to her writing talent had that magazine accepted her work.

For fiction, clearly, was not yet an area which O'Connor had thoroughly explored as a possible career. Gooch carefully outlines the several courses in English Literature O'Connor took, pointing to important early readings in her textbook, including stories by Faulkner, Joyce, and Poe. It was a social science course, however, that was ultimately to change her life. That course, an Introduction to Modern Philosophy, was taught by George Beiswanger, who had received his PhD at the University of Iowa. He had also worked as an editor for

Theatre Arts Monthly and written on dance in *Dance Observer*, as well as taken part in an arts symposium at Black Mountain College. Later in O'Connor's life, philosophical theory, particularly of the religious sort, would occupy a great deal of her energy. But in this course she sat through discussions of Descartes and other Enlightenment thinkers with a "persistent, subtle scowl." "What kept me a sceptic in college was precisely my Christian faith," she confided in a letter of 1962. Yet Beiswanger clearly saw her abilities, particularly from her classroom arguments with him. Not only did the student receive an A, but he encouraged her to apply for graduate school at his alma mater. She applied to both Duke University and Iowa, considering a career in journalism. The latter accepted her with full tuition, to which she readily agreed.

From almost the first moment of entering the Iowa campus, O'Connor found her way to the office of Paul Engle, then director of the Iowa Writers' Workshop. Their hilarious first encounter is worth describing:

> Sitting in his office early in the fall of 1945, Paul Engle...heard a gentle knock at the door. After he shouted an invitation to enter, a shy, young woman appeared and walked over to his desk without, at first, saying a word. He could not even tell, as she stood before him, whether she was looking

in his direction, or out the window at the curling Iowa River below. ...[Engle] introduced himself and offered her a seat, as she tightly held on to what he later claimed was "one of the most beat-up handbags I've ever seen."

When she finally spoke, her Georgia dialect sounded so thick to his Midwestern ear that he asked her to repeat her question. Embarrassed by an inability, a second time, to understand, Engle handed her a pad to write what she had said. So in schoolgirl script, she put down three short lines: "My name is Flannery O'Connor. I am not a journalist. Can I come to the Writers' Workshop?"

A couple of days later, after Engle read a few stories she had sent him, O'Connor was accepted into the program, and an important new chapter in American literary history began.

It was at the Iowa campus that Flannery O'Connor truly discovered herself. Changing her name from Mary Flannery O'Connor in order to avoid "the lilting double name that exaggerated her oddity as a Southern lady in Iowa City," Flannery soon settled in to her home at Currier House, beginning a series of "close reading" literary classes with Engle, Paul Horgan, Austin Warren, Andrew Lytle, and guest lecturers John Crowe Ransom and Robert Penn Warren. It was there she wrote early stories such as "The Geranium," "The

Crop," "The Barber," and others. In 1946 she began the story "The Train," finishing it in early 1947, soon after expanding it to become the first chapter of her novel *Wise Blood*. In May of that year, O'Connor was awarded the Rinehart-Iowa Award for an early version of the novel.

As a postgraduate student the next fall, O'Connor moved out of Currier House and became friends with several individuals with whom she would communicate throughout her life, including the story writers and novelists Jean Williams, Robie Macauley, and Walter Sullivan. She also met poet Robert Lowell, who gave a reading in Iowa City's Old Capitol building.

In early June of 1948, O'Connor arrived for her first stay at Yaddo, the writers colony located at the former Trask estate in Saratoga Springs, New York. Among the many noted figures visiting during O'Connor's stay were Patricia Highsmith, Frederick Morton, Clifford Wright, Elizabeth Hardwick, Malcolm Cowley, and Robert Lowell, who quickly became "Flannery's champion." Here, working on and reworking *Wise Blood*, O'Connor, despite her monastic writing habits which kept her at arm's distance from the wild behavior of Lowell (his romancing of Elizabeth Hardwick was the talk of the colony), had finally found her milieu, determining to remain at Yaddo over the Christmas holidays instead of returning home to her mother.

The postwar anti-Communist hysteria of the "Red Scare," however, found its way to the isolated institution's doors. General Douglas MacArthur's accusation that Agnes Smedley had run a spy ring out of Shanghai startled the residents, since she had been a close friend of the Yaddo director and "monarch," Elizabeth Ames. An FBI check of Communist sympathies at Yaddo quickly followed. Clifford Wright, believed by Ames to be an FBI informant, was sent packing. Lowell, also one of the directors of Yaddo, held an "inquisition" against Ames, accusing her of arbitrary decisions, even involving a reluctant and distanced O'Connor, who announced that she would be leaving the next Tuesday.

Left without a place to go, O'Connor suddenly found herself in Manhattan, staying for a while first with Elizabeth Hardwick, and moving later to Tatum House, a YWCA residence on Lexington Avenue. Lowell, in turn, helped her make contacts, introducing her to translator Robert Fitzgerald and his wife Sally, who, through their shared Catholicism and intellectual abilities, would become lifetime friends of O'Connor, with Sally later editing O'Connor's letters and essays, and creating a chronology of O'Connor's life in the 1988 Library of America edition of O'Connor's *Collected Works*.

Lowell also introduced her to Robert Giroux, in those days an editor at Harcourt Brace, the publisher, ultimately, of *Wise Blood*, who, later as a publisher at Farrar, Straus, and Giroux, would promote O'Connor's other works.

Lowell's increasing madness during this period, however, and his ultimate rebuke from the Yaddo directors for his charges against Ames, left O'Connor once again in the lurch, a woman with little money and a mother fearful of her living alone in Manhattan. In March the author returned home, staying through Easter, with the intention of returning to New York.

When O'Connor did return, she faced a muggy summer, and, according to Gooch, spent most of her time in her humble room, revising the last sections of *Wise Blood*, only rarely getting out into the New York streets. As O'Connor herself describes these outings: "I finally ended up eating at the Columbia University student cafeteria. I looked enough like a student to get by with it, and it was one of the few places I suspected the food of being clean." In August, the film *Mighty Joe Young* opened at the Criterion Theatre in Times Square, flanked by a publicity stunt in which a man in an ape suit greeted theater-goers, an incident that made its way into her first novel.

An invitation to stay as "a paying guest" at the Fitzgeralds' large country house in Connecticut saved her from further suffering in the city, of which, she later admitted, she knew only that there was an "uptown" and a "downtown." But the daily business of family life with three children, with another on its way, clearly made for some distressing interruptions in her writing time. During a trip back to Milledgeville in December, O'Connor became seriously ill and was hospitalized for an operation for a floating kidney, a disease described as "Dietl's crisis." And, although she made good progress in writing upon her return to the Fitzgeralds, she described the heaviness in her "typing arms." So serious did the pain become that Sally took O'Connor to a local doctor who diagnosed the joint pains as rheumatoid arthritis, recommending a complete examination when she returned to Milledgeville for Christmas. A few nights after O'Connor's return home, Regina called the Fitzgeralds to announce that Flannery was dying of lupus, insisting that they keep the fact a secret from her daughter.

2

Gooch aptly compares O'Connor's return to the South to that of Asbury Fox's return home in O'Connor's story "The Enduring Chill." Fox's "illness," although he believes it to be a deadly one, is later discovered, ironically, to be undulant fever, a fever which will destroy his life without truly killing him. O'Connor's illness was of a far more serious nature, and even though she was told it was only arthritis, she described her feelings to a friend that belied her fears:

> I am languishing on my bed of semi affliction, this time with AWRTHRITUS or, to give it all it has, *the* acute rheumatoid arthritis, what leaves you always willing to sit down, lie down, lie flatter, etc....
> I will be in Milledgeville Ga. a birdsanctuary for a few months, waiting to see how much of an invalid I am going to be...but I don't believe in time no more so its all one to me.

It was during the painful hospital stays, in Atlanta and back in Milledgeville, of this period, however, that O'Connor finally came to comprehend the major character of *Wise Blood*, Hazel Motes, in her own illness—as she described it, spelling out the book. In June of that year, after having been rejected by Rinehart, Harcourt Brace accepted the book, with Giroux sending a list of suggested additions and corrections. Through Robert Fitzgerald's intercession, the book was also read and edited by Southern novelist Caroline Gordon, who became another of the author's literary friends and a reader of all O'Connor's later work. Gordon's editorial influence upon O'Connor's work was evidently quite significant and appreciated by the writer, yet, as an editor, I would certainly have questioned editorial changes such as that Gooch describes wherein the color of Emery Enoch's tie was changed from "greenpeaish" (a perfect O'Connorism) to "the color of green peas," a far more standard metaphor.

On May 15, 1952 *Wise Blood* was, at last, published.

Hazel Motes from the very beginning of the fiction, is a man defined by his eyes. On the train ride to Taulkinham, Mrs. Hitchcock sees the ex-soldier, dressed in his "glaring blue" suit and broad-brimmed hat, "a hat that an elderly country preacher would wear," as a figure with his eyes trained on something outside of her own vision. "...His eyes is what held her attention longest. Their settings were so deep that they seemed, to her, almost like passages leading somewhere and she leaned halfway across the space that separated the two seats, trying to see into them."

Just by Hazel Motes' name, the reader recognizes that the deep-set eyes that Mrs. Hitchcock observes, in part, account for the fact that she cannot see into them. Not only are they the color, O'Connor tells us, of "pecan shells," a "hazel-like" color, but they are "hazy" and, as his last name hints, they contain "motes," specks that, symbolically speaking, do not allow him to properly see. This image, in turn, suggests the famous Biblical passage repeated in both Matthew and Luke:

And why beholdest thou the mote that is in thy brother's eye, but considerest not the beam that is in thine own eye?

Or wilt thou say to thy brother, Let me pull out the mote out of thine eye; and behold, a beam *is* in thine own eye?

Thou hypocrite, first cast out the beam out of thine own eye; and then shalt thou see clearly to cast out the mote out of thy brother's eye. (Matthew 7:3-5)

With this warning against hypocrisy, O'Connor sets the tone for her tale of a man destined to become a preacher, yet who rejects the religion of his father and grandfather. Clearly affected by his military experiences, the death of his father (who does not arise from his coffin as he has promised), and the cultural and sociopolitical changes in his state and small hometown (he is convinced that the train porter is a Parnum "nigger" from his now empty hometown of Eastrod, pretending to be born and raised in Chicago), Motes is determined to promulgate a new faith, "The Church without Christ."

The dilemma of preaching for a church of disbelief in a world where most individuals perceive themselves as eternally saved results in a comic situation, leading to a world in which, as Haze puts it early in the book, "If you're been redeemed...I wouldn't want to be," a predicament played out in the works of the devout Catholic writer again and again. Indeed, through O'Connor's serious engagement of this dark comedic existentialism, Motes' predicament—wherein the more he fights against his lost faith, the more he reveals his own Christian temperament—becomes a terrifying tale of redemption.

Without even trying, Motes immediately attracts disciples: first Enoch Emery, a frictional rock of faith. In his name, Enoch, the eldest son of Cain—who was the murderer of his brother Abel—is a sort of reverse image of God's chosen, recognized even by the waitress of the zoo's Frosty Bottle stand as a "pus-marked bastard...a goddamned son a bitch." She recognizes Motes, on the other hand, as "a clean boy." Again, however, Motes perceives his purity in oppositional terms: he is clean because there is no Christ.

The relationship between Enoch and Haze, like Christ's relationship with several of his disciples, is an inexplicable one, with Enoch immediately sensing some change in his life and attempting to please the new stranger in Taulkinham. Like Motes, Enoch, coming from the country, finds city life lonely, a place in which people are unfriendly. He recognizes in Motes a potential friend and a kind of older brother with whom he might bond. Yet O'Connor goes out of her way to make their relationship even more complex, presenting it as a kind of sacramental kinship in which Enoch is determined to award Motes with something of significance. In that sense, their relationship, without having anything directly to do with sex, is based on an immediate male-to-male attraction, at least on Enoch's part, and made even more sexually ironic when we realize the gift he chooses is a shrunken man, in Enoch's eyes a kind of immortalized baby. That latent sexuality energizes their relationship in the same way that Motes is determined to sexually seduce Sabbath Lily Hawks, the second of his disciples, a kind of Mary Magdalene and Mary, the Mother of Jesus, rolled into one.

If Enoch is perceived as an "unclean" figure, Sabbath Lily and her father, also a preacher, are true hypocrites, the old man pretending that he has blinded himself in order to proclaim his faith. In truth, they are both sham artists, attempting to make a meager living from their prayers of salvation. For her part, Lily is determined to marry the preacher because he is "good to look at." More sexually experienced than Motes, she has a difficult time engaging him until she moves in with him, Motes desiring to rid himself of her even then.

Predictably, what most intrigues Motes about the pair is the father's presumed blindness, and he goes out of his way to find out what is "*behind* the dark glasses."

Just as people cannot properly see into Motes' eyes, so Motes cannot glimpse the secret of Hawks' vision. Indeed, unlike other preachers, Hawks makes no attempt to convert Motes or invite him to join his church.

Motes' own attempts at converting the Taulkinham crowds to join his "Church without Christ" are a complete failure. That is, until Hoover Shoats, another of O'Connor's Christian hypocrites, speaks up as having been converted by Motes. But his claim that he previously "met the prophet," who completely changed his life, infuriates the honest Haze, who turns on Shoats and the crowd both, bellowing, "Blasphemy is the way to the truth."

When he discovers, the next evening, that Shoats has found a new boy in his preaching scheme, a man who looks to be the twin of Motes, he has no choice but to destroy his double if he and his message are to be heard.

In some ways, Motes' faith in the "Church without Christ" is so fervently straightforward, so humanly honest in its utter rejection of faith and miracles, that no one can believe him, for there is nothing he offers to believe *in*. Just as ironic is Enoch's robbery from the Museum of "the shrunken man," which he delivers to Motes' room soon after Sabbath Hawks has taken up quarters there. Her language and her actions create a symbolic scene that stands against everything that

Motes has preached. Calling Motes the "king of the beasts" and insisting he "Make haste," it is inevitable that Sabbath takes up Enoch's gift of the shrunken man as if it were a baby to nurse, taunting Motes with the very image of the Nativity. Haze flings the object out the window!

Shaken by events but having the courage of his convictions, unlike the fake preacher Hawks, Motes puts lime into his eyes, symbolically removing his motes and snaring the Hawk simultaneously.

Enoch, meanwhile, filled with the wonder of "expectation," attends the premiere of *Gonga, Giant Jungle Monarch*. Escaping with a gorilla suit "awarded by its god," he dons the costume and slouches through the countryside like Yeats' rough beast towards Bethlehem to be born anew.

3

The forces at work in O'Connor's first fiction are fierce oppositions, ironies that point to possible redemption rather than awarding those who believe themselves saved. It is a pattern she will repeat in the rest of her writings, a vision that, as she admitted back in Iowa, arises from a Third Century point of view of Christianity.

Moving with her mother to Andalusia, O'Connor

settled in a room on the first floor. With treatment she was soon able to work for a few hours every morning, spending the rest of the day reading philosophi-

cal and theological books, corresponding with friends, caring for her numerous peacocks and peahens, and receiving, on a regular basis, several visitors, including the textbook salesman from Harcourt Brace, Erik Langkjaer (perhaps the major love—albeit a nonsexual one—of her life). O'Connor also traveled to the Fitzgeralds' friends Brainard and Frances Cheney's home, Cold Chimney's, a house described by Gooch as a "refuge for many of the leading figures in the 'Southern Renaissance,'" including Caroline Gordon, Robert Penn Warren, Randall Jarrell, Cleanth Brooks, Andrew Lytle, Eudora Welty, Allen Tate, Katherine Anne Porter, Jean Stafford, Peter Taylor, Eleanor Ross, Malcolm Cowley, Russell Kirk, Robert Lowell, and Walker Percy. Gooch notes these activities to make it clear that O'Connor, despite the isolation brought about by her illness, was anything but a recluse. Most of these quite intense friendships had already been reported in O'Connor's letters and through Sally Fitzgerald's extensive chronology, but it is useful to have O'Connor's social world spelled out in a single book.

Gooch also notes several events in Andalusia and Milledgeville as sources for the stories O'Connor was writing during these years, pointing in particular to newspaper articles, Langkjaer's relationship with Flannery, the hiring by Regina of a Polish family, the Matysiaks, and O'Connor's relationship with her mother. What is apparent after reading Gooch's biography is how much O'Connor depended on her local community for her writing; but equally important, I would argue, is how the author transformed those local events—or perhaps reconceived her daily encounters as satiric and spiritual fables. It is quite apparent that O'Connor could not have survived those years without the help of her mother, but it is also quite evident that Regina often stood like a thorn in her side, entreating her daughter, again and again, to write about nicer subjects and people. During a visit from Robert Giroux, the publisher describes just such an occasion. During breakfast with mother and daughter, he was asked by Regina: "Mister Giroux, can't you get Flannery to write about nice people?"

Giroux said, "I started to laugh. But Flannery was sitting utterly deadpan. I thought, 'Uh, oh. This is serious to her.' Flannery never smiled, or raised her eyebrow, or gave me any clue."

The "small, managing indomitable mother," as Giroux later described Regina to Elizabeth Bishop, is both an important source for many of O'Connor's forbearing and unbearable mothers, and someone O'Connor saw as a force with whom she had to daily reckon, just as in her youth she had fought against the nuns and her guardian angel.

4

Despite her illness, by June 1953 O'Connor was ready to return to the Fitzgeralds', also making a day trip with Caroline Gordon to New York City. This time, the slightly older children were full of mischief, made even worse by a Yugoslav "shepherdess" brought to the US to help with the children and pets. Accordingly, life in the Fitzgerald home was more chaotic than before, and O'Connor surely found it difficult to write. Of the greatest importance, however, was a piece of information that would change her perception of everything. Gooch effectively describes the scene:

> On the way back, on a lovely summer's afternoon, she [Sally] glanced over at her passenger... [having] made up her mind, following much inner

struggle, that Flannery should know of her illness. At that instant, Flannery happened to mention her arthritis. "Flannery, you don't have arthritis," Sally said quickly. "You have lupus." Reacting to the sudden revelation, Flannery slowly moved her arm from the car door down into her lap, her hand visibly trembling. Sally felt her own knee shaking against the clutch, too, as she continued driving....

"Well, that's not good news," Flannery said, after a few silent, charged moments. "But I can't thank you enough for telling me.... I thought I had lupus, and I thought I was going crazy. I'd a lot rather be sick than crazy. ...But don't ever tell Regina you told me, because if you do she will never tell you anything else. I might want to know something else sometime."

What with the continued difficulties with the Slavic nanny, Sally being pregnant with a fifth child and turning ill, and Flannery's own contraction of a virus, O'Connor arranged for Sally's care and returned to Georgia. The lupus had been reactivated by the viral infection, further sealing O'Connor's future.

By 1954, as Erik Langkjaer reported, O'Connor was "using a stick" to help in her walks, which would be followed by her need for crutches. Yet O'Connor continued to write new stories, and by the end of that year, she promised Sally Fitzgerald a forthcoming volume of tales. By May 1955, O'Connor found herself seated before an NBC camera in New York City to discuss with Harvey Breit her upcoming collection, *A Good Man Is Hard to Find*. The book was published on June 6th.

Even in her first work, *Wise Blood*, one perceived that O'Connor's writing, at times, could be comically violent, but now, facing her own mortality, O'Connor's dark humor entered a new phase. Particularly in the title story, Flannery proffers a work in which all characters might be said to be fiends. As in so many of her fables, the major struggle in *A Good Man Is Hard to Find* is between the self-righteous societal figures, particularly represented by The Grandmother, and those outside of societal values, exemplified by The Misfit and his gang. But there is a second and more subtle battle played out in this tale between The Grandmother and the family: her son Bailey, his wife, and their two children, John Wesley and June Star. Had O'Connor written this tale a couple of years later, after she had seen Tennessee Williams' 1955 *Cat on a Hot Tin Roof* with Caroline Gordon in New York, one might suspect that the two children of this tale were based on what Maggie the Cat describes as her sister-in-law's "no-neck monsters." For the children here are true terrors, selfish, overweight brats whose major activities include dismissing the world around them and reading comic books. In his diffident hatred of his family, however, Bailey is no different, dismissive of any imagined past his mother might conjure up and determined just to survive their trip to Florida. O'Connor doesn't even name the  mother, who is described as "a young woman in slacks, whose face was as broad and innocent as a cabbage and was tied around with a green head-kerchief that had points on the top like rabbits' ears." The Grandmother, another figure clearly inspired by Regina, is a busybody, do-gooder, who has an answer for everything and believes that her values, particularly those inspired by the past, are superior to the modern world in which she has discovered herself. It is her determination to revisit a Southern Plantation she had seen earlier in her life that takes the family down the dirt road to their doom. Even her sudden revelation, as the car is propelled off the road in an accident, that the mansion she had witnessed as a child was in Tennessee, not in Georgia, does not alter for a moment her faith in her own righteousness, a belief she is convinced can be imposed upon people if spoken insistently and strongly enough. As The Misfit they discover upon this ill-fated journey takes the family away to shoot them, one by one, The Grandmother repeats over and over how she can see The Misfit is "A Good Man" at heart, who only needs to rediscover God through prayer. Unable to recognize true evil, she insists up until the moment of her death that he can be redeemed. The utterly cynical statements of The Misfit and Bobby Lee at tale's end reveal to the reader how absurd she has been in her empty faith and her shallow prescriptions for life.

> "She would of been a good woman," The Misfit said, "if it had been somebody there to shoot her every minute of her life."
> "Some fun!" Bobby Lee said.
> "Shut up, Bobby Lee," The Misfit said. "It's no real pleasure in life."

The parents of the young boy in "The River" are as ineffective as Bailey and his wife. But these figures are perhaps even more detestable in their endless partying, followed by mornings of drunken sleep. Their young son seems expendable, a child who has little to do in his life "but eat," and they are happy to surrender him to the hired black woman who intends on taking him to an old-fashioned Southern Baptism.

So dissociated from life is the child that, overhearing that the minister who he will soon see is named Bevel Summers, he tells his sitter, Mrs. Connin, that his name is Bevel, thus becoming a new being even before he is ultimately "reborn" in the river, immersed in the water as a symbol of new life.

The world where Mrs. Connin takes the child does, in fact, represent a "new life," a world completely different from his, and when he arises the next morning to discover his parents in a drunken stupor once again, he steals away from the house by himself, returning to the river to "Baptize himself and to keep on going this time until he found the Kingdom of Christ." The only witness to his death, inevitably, is a man named Mr. Paradise.

In "A Circle of Fire," another Regina-based figure, Mrs. Cope, must indeed "cope" with her hired hands, particularly the Pritchards, her current head workers. As I previously mentioned, her daughter is a Flannery-like figure, her head buried in a book throughout most of the story—except when three strangers arrive, one of them, Powell, whose family once worked on the place.

The boys have escaped their homes in Atlanta (a city despised by many of O'Connor's figures) to return to an idyll that Powell has often described to them of fresh air and riding horses. At first, Mrs. Cope attempts to placate the young men, inviting them to stay. But it quickly becomes apparent through their manners and refusal to eat what she serves that they are not at all "Good Country People," that, in fact, they are dangerous in their carelessness and sexuality. Mrs. Cope is terrified of fires, and the boys smoke, tossing their cigarettes into the grass. Her tormented daughter, moreover, is fascinated by the young men. Mrs. Cope orders them off her land, but they refuse to leave, becoming interlopers who threaten the ordered world she has created.

Like Hedda Gabler, the daughter escapes to the woods with a pistol, intending to enforce the exit her mother has been unable to accomplish. But when the boys come close to her, she grows silent with wonderment as she watches them naked, bathing in the cow trough. The boys are clearly torn in their desires to live in this rural Eden and, since it cannot belong to them, to destroy it, setting the woods afire as the girl runs home terrified of the possible desolation of her future life: "Mama, Mama, they're going to build a parking lot here!" In that mix of new sexuality and loss, she hears the whoop of the boys as if they were the Biblical boys Shadrach, Meshach, and Abednego, who, having refused to bow before the golden idol, survive Nebuchadnezzar's fiery furnace:

> She stood taut, listening, and could just catch
> in the distance a few wild shrieks of joy as if the

prophets were dancing in the fiery furnace, in the circle the angel had cleared for them.

An opposition between mother and daughter is also at the center of O'Connor's great story "Good Country People." Mrs. Hopewell does indeed "hope well," facing all of life's difficulties with her favorite clichés, "Nothing is perfect" and "That is life!" Her major sorrow, however, is her overeducated daughter, Joy, a woman with an artificial leg, who has renamed herself Hulga, in part just to irritate her well-meaning mother.

When a traveling Bible salesman arrives, Mrs. Hopewell, although having no intention of buying a Bible, politely invites the young man to dinner and, later, allows him to stay in the house. In her world of empty homilies, Mrs. Hopewell sees the young man as "Good Country People," the salt of the earth, "honest" and "genuine." Hulga, detesting her mother's refusal to see what she perceives of reality, dares the situation by arranging with the salesman, for the next day, a sexual encounter in a barn.

But the irony here is that it is not only the ridiculous Mrs. Hopewell who is duped. When the Bible salesman has deposited Hulga in the hayloft, Hulga is shocked when the boy whom she sees as a complete innocent offers her a drink out of a flask embedded in one of the Bibles, and, after cajoling her to explain how her artificial leg is attached, steals the leg, leaving her in the helpless lurch.

Although O'Connor strongly denied it, several of her critics, Gooch included, and even the traveling salesman, Erik Langkjaer, have suggested this tale is based, in part, on the friendship between her and Langkjaer. If so, the story reveals that, despite her often sardonic viewpoints, O'Connor recognized a kinship with her mother in their inability to see the "real" state of things.

"The Displaced Person" is also a story strongly based on events at Andalusia. Like Mrs. McIntyre, convinced by a local priest to hire a family displaced by World War II, Regina had hired a Polish family to work on the farm. In O'Connor's tale, the good work done by Mr. Guizac and his wife, while first greatly admired, is rewarded with fear and doubt, particularly since Mr. Guizac has little of the Southern prejudice against blacks that his employer does, and is quite willing to suggest a marriage with a family member still in Poland to a meek and uneducated black worker on the place.

As in many of the stories in *A Good Man Is Hard to Find*, a secondary cast of characters is central to the action, in this case the Shortleys who previously ran the farm, but who in their daily gossip and lack of ambition are quickly shown up by the newcomer. Their hatred of the outsiders, accordingly, is even more fervent than Mrs. McIntyre's, who cannot make up her mind to ask the displaced family to leave. When she finally gets the courage up to fire Guizac, she enters the barn just in time to witness Mr. Shortley accidently (?) driving his tractor over the Polish worker. With Guziac's death and the Shortleys' departure, Mrs. McIntyre grows ill, herself becoming a kind of displaced person on her own land, a Protestant now regularly visited by the priest explaining to her the doctrines of his church.

5

Unlike *Wise Blood*, which had received mostly negative reviews, *A Good Man Is Hard to Find* received a great deal of praise in the *Herald Tribune Book Review, The New York Times* and the *Times Book Review* (written by Caroline Gordon). *The New Yorker*, on the other hand, called the work brutal, and the *Times Literary Supplement* described it as "intense, erratic and strange." Yet it was clear that O'Connor had begun to find an audience and appreciative readers.

During this same period, O'Connor also received her first letter from a woman who would later become her closest and most regular correspondent, Betty Hester. With Hester and others, O'Connor would explain, as Gooch describes it, "her artistic intentions," building up a series of expressed concerns that she would soon use to good example in her several university lectures and in essays such as "The Church and the Fiction Writer," "Some Aspects of the Grotesque in Southern Fiction," "The Regional Writer," and "The Catholic Novelist in the Protestant South."

When Hester felt compelled to reveal to O'Connor her "history of horror," that she was dishonorably discharged from the military for "having been intimately involved with another woman," O'Connor's response, as Gooch describes it, "was immediate and caring":

> "I can't write you fast enough and tell you that it doesn't make the slightest bit of difference in my opinion of you, which is the same as it was, and that is: based solidly on complete respect." As to Betty's point about scandal, Flannery argued, "I'm obscure enough. Nobody knows or cares who I see. If it created any tension in you that I don't understand, then use your own judgment, but understand that from my point of view, you are always wanted." Flannery did suggest that they not tell Regina as "she wouldn't understand." Given the nature of their friendship, she parsed the matter theologically. "Where you are wrong is in saying

that you *are* a history of horror. The meaning of Redemption is precisely that we do not have to *be* our history."

In 1956, through the auspices of the new president of Georgia State College for Women, Robert E. Lee, Flannery met Lee's sister, Maryat Lee, a larger-than-life six-foot-tall woman, educated at National Cathedral School in Washington, D.C., who finished her MA at Union Theological Seminary under the direction of Paul Tillich, and who worked for a while for anthropologist Margaret Mead. Maryat had also written a street play in Harlem, *Dope!*, covered by *Life* magazine and selected in the 1952-53 edition of *Best Short Plays*. A bit like Rosalind Russell's version of Auntie Mame, Maryat showed up in Milledgeville "outfitted in pants, boots, a black overcoat, and an imposing Russian lamb's wool hat," bearing brown bags with cans of beer, illegal in that part of the state. Both she and O'Connor feared for their meeting. Maryat worried, since she had not read or even previously heard of O'Connor, that she would be encountering "a local lady writer." The encounter at Andalusia did not begin well, with Regina disapproving of Maryat's worn, pink sneakers and remarking that she had to keep doors locked because of "the niggahs." As the politically liberal Maryat was about to respond, however, O'Connor came thudding upon her crutches into the room and swept Maryat away into the backyard, where she explained her illness and the necessity of remaining with her mother, as well as sharing with the newcomer her dream of turning the henhouse into an office.

When Maryat finally read some of her stories, including "You Can't Be Any Poorer Than Dead," the original title for *The Violent Bear It Away*, she was, as she writes, "excited, relieved, impressed—and mystified." Thus began a correspondence between the two of over 250 epistles, many of the letters signed by or addressed to the two significant figures of O'Connor's novel with whom they identified, Maryat predictably siding with the intellectual rationalist, Rayber, O'Connor with the boy-would-be-prophet Tarwater.

Even the news that Maryat's marriage to the Australian David Foulkes-Taylor had gone astray when he met a man to whom he was attracted, and that in Tokyo, Maryat herself had fallen in love with film critic Donald Ritchie, did not alter their friendship. Only when Maryat, who in the 1970s would admit to bisexuality, wrote Flannery that she was in love with her, was there a temporary chill. Again, O'Connor did not, as Gooch describes it, "blink" about the issue of lesbianism, but she did "transpose the discussion into a more spiritual key." Speaking of the grace in the blood of Christ, O'Connor concluded her discussion: "Even if you loved Foulkes and Ritche and me and Emmet and Emmet's brother and his girl friend equally and undividedly, it all has to be put somewhere finally."

When Maryat reacted by describing O'Connor's comments as full of "pious clichés, not flesh and blood," the communications ceased for several months; but when Maryat resumed the letters, O'Connor assured her, "I am not to be got rid of by crusty letters."

During these same years, O'Connor enjoyed great creativity, writing several of the stories that would appear in her last volume, *Everything that Rises Must Converge*, but her main frustration was working through her promised novel. She had found it easy to deal with her Tarwater figure, but felt ill-at-ease with Rayber, and believed that she had some 50 pages yet to complete, without any certainty that she was up to the task.

Further clouding the waters was a planned trip, to be paid for by her cousin, Katie Seemes, to Europe on the occasion of the Lourdes Centennial. As she fumed over the enforced vacation which she feared would be made up of "fortress-footed Catholic females herded from holy place to holy place," ending in "holy exhaustion," her doctor advised that she cancel the trip because of hip deterioration, a side effect of lupus. Gooch describes O'Connor as being secretly relieved, but her cousin again intervened, offering Flannery and Regina a less exhausting itinerary, in which they would stay

 with the Fitzgeralds, now ensconced in Italy (where Robert was translating *The Odyssey*), who would accompany them to rejoin the pilgrims gathered in Paris, O'Connor had little choice but to agree.

On April 21, O'Connor and her mother flew to Idlewild Airport in New York, where they were met by a limousine that took them to Roger Straus and Sheila Cudahy, the publishing house that Robert Giroux had recently joined, where she signed a new contract for the novel. The next evening the two women were off to Italy.

After four days at the Fitzgeralds' villa, Flannery, Regina, and Sally flew to Paris, then traveled south to the region of Lourdes. Flannery had not wanted to enter the baths at Lourdes, as she had insisted before leaving on the trip that she was going as "a pilgrim, not a patient." But after Sally's insistence that Katie Seemes would be highly disappointed if O'Connor did not take part in the ritual, Flannery capitulated. Joking about the medieval hygiene of the place, she later wrote Betty, "Nobody I am sure prays in that water."

From Lourdes the group flew to Barcelona, then

left Spain on May 3rd for Rome, the highpoint of O'Connor's trip. For in Rome it was arranged for the travelers to attend a general audience with Pope Pius XII, at which time, witnessing her on her crutches, he granted her a special blessing.

The return to Georgia meant that O'Connor had to face the completion of her novel, now called *The Violent Bear It Away*, which she was determined to do with new vigor. The book, so many years in the making, finally reached the public on February 8, 1960.

In some respects, the new novel was a retelling of *Wise Blood*. Tarwater, a boy a few years younger than Hazel Motes, is raised by his preacher grandfather in rural Georgia to become a prophet of the church. In this case, however, the boy has been stolen from his family home, just as, previously, the old man tried to steal away the boy's uncle, Rayber, whose short time under the preacher's tutelage, has, he feels, tainted his entire life. He is now a rationalist, a schoolteacher who will have nothing to do with religious faith.

In the first few pages of this book, the grandfather dies, and Tarwater, a stubbornly independent child determined to find his own calling in life, is faced with the old man's request for burial. In a highly Faulknerian flourish, the body is left to rot as the young boy retreats to the preacher's still, drinking himself into unconsciousness. Awakening in a funk, Tarwater sets the house, with the old man in it, on fire and heads for the city and his uncle Rayber, the only relative remaining.

Through dreams and personal memories revealed in the first two chapters of the book, we quickly discover what life was like for Tarwater living with the old man.

Rayber's own son, Bishop, is an idiot, and when Tarwater shows up at his door, he is, at first, convinced of a new possibility in his life, a kind of redemption for his inability to deal with Bishop and his failed attempt to kill his own son early on. Imagining for himself a role similar to Holden Caulfield in *The Catcher in the Rye*, "catching thousands of little kids" from falling off a cliff, Rayber clearly intends, as we would describe it today, to "recondition" his nephew, bringing him out of the darkness of his religious mania into the light of the rational world.

But just as Motes was drawn deeper and deeper into faith the more he fought against it, so does Rayber, through his sociological jargon, clichés, and just plain American innocence, push the desperate Tarwater away, finally finding himself giving up on his end of the conversion. The book's title emanates from Matthew 11:12, "From the days of John the Baptist until now, the kingdom of heaven suffereth violence, and the violent shall bear it away." Throughout O'Connor's powerfully violent work—a book O'Connor herself described to Maryat as "grey, bruised-black, and fire-colored"— there are numerous terrifyingly surreal events. Perhaps the most cinematic (and we must remind ourselves that O'Connor was a master of visual imagery) is the revival meeting to which Tarwater, followed by a half-dressed Rayber, is drawn one night. There a young girl, Lucette, having traveled the world with her parents, powerfully preaches in a mix of Biblical poetry and lunatic-like incantation ("Leave the dead lie. The dead are dead and can stay that way. What do we want with the dead alive?"), exclaiming at the end as she points to Rayber, "a damned soul before my eye!"

Strangely, or perhaps we should say understand-ably, the most innocent figure in this tale, Bishop, is completely mesmerized by the slightly abusive elder boy, following him everywhere in a manner that is even more sexually charged than the relationship be-tween Motes and Enoch Emery. And like Enoch's final transformation, that relationship also ends in a kind a redemption when Tarwater takes the child out on the lake and, in baptizing him, frees him also into death.

Yet for Tarwater the baptism has been an accident, something against which he has desperately fought, and his only possible escape is to go back to where he has come. Yet even as he attempts to retreat to the source of his compulsion, he is determined to remain independent, to simply live off the land without becoming a prophet. His rape by a passing homosexual changes everything.

As O'Connor argues, in what Gooch describes as her "extreme theology," "Tarwater's final vision could not have been brought off if he hadn't met the man in the lavender and cream-colored car." When the Fitzgeralds suggested that perhaps the character was presented as too broadly stereotypical, O'Connor argued that she had seen just such an individual "with yellow hair and black eyelashes—you can't look more perverted than that."

In his anger for the violence against him, like the boys in "A Circle of Fire," Tarwater takes up his matches, and in mad pyromaniac dance, lights the woods afire.

But his final conversion comes only after he discovers that, instead of his ridding the world of his grandfather's body through incineration, the neighboring black laborer Buford had buried him, giving him a decent Christian funeral. The deep hunger Tarwater has long felt swells: "His hunger was so great that he could have eaten all the loaves and fishes after they were multiplied," O'Connor writes. And suddenly in the fiery whirl of the treeline, he understands his destiny as being connected with all those that have come before him, Daniel, Elijah, Moses. Returning to the city, Tarwater has becomes a true prophet of God.

For a non-believer like myself, this fiction is not an easy read. Yet, strangely, I find it her most powerful work, in part because of the intricacy of the story, which follows the mindsets of its various characters, its fantastic apocalyptic imagery, and its comically surreal dialogue. Finally, one must remember what O'Connor herself insisted: her works were not psychological realist pictures of life in the South, but, as Hawthorne described his fictions, romances, a possibility for fiction that lay outside of a presentation of social forces. Allying herself with the "grotesque," O'Connor writes in "Some Aspects of the Grotesque in Southern Fiction":

> In these grotesque works, we find that the writer has made alive some experience which we are not accustomed to observe every day, or which the ordinary man may never experience in his ordinary life. We find that connections which we would expect in the customary kind of realism have been ignored, that there are strange skips and gaps which anyone trying to describe manners and customs would certainly not have left. Yet the characters in these novels are alive in spite of these things. They have an inner coherence, if not always a coherence to their social framework. Their fictional qualities lean away from typical social patterns, toward mys-

tery and the unexpected.

The reviews for *The Violent Bear It Away* were, predictably, given the dominant values of the realist fiction of the day, quite negative, describing the author as a "literary white witch," as belonging to "The School of Southern Degeneracy." Invoking images of the "Hillbilly South," the *Time* review even went so far as to accuse the author for being negative because she suffers from lupus "that forces her to spend part of her life on crutches." O'Connor, so Gooch tells us, felt particularly violated by that review: "My lupus has no business in literary considerations."

6

Over the past few years, O'Connor had written a sizable number of new stories, but she now found herself, in 1962, at a kind "creative impasse," and, as Gooch describes it, she began to reappraise her life.

The year before she had looked forward to a hip operation that might have allowed her to walk without crutches. Her current regimen of cortisone and Novocain lasted only temporarily. But her doctor advised against the surgery in fear that it might reactivate her lupus. Her relationship with Betty Hester was also strained when her friend announced her intentions to leave the church, a decision which O'Connor attributed to Betty's reading of Iris Murdoch.

Although she was certainly heartened by Farrar, Straus, and Cudahy's decision to reissue *Wise Blood*, O'Connor could not bring herself to write a new note to the book and, instead, wrote a disclaimer, describing the work as "a comic novel about a Christian *malgré lui*, and as such, very serious," words which, as any publisher might realize, would scare away most readers.

O'Connor did travel, reading and lecturing at several Southern universities, including East Texas State, the University of Southeast Louisiana, and Loyola, the New Orleans trip including a meeting with Alabama novelist Walker Percy.

Yet work on a new novel, "Why Do the Heathen Rage?," was at a standstill. As she wrote her friend John Hawkes, "I have been working all summer just like a squirril on a treadmill, trying to make something of Walter and his affairs and the heathens that rage, but I think this is maybe not my material (don't like that word)."

In a doctor's waiting room that fall, however, the writer's block finally ended. There in the room she found her country women that make up the marvelous story "Revelation," a story she completed within eight weeks. Planning a new collection of stories, she wrote Giroux, asking for the addition of the new work.

Already in winter 1963 O'Connor had a fainting spell on account of a low blood count. But as Gooch quite forthrightly declares, "In truth, she had begun the long, slow process of dying." In February she was told that she needed a hysterectomy to remove a fibroid tumor, an operation that was, at first, declared a great success. But in two weeks time she was back in bed, and by late March she clearly comprehended that "something was gravely wrong." Forced to take a new regimen of drugs, O'Connor found her body covered with the lupus rash. Unable to use the typewriter, she was forced to begin writing stories in her head, including a rewriting of her early tale, "The Geranium," which in *Everything That Rises Must Converge* would become "Judgment Day."

In early July she returned home, but had little energy to crawl out of bed. Receiving the local priest for communion, she asked that he also give her the sacrament of Extreme Unction. For the rest of the month, she struggled to type up "Judgment Day" and another new story, "Parker's Back." But soon, even those few hours were impossible to maintain. After three coronary arrests, her doctor refused to make further house calls, putting her on a heavy dose of antibiotics. On July 28th O'Connor wrote her last letter, a note to Maryat beginning "Dear Raybat" and ending "Cheers, Tarfunk."

On August 3rd, O'Connor died.

Her funeral was scheduled for the very next morning, and, accordingly, many of her closest friends, including the Fitzgeralds, discovered that she had died days later through newspaper obituaries.

Many critics argue that O'Connor's greatest work was the collection published shortly after her death, *Everything That Rises Must Converge*. And several of these stories are, indeed, masterworks. Yet I find that O'Connor's major concerns are repeated here rather than further developed, making all of her writing of one brilliant piece.

Like Hulga in "Good Country People," the young son, Julian, of the title story is a frustrated intellectual, out of place in the homey world of clichés and myths in which his mother lives. Yet, despite his education, he has found no employment and is dependent upon the small income of his mother.

Several of O'Connor's fables skirt issues of race relationships, but in the Teilhardian-titled tale she meets the issue head-on as Julian's bigoted mother is forced to come face to face with a black woman, whose head is topped with the same hat. While the son's smug pleasure in his mother's discomfort might delight O'Connor's liberal readers, the tragic results of that encounter are equivocal, as Julian's mother, attempting to award the black woman's child with a penny, is accosted by the stranger. Delighted by the "lesson" he imagines his mother has received in the encounter, Julian must suddenly face her flight and death by heart attack. The final lines ironically put him and the absurd situation in its place: "The tide of darkness seemed to

sweep him back to her, postponing from moment to moment his entry into the world of guilt and sorrow."

Similarly, the Regina-like Mrs. May of "Greenleaf," unforgiving of the behavior of her worker, Mr. Greenleaf, and his two sons farming nearby, ends in a come-uppance that does not expiate the actions of the other characters. The Greenleaf boys' bull has entered Mrs. May's property, and she wants it immediately removed, convinced they are lazy no-gooders and unable to keep up an excellently-run farm like her own. Yet even upon her discovery that their farm is far more up-to-date and cleaner than hers, the bull on the loose seems to justify all her petty doubts about those she deems socially inferior. Her huff-and-puff philosophy, however, seems almost to wear her out, as, determined to rid her farm of the bull, she drives her car to the center of the field only to suddenly find herself inordinately tired. Her sleep might almost be seen as the exhaustion of a whole way of life, a life of determined independence founded on small-minded striations in the social fabric of her community. And her final goring by the bull is not only a kind of ritual killing of this small-minded matador, but a revelation of the sexual prowess of a new generation (a "green leaf").

> She did not hear the shots but she felt the quake of the huge body as it sank, pulling her forward on its head, so that it seemed, when Mr. Greenleaf reached her, to be bent over whispering some last discovery into the animal's ear.

In many respects, "Revelation" is a kind of interweaving of the two themes I have noted above. Once again we witness a battle between an intelligent offspring, this time represented as a young woman awaiting a doctor's appointment, and her well-meaning but cliché-spouting mother. Into this minefield steps what may be O'Connor's most opinionated character ever, Mrs. Turpin, who not only shares the well-dressed mother's jargon, but has created a complex social-stratification topped by wealthy individuals and bottomed by "white trash." As Mrs. Turpin insists throughout the tale, she would rather be a "nigger" than a trashy white woman.

The pleasure of this story is O'Connor's dead-on dialogue, both in Mrs. Turpin's inner thoughts and the two ladies' comments. So settled are they in their absurd formulas of life that by story's end the reader may want, as Mary Grace does, to slug Mrs. Turpin in the face. Yet it is not so much what Mary Grace does, but what she *says* that astounds and troubles the older woman. The girl's cry, "Go back to hell where you came from, you old wart hog," shakes Mrs. Turpin's sense of reality more than any possible event she might have encountered and simply judged.

For one of the few times in O'Connor's work, moreover, this violent act does not result in death or potential destruction, but ends in a beatific revelation for Mrs. Turpin, whose entire system of societal values is suddenly overturned as she witnesses, in an apocalyptic vision, the true meaning of a forgiving Christ:

> There were whole companies of white-trash, clean for the first time in their lives, and bands of black niggers in white robes, and battalions of freaks and lunatics shouting and clapping and leaping like frogs. And bringing up the end of the procession was a tribe of people who she recognized at once as those who, like herself and Claud, had always had a little of everything and the God-given wit to use it right. ...They alone were on key. Yet she could see

by their shocked faces that even their virtues were being burned away.

In some senses, one could almost use that vision to describe the entire range of blacks, freaks, lunatics, and "good people" who inhabit O'Connor's fiercely satirical fictions, all of them redeemed in the blood of the lamb.

LOS ANGELES, AUGUST 3, 2009 (THE 46TH ANNIVERSARY OF O'CONNOR'S DEATH); SEPTEMBER 1-7, 2009

The method I used to organize the above essay reflects the process of my reading. I read Gooch's O'Connor biography in sections, each time reading up until his announcement of the publication of a new O'Connor book, then pausing to read the work itself. Accordingly, I metaphorically "lived through" the author's life and writing for a period of approximately two months. The writing, as is apparent from the dates, also took about a month longer to explore the mind of Flannery O'Connor. Most of the facts of her life are directly repeated from the Gooch biography, but I have incorporated a few other details from her letters and Sally Fitzgerald's chronology published in The Library of America's Flannery O'Connor: Collected Works. *The comments on her fictions are, for the most part, my own. In this one instance, I did not wade through the mass of*

essays and books written about the author for further elu-
cidation and critical support; rather, I felt it important to
react to these powerful works in a personal, unscholarly
way. Accordingly, my own perceptions may not be par-
ticularly original and are certainly not exhaustive, but
are merely meant to present immediate responses to her
writing.

I should add that, although I never met O'Connor
(I was only 17 at the time of her death), I read her work
as early as 1966 or 1967 at the University of Wiscon-
sin, and I taught a couple of her books in a course titled
"Avant-Garde Contemporary Fiction"—along with fig-
ures such as Djuna Barnes, John Hawkes, and Jane and
Paul Bowles—as a graduate student at the University of
Maryland in the early to mid-1970s.

A couple of insignificant parallels also bring me spiri-
tually closer to O'Connor. She attended the University of
Iowa a couple of years before my birth, when my father
was a student at the University of Northern Iowa in Ce-
dar Falls. But only two or three years after she left Iowa,
my family moved to a small town quite near Iowa City,
an area where I grew up and remained throughout high
school. Working on his Master's Degree in the summers,
my father suffered courses in the same overheated Quon-
set huts where O'Connor had taken some of her writing
courses. The head of the writing program, Paul Engle,
moreover, was later well-known in our home as a poet:

for a few years in the early 1960s my parents, themselves not readers of poetry, chose his books such as An Old-Fashioned Christmas *and* A Woman Unashamed and Other Poems *as Christmas gifts for their literarily pretentious son.*

Finally, Sheila Cudahy, the third publisher of Farrar, Straus, and Cudahy before editor Robert Giroux replaced her, was also a writer of fiction and poetry and a translator of Natalia Ginzburg. In 1993 or 1994 Cudahy sent me a new collection of her tales, Crow Time, *which my Sun & Moon Press published in 1995.*

LOS ANGELES, SEPTEMBER 8, 2009
Reprinted from *EXPLORING* fictions (September 2009).

Rara Avis

ARISTOPHANES **THE BIRDS**, IN **THREE COMEDIES**,
EDITED BY WILLIAM ARROWSMITH (ANN ARBOR: THE
UNIVERSITY OF MICHIGAN PRESS, 1969)

WALTER BRAUNFELS **DIE VÖGEL/THE BIRDS**, LA
OPERA, CONDUCTED BY JAMES CONLON / THE PERFOR-
MANCE HOWARD FOX AND I ATTENDED WAS THE LOS
ANGELES PREMIERE, APRIL 11, 2009

ON APRIL 11, 2009 my companion Howard and I attended the Los Angeles Opera premiere of composer
Walter Braunfels' *The Birds*, an opera performed as part
of their "Recovered Voices" series devoted to bringing
attention to "lost operas," operas banned by the Nazis
and neglected since.

Braunfels was certainly not the typical banned artist. Although part-Jewish, Braunfels had converted to
Christianity after serving in World War I, an experience
which transformed his view of life. The opera, begun
before the war and finished after, premiered in Munich
in 1920 and received at least 50 performances over the

next few years. With its Wagnerian and Strauss-like harmonies, and its restatement of Germanic Romantic values, the opera, indeed, might have nicely served the Nazi cause had it not been that Braunfels was adamantly anti-fascist, refusing to write an anthem for Hitler. His music, accordingly, was labeled as "Degenerate" (*Entartete Kunst*), and he was removed from his position as co-director of the Hochschule für Musik Köln (the Cologne Academy of Music); Braunfels waited out World War II in Switzerland, returning to a postwar world in which his music appeared old-fashioned and completely out of touch with its time.

Yet, as several music critics have observed, there is a shimmering beauty to *The Birds* that creates a comforting sense of homage to Wagner and Strauss which easily enchants its audience. Based loosely on Aristophanes' hilarious satire of Athenian society, Braunfels' version follows the journey of Good Hope and Loyal Friend to visit the leader of the birds, Hoopoe, paralleling Pisthetairos' sudden inspiration—stimulated, in part, by his fear that he and his friend will be killed by the skeptical avians if the birds regain their rightful place as rulers of the heavens by rising up against the gods and building a heavenly walled city in the sky. As in Aristophanes' play, Cloudcukooland is built and the birds, delighted with their success, award Pisthetairos (Braunfels' Loyal Friend) with their friendship and wings.

In Aristophanes' work, however, the building of the great city brings on a plague of visitors, each satirizing an aspect of Athenian society; Good Hope in the ancient version of the play is all but lost as Pisthetairos, one by one, mocks and wittily dismisses his "enemies," and, even outfoxing Zeus, marries the figure who translator William Arrowsmith describes as "Miss Universe."

From the evidence of his Act I, Braunfels may have originally intended to more closely follow Aristophanes, but Act II of his opera diverts the focus of the work away from Loyal Friend's grand schemes by having Good Hope fall in love with the song and being of the Nightingale, resulting in one of the most memorable of the opera's duets, in this performance sung by tenor Brandon Jovanovich and soprano Désirée Rancatore. Braunfels further imbues Cloudcukooland with Utopian possibilities by adding a marriage ceremony and dance between Miss Dove and Mr. Pigeon (Yvette Tucker and Seth Belliston).

Omitting the series of visiting troublemakers to Cloudcukooland, Braunfels focuses instead on the mythic possibilities of the bird kingdom and the

birds' *hubris* in attempting to rise up against the gods. Whereas Aristophanes' Prometheus comes to Cloud-cukooland to warn his human friend, Pisthetairos, suggesting how he might outwit Zeus, Braunfels' Prometheus (brilliantly sung by Brian Mulligan) is more like Strauss' John the Baptist, a prophet crying in the wilderness.

The terrifying storm of lightning Zeus reigns down upon the upstart kingdom reduces the birds and humans involved to the twittering, fearful creatures they had been at the beginning of the work. The Utopian world sought by Good Hope and Loyal Friend has been destroyed, perhaps Braunfels' presentiment that the Weimar Republic would not survive. Certainly he would not be the first German-language writer to pre-

dict the dangers that lay ahead; two years after the premiere of *The Birds*, Austrian writer Joseph Roth wrote a scathingly realistic portrait of the conspiracies of the radical right in his novel *The Spider's Web*.

Yet Braunfels' work—with Good Hope's final insistence that his encounter with nature has changed him, healed him perhaps, an experience that will remain with him forever—merely reiterates the Germanic Romanticism that lay behind so many of the Nazi ideals. And in that sense, the dream of a militaristically-determined city-state, as presented in Braunfels' conception, may reveal the desire of another generation.

LOS ANGELES, APRIL 16, 2009
Reprinted from *US Theater, Opera, and Performance* (April 2009).

Beverly Hills Housewife

ON SATURDAY, January 3, 2009, the world lost one its "great ladies"—as Earl Powell III, the former director of the Los Angeles County Museum of Art, once described Betty Freeman. She died in her Beverly Hills home at the age of 87 of pancreatic cancer.

Born as Betty Wishnick, the daughter of a wealthy chemical engineer, Betty grew up in Brooklyn and New Rochelle, New York before studying music at Wellesley College. Upon graduating, she married the investor Stanley Freeman, moving with him to Los Angeles, where they had four children.

Like so many wealthy citizens of Beverly Hills, Betty could have easily spent the rest of her life as the "housewife" type, as David Hockney had portrayed her, a woman living in relative ease in her well-appointed home. And, in fact, Betty remained in that famed house for the rest of her life.

Yet Betty was anything but the iconic image Hockney had portrayed in his 1966 painting. In 1964, two

years earlier, she met the American composer and inventor of unusual instruments, Harry Partch, who was living in his car. Freeman provided him with a studio and covered his living expenses for ten years until his death in 1974. She had already taken a great interest in contemporary music, and in 1961 contributed to the bail-out of Fluxus composer La Monte Young, who had been arrested on marijuana charges in Connecticut. He responded by dedicating a work to her.

The same year that she encountered Partch, she became the producer of a new music series at the Pasadena Museum of Art (now the Norton Simon Museum of Art). In 1969, she underwrote Partch's opera *Delusion of the Fury* at the University of California, Los Angeles. And so began a philanthropic endeavor that included support to most of the great experimental composers of her time, including Elliott Carter, Philip Glass, John

Cage, Pierre Boulez, Harrison Birtwistle, Steve Reich, Lou Harrison, Kaija Saaiaho, and John Adams, whose opera *Nixon in China* was dedicated to her.

While producing a documentary about Partch in 1972, she was asked to help with the photographs, which resulted in a new career of photographing noted musicians, works later shown in galleries and published in several books.

In the early 1980s Betty began celebrating her musician friends through salons in her Beverly Hills home. My companion Howard and I attended several of those events, including one for John Adams, another celebrating a series of pieces written for singer Joan La-Barbara, a performance of works by Gordon Getty, and others. Being able to hear the composer and performers in the intimate space of a large living room was a memorable experience, and Howard and I always felt saddened when we were unable to attend. After these Salotti, Betty's second husband, the Italian artist Franco Assetto, would serve up large bowls of pasta and salad, accompanied by various drinks. Guests would mingle, discussing what they had just heard with one another, the composers, and performers. It was at one such event that I first met director Peter Sellars. The salons ended with Assetto's 1991 death.

Over the years Betty became a dear friend who, at times, would invite us over for small dinners, usually

 with one or two others. I recall that one evening she invited us upstairs to her bedroom to listen to *Nixon in China*.

While Freeman was a magnanimous individual, with the ability to inspire a true dedication to the new, she was not without her eccentricities. People who attended more traditional concerts with her found her intolerant of older work. And in the last years of her life she had seemingly abandoned American composers for contemporary European figures, which understandably upset many friends.

In October or November of 2006, Betty called me, suggesting a luncheon to discuss some new projects she was considering publishing. The day of the luncheon she called, saying she had just broken her foot! We met, accordingly, at her home a few weeks later on December 28.

The glorious Beverly Hills home had been radically altered. We dined on excellent take-out food, but the kitchen was overwhelmed by piles of dirty dishes. Obviously, the maid had not been in for several days. The grand hallway was filled with piles of photographs and various applications for musical aid.

She took me upstairs to her study. She had three

books which she was interested in publishing. One was a semi-critical study of the art of her friend Sam Francis, the second a collection of interviews by music critic Alan Rich of the figures who had appeared in her Salotti, and the third a book of reproductions of visually entertaining faxes sent to her over the years by director Robert Wilson.

I explained to her that I was not the right publisher to do the Francis book, but that the other two were interesting projects, particularly the interviews with the musicians. She seemed, however, more engaged in placing musicians within the context of her salons (each section was introduced by the salon invitation, often hand-corrected and of little visual interest) than in Rich's interviews with the artists.

A call to Alan Rich revealed that he had been somewhat frustrated by Betty's focus, and that he would rather move ahead with the book without her. I had lunch with him a few weeks later, and we signed an agreement for the work in which we would explain the context of these interviews in an introduction rather than reproduced invitations.

Betty was still interested, however, in publishing the Wilson book—which she wanted to be published in the size of the large 8" x 12" faxes (an idea from which I tried to dissuade her)—and called me in late March of 2008, proposing another meeting which, unfortunately, because of my procrastination and my own illness soon after, never took place.

Our last encounter with Betty was at the opening on May 9, 2007 of *Dan Flavin: A Retrospective* at the Los Angeles County Museum of Art. Betty, in a wheelchair propelled by a young man, was radiating with joy before the artist's fluorescent tubes of blood-red lights. "Isn't this just glorious?" she rhetorically asked. She literally glowed against the banks of Flavin's lights, convincing me, in fact, that everything was glorious. I leaned over to kiss her as she almost giggled with delight.

Betty was one of the most gracious women I have ever known, a woman who had a passion for life, and who was a grand and original philanthropist who contributed to music and art not only with money, but with her heart.

LOS ANGELES, JANUARY 13, 2009
Reprinted from *Green Integer Blog* (January 2009).

Why the Hell Did You Come?

HARRY PARTCH **PARTCH DARK, PARTCH LIGHT,**
PERFORMED BY THE PARTCH GROUP AT REDCAT (ROY
AND EDNA DISNEY/CALARTS THEATER) IN THE WALT
DISNEY CONCERT HALL ON MAY 29, 2009

A TRUE AMERICAN musical maverick similar in some respects to Charles Ives, composer Harry Partch was born, the son of Presbyterian missionaries, in Oakland, California in June 1901. Much of his youth was spent in

isolated Arizona and New Mexico towns, where, reportedly, he heard and sang songs in Spanish, several American-Indian languages, and Mandarin, sung to him by his mother, who had spent time in China.

He attended the University of Southern California in Los Angeles with the intention of a musical career; but in 1925 he discovered the book *On the Sensations of Tone* by the German physician and physicist Hermann Helmholtz, a study of the psychological effects of musical tones, and soon after dropped out of school to study by himself, exploring the musicality of speech and constructing his own instruments that "underscored the intoning voice." As Partch wrote:

> I came to the realization that the spoken word was the distinctive expression my constitutional makeup was best fitted for, and that I needed other scales and other instruments. This was the positive result of self-examination—call it intuitive, for it was not the result of any intellectual desire to pick up lost or obscure historical threads. For better or for worse, it was an emotional decision.

His first instrument was the "Monophone," an "adapted viola," which later joined with numerous others including The Diamond Marimba, The Quadrangularis Reversum, the 11-key Bass Marimba, Bamboo Marimbas (nicknamed "Boo" and "Boo II"), Cloud Chamber Bowls, an instrument he called "The Spoils of War" (which included Cloud Chamber Bowls, artillery shell casings, metal whang-guns, and wooden piecings), The

Gourd Tree and Cone Gongs, a xylophone augmented with tuned liquor bottles and hubcaps (The Zymo-Xyl), Kitharas, and Harmonic Canons (played with fingers, picks or mallets).

Receiving a Carnegie grant in the early 1930s, Partch traveled to London, meeting the great Irish poet William Butler Yeats, who game him permission to set his translation of Sophocles' *Oedipus* as an opera. Transcribing the inflections of the Abbey Theatre actors, Partch performed his piece on Monophone, intoning "By the Rivers of Babylon." Yeats was delighted by the effects.

Yet the grant soon ran out, and the following year, 1935, Partch returned to the US at the height of the Great Depression, and lived for nine years wandering as a hobo, doing odd jobs and designing his instruments.

Important works of this period were "Dark Brother," performed at the concert I saw by the Partch Group, and a piece from Thomas Wolfe's "God's Lonely Man," which reiterates Partch's own sense of isolation and separateness. Most of Partch's relationships were with males, and his feelings of disengagement with the whole of society were obviously intense.

Yet many of the works of this period are brilliantly comical, including the "Yankee Doodle Fantasy," sung in accompaniment with tin oboes and other instruments, that satirizes patriotism, serious club women, and even his 43-tone note system. Similarly lighter Partch pieces, two based on James Joyce's *Finnegans Wake*, "Isobel" of 1944 and "Annah the Allmaziful" of the same year, were, along with his utterly charming tribute to Lewis Carroll's "Jabberwocky," ("O Frabjous Day!"), highlights of the evening.

One of Partch's most strange yet arresting works is his *Barstow: Eight Hitchhiker Inscriptions*, based on messages left by hitchhikers just outside the Mojave Desert junction of Barstow:

> The scribbling is in pencil. It is on one of the white highway railings just outside the Mojave Desert junction of Barstow, California. I am walking along the highway and sit down on the railing to rest.
>
> Idly I notice the scratches where I happen to drop. I have seen many hitchhikers' writings. they are usually just names and addresses—there are literally millions of them, or meaningless obscenities, on the highway signs, railings, walls.
>
> But this—why, it's music. It's both weak and strong, like unedited human expressions always are. It's eloquent in what it fails to express in words. And it's epic. Definitely, it is music....

Indeed, upon first hearing each of these numbered pieces, presented in a *sprechstimme*-like performance by guitarist John Schneider, the words are almost laughable. But Partch allows us after the original statement to hear the echoes of those words, by repeating them with emotionally-charged aftertones and dramatic additions ("ha-ha-ha," "dum-de-dum," etc.) that

transform them into haunting expressions of fear and joy. The first one, for example, begins with a young man returning to Boston, Massachusetts, wishing he were dead, yet oddly adding, "Today I Am a Man." Is his manhood defined by his desire for death or by some sexual encounter that he has recently had? There is no one answer; but the echo of the two, filled in by Partch's joyful exclamations, alters the whole, and suddenly what might have been simple banality is awash with glorious possibilities.

Similarly, the young girl of "Considered Pretty," whose name and Las Vegas address appear merely to be a sexual invitation, is transformed by the final statement: "objective matrimony," while the sly admission that she is "considered pretty" pulls at our hearts when connected with her obvious desires.

"Jesus Was God in the Flesh" begins as a simple

announcement of belief, repeated over and over like a prayerful charm song instead of a statement of faith. "You Lucky Woman" recounts the self-described charms of a passing man, whose braggadocio might be completely disgusting were it not for his final challenge to the opposite sex that "all you have to do is find me." And the final piece "Why in Hell Did You Come?" is shouted out almost in irritation for those hitchhiking complaints of the writer and others suffering the itinerant life. Yet in that ironic cry we hear the numerous echoes of drifters catalogued by John Steinbeck, Woody Guthrie, and others.

The evening began with *Eleven Intrusions* of 1950, written while Partch was staying in Gualala, on California's northern coast, at a ranch owned by pianist Gunnar Johansen. There, among the redwoods, Partch created many of his instruments and worked in relative splendor in comparison to his earlier days. But the isolation apparently became oppressive, and these Japanese-inspired works, almost haiku-like studies—each piece generally performed by two instruments that present a sequence of microtonal dissonances—of a rose, a crane, a waterfall, the wind, the street, the lover, soldiers, and other concerns, reveal the darkness of a life that formerly seemed to be able to survive great deprivation.

This was, I am sorry to say, my first encounter with the music of Harry Partch, a man who, as I describe above, was rescued later in his life by my friend Betty Freeman. It will not, however, be my last Partch concert. And the day after this event I listened with wonderment to Partch's "Two Studies on Ancient Greek Scales" and, again, to *Barstow* on the record *Just West Coast* with great pleasure.

LOS ANGELES, MAY 31, 2009
Reprinted from *USTheater, Opera, and Performance* (June 2009).

Barnyard Philosophers

LEE BREUER (TEXT AND DIRECTION) **PATAPHYSICS PENYEACH: SUMMA DRAMATICA** AND **PORCO MORTO** / PERFORMED AS PART OF THE UNDER THE RADAR FESTIVAL, NEW YORK / MABOU MINES / THE PERFORMANCES I SAW WERE AT A MATINEE ON SUNDAY, JANUARY 18, 2009

AFTER THE WEAK performances I had witnessed one night earlier in a Broadway theater, I was delighted to catch actor Ruth Maleczech's marvelous acting as Sri Moo Parahamsa, the first bovine to lecture at the Gifford lectures of William James in Scotland. As if she herself had four stomachs, each with a different voice attached, Maleczech divertingly argues, in pure pataphysical nonsense, that the post-performance animal should take acting lessons, and proceeds, in a heady mix of scientific jargon and an oddly logical argument based on the existence of the "triune brain," to say that all animals should "Know Thyself":

As an academic, a mammal, and a cow, I know I
  have a soul
And since I do not have a neocortex, it must not
  reside therein
It's my thesis—and I'll go to the mat with a lizard
  on this point—that *psyche* lives in the *limbus*
    Reality is not real, it is virtual
    Each mind has its game and virtualities
      are subject each to their own laws
    The neocortex to the laws of reason,
      the reptilian spinal stem adheres to
      chaos theory
    and as for the hedonic—limbic laws are,
      in the vulgate vernacular, *showbiz*
    "Know Thyself" says the Delphic oracle
    Well, to "know itself" the post-
      performance animal should take an
      acting lesson

The school, of course, is her own: The Institute for the
Science of the Soul, a fully accredited acting conservatory ranked in the top 10 by *US News and World Report*!

  A zany satire on various acting methods ("A Strasberg, a Meisner and an Adler may differ in approach, /
But Methodists generally agree that the spiritual script
breaks into actions and objectives"), "Summa Dramatica" ends with a recovering animation, Marge Simpson,

testifying on screen to the value of Sri Moo Parahamsa's Institute, letting loose a hilarious send up of phrases such as "truth is beauty." This delicious monologue (or, if we count Marge as a "true" character, we must describe it as a dialogue) ends with the new barnyard post-performance conclusion that "The Greeks have been in denial for 3,000 years / The Truth is not beautiful."

Poor Porco, the wonderful puppet of Breuer's loony imagination, has just committed suicide, and in a valedictory ode from the grave admits that he could no longer stand living, obsessed as he had become with the great Grey Lady, *The New York Times*. Although he attended the famed bovine-run "Institute" for a while, he left it doomed by the "Sick Fiction Syndrome," destined to end its days as a replay of a subplot to *The Lion King*.

Breuer's satire here at times seems so broad-reaching that it does not always hit its mark, but when Breuer's language does hit home, it takes us all aback, as we are shamed by our easy acceptance of mediocre journalism as a "true" presentation of life. Recalling his feelings upon first meeting The Grey Lady, Porco proclaims:

What did I feel, Grey Lady I felt vivid!

O the torture, the spins, the needles, the pins. The
    creative dilemmas....
What music of my heart should underscore what
    angle of your face?
What did I feel Grey Lady? I felt "life-like"
The Times was a beautiful vagina that in my
    hubris I engorged with every *cunilingual* wag
    of my tongue
Your vibrations were histronic!
There was drama in the air—tragedy—and it was
    generational
The New York Times was going through
    menopause

...

Later:

I am a New York Times creation, American un-
    emancipated
I am a tabloid's love slave.

How hilarious, accordingly, to have read a few days
later, in the Grey Lady herself, a review expressing the
following:

So there's this pig, see, and he lives for The
New York Times. After a romantic affair with the
Gray Lady, they commit suicide together with a

"Diamond Sutra dagger," but not before the pig, played by a puppet, offers a few sweet nothings to a stack of newspapers.

...If you're trying to figure out what is going on here in "Porco Morto,"...you're not the only one.... It stars animal puppets and features a lot of bad puns, pretentious jargon ("normative soulfulness"?), some jokey video and barely coherent mockery of commercialism and this news organization.

Luckily Porco's no longer around to engage in conversation with his former love. Breuer couldn't have written a sillier response. As Mac Wellman once admitted, the surreal events of his plays are generally based on news articles; "you couldn't make them up!"

I was happy to admit, upon Sri Moo Parahamsa's urging: "I pledge allegiance to the hype."

LOS ANGELES, FEBRUARY 15, 2009
Reprinted from *US Theater, Opera, and Performance* (February 2009).

Stage and Street

STEFAN BRECHT **THE THEATRE OF VISIONS: ROB-ERT WILSON** (NEW YORK: SUHRKAMP VERLAG, 1978)

STEFAN BRECHT **QUEER THEATRE** (NEW YORK: METHUEN, 1986)

STEFAN BRECHT **POEMS** (SAN FRANCISCO: CITY LIGHTS, 1978)

STEFAN BRECHT **8TH AVENUE POEMS** (NEW YORK: SPUYTEN DUYVIL, 2006)

THEATER HISTORIAN AND POET Stefan Brecht died, at the age of 84, on April 13th of this year. The son of German playwright Bertolt Brecht and actress Helene Wiegel, Stefan was born in Berlin, and came to the United States at the age of 17, when his family escaped Nazi Germany by moving to Santa Monica, California, where they joined the growing German émigré community. When his family returned to Germany after Bertolt Brecht was forced to testify before the House Un-American Activities Committee, Stefan remained in California, attending UCLA and, later, Harvard,

 where he received his PhD in Philosophy.

In 1966 he moved to New York City with his wife Mary McDonough Brecht and his two children, quickly becoming involved in the burgeoning experimental theater groups in lower Manhattan. Brecht performed with the theatrical performance artists Robert Wilson and Charles Ludlam in his Ridiculous Theatrical Company.

In 1972 Brecht published a book detailing several of Wilson's performances titled *The Theatre of Visions: Robert Wilson*, printed in English by the German publishing house Suhrkamp Verlag, thus beginning what was to have been a nine-volume series of presentations of what he described as "original" theater: "The Original Theatre of the City of New York: From the Mid-60s to the Mid-70s." The mind boggles just thinking about Brecht's grand project, outlined as follows:

Book 1. The theatre of visions: Robert Wilson.
Book 2. Queer theatre.
Book 3. Richard Foreman's diary theatre. Theatre as personal phenomenology of mind.
Book 4. Morality plays. Peter Schumann's Bread

and Puppet theatre.

Book 5. Theatre as psycho-therapy for performers.
  A. Joe Chaikin's Open Theatre. The Becks'
     Living Theatre.
  B. Richard Schechner's Performance Group.
     Andre Gregory's Manhattan Repertory
     Company. With notes on Grotowski
     and Andre Serban.

Book 6. The 1970s hermetic theatre of the
  performing director. Jared Bark, Stuart
  Sherman, John Zorn, Melvin Andringa.
  With appendices on Ann Wilson, Robert
  Whitman and Wilford Leach.

Book 7. Theatre as collective improvisation. The
  Mabou Mines.

Book 8. Black theatre and music. With notes on
  the Duo Theatre and M. Van Peebles.

Book 9. Dance. Merce Cunningham, Yvonne
  Rainer, Meredith Monk, Douglas Dunn.
  With a note on Ping Chong.

One can only imagine, had he accomplished this project, how much richer would be the history of our cultural heritage. As it happened, Brecht was able only to complete three of these volumes, *The Theatre of Visions: Robert Wilson, Queer Theatre,* and *Peter Schumann's Bread and Puppet Theatre.* At the time of his death he was working on the Richard Foreman study.

To call these books "studies," however, would be inappropriate. Each of the volumes differs from the others, but all combine painstaking detail with an often irritating style that frequently overwhelms the works he is attempting to describe.

The Robert Wilson book, for example, consists of minute-by-minute descriptions of the performances, along with charts and maps, and Wilson's own notes that take us through each production. These detailed descriptions, moreover, share each page with long footnotes describing events in even greater detail and explaining variations in the text.

Brecht's description of Wilson's renowned *Einstein on the Beach*, for example, begins:

K 151
18.31
On the horizontal grey rectangle of the drop, (ft 52: American premiere of Robert Wilson's and Phil Glass' *Einstein on the Beach*: November 21, 1976, at the New York Metropolitan Opera. I am here describing the second performance, in the same place, the following Sunday, Nov. 28th, but include data re the first), doubly framed in black, enormous, at the lower right a smaller, fatter, almost square rectangle, pasted to it, projector light that seems to spill over, a white rug, on the floor beneath the two women seated in front of

it, a Caucasian, the dancer Lucinda Childs) and a Negro (Sheryl Sutton, a Wilsonian performer),the latter immobile, hands in lap, the former, within the maintained pose, shifting: contrast of self-contained quietude in concentration to tension imperfectly imposed on nervous agitation. (ft 53: Wilson has maintained them in this contrast, analogous, relative to light, to that of back to white, through the play except for the concluding >knee< (tho' act IV is such as to preclude its being in evidence). Self-contained black is to Wilson not negative. It is his own color.) *A sustained organ note, the space-filling sound of a present awareness, accompanies it (in the pit, by pale-green lights, the console awareness of an electric organ is visible).*

All that in the very first moment of the work! After 59 pages of that kind of writing, on some of which there is only one line of text, the rest given over to footnotes, one feels utterly exhausted, although perhaps one can conjure up the "vision" at the heart of Wilson's piece. Yet Brecht's conclusion to all his attentive description is a simple thumbs-down dismissal of the work:

> Wilson failed to find images for what was on his mind. The themes he hit on do not relate to the content. He changed his style to divorce the spectacle from its content. Watching it, we see the

meaningless alternation of meaningless themes, and perhaps the theme of failure.

Arguably, it may be beneficial to have such a thorough historian treat his work with a kind of love-hate relationship. For all of his obvious devotion to the experimental theater on which he writes, Brecht never makes easy assumptions.

For example, in *Queer Theatre*, he maintains that as the gay theater got better, as it more artfully organized its childish yet energized low comedy and burlesque into formal artifice, the works became more popular but less interesting, that, in some senses, although they were better structured, the plays "fell apart."

After a description of the work of Jack Smith, notes on the earliest productions of the Theatre of the Ridiculous, an analysis of "the gesture of hatred" works of John Vaccaro and the "gesture of compassion" works of Charles Ludlam, and a brief summary of Ronald Tavel's career, Brecht ends this fascinating work with three pieces on The Hot Peaches, a discussion of Larry Ree's Original Trockadero Gloxinia Ballet Company and Les Ballets Trockadero de Monte Carlo, and a piece on John Waters.

In this volume Brecht has replaced his detailed scenarios with broader, but even more baroque, personal evaluations of the works he has seen:

Still in the flush of his first imperfection broadcasting untellable riches, Charles [Ludlam] immediately without hesitation entered his Classic period, putting on *Whores of Babylon* (by Bill Vehr) and then *Turds in Hell* (based on an idea of Bill's), grandiose Christian moralities, personal pictures of homosexual misery in the grand format of existential maps. The party-going camouflage of naive fun shed, no longer in a living-out on stage, their opulent disorder, aristocratic crudity, unostentatious shamelessness was the adequate form of a content in ideal beauty, which is why i use the word >classic< in spite of these plays being Romantic outcries of panic anxiety and disgust. Their poetic despair of an awful misogyny is passionate *in* their images and their just disorder.

He then goes on to more specifically describe the play at hand.

If the overlying metaphors of the paragraph above seem to present a kind of thicket of words through which one must make his or her way to get to the heart of Brecht's observations, there are other times in his writing that one feels Brecht's academic training crowding out any heady gush of lively expression:

Sentimentality is a predisposition to uncircumspect, though conventionally prescribed, feelings of tenderness of a mind and approving, through possibly compassionate sort, more indulged in for their own sake, i.e. with a hypocrisy, because they feel agreeable and reflect credit on oneself, than stimulus to generous action.

More often, however, some of these impacted sentences quite brilliantly reveal the theater to which he is attending:

Remarkably, this sentimental appeal of Ludlam's clean and pure sentimental poses,—not camped up, neither exaggerated nor twisted, nor played in quotational style,—was not destroyed either by their being recognisable derivatives from films shown at night on TV, and from old films at that, that is, in a style of expression gone out of style in art and in life, given up together with the ideal of woman as fulfilled by her sacrifice of herself to man and procreation, nor by their isolation in an ornate setting of stridently ambiguous poses of enviously competitive, ridiculing adoration of woman as powerful sex-object.

Similarly, a comment on playwright Ronald Tavel tells the reader a great deal about most of this author's works, including some of his early Andy Warhol movie scripts:

> The dialogue [of *Shower*] was an exercise in the pseudo-wit of smutty puns, the author's attempt to elevate the speech of the boroughs into art, an art that would provide a kind of entertainment. This art, though like Oscar Wilde's an art of speech, is literary rather that theatrical in that, a play on language, it focuses the audience on language rather than character, and does not create tension or advance action. The puns hinge on meaning, a not too clever double entendre, but Tavel is stuck on sound, addicted to alliteration.

Accordingly, Brecht sums up Tavel as a writer of "cleverness," focusing, in place of a ridiculous theater (a term first coined by Tavel), on what he calls a "disgusting use of language."

In short, although one is seldom given an easy go of it, Brecht takes us through the various stages of experimental New York theater in a way no one previously has been able to accomplish. And what a joyful, if some sometimes carping, trip that is!

One might add that what this artist attempted to do for the theater taking place mostly in lower Manhattan, he attempted to capture for that same area's streets in his two collections of poetry, *Poems* of 1975 and 1978, and *8th Avenue Poems*. These are not carefully sculpted poems but often raw expressions, not without their own sentimentality, of city life.

> a hum in the air envelops the wheeling flocks of
>   pigeons above the gliding cars,
> as a newspaper page in the lesser format of the
>   tabloids
> with agility slips off the sidewalk.

From another poem:

>   dream, befittingly disquieting,
> the morning's sea throwing the dream's transtem-
>   poral fluidity into city
>   street's straight line, eerily dissolves
> the night's phantom solidity of matter
> into aspect of time....

In a sense, through his very personal encounters, both everyday and cultural, with the American scene, and despite his European upbringing, Brecht was the most American of Americans. In a poem title "Addendum" he writes:

I walk here and I don't have to
and I wasn't meant to, the houses about me always
perfectly clear. No thread ties me to them, eyes only
that see and they sink into me
and the traffic too and the people
and never become mine
and don't touch me.
. . . .
Yet I feel perfectly at home here.
So you see I am not even afraid
nor merely discontent,
but simply unnourished, myself not stirring ever
an old man virginal.

This is the truth.

At the performance at Mabou Mines I describe in
the essay above, I introduced myself to Stefan Brecht and
his current wife, Rena Gill, who were attending the play.
Suffering from the progressive brain disease Lewy body
dementia, Brecht looked frail, his head and arms heavily
shaking. Upon hearing of his death last month, I again
mused on what a great loss to the theater world it was
that Brecht had not been spared to complete his books.

NEW YORK, MAY 10, 2009
Reprinted from *US Theater, Opera, and Performance* (October 2009).

 *In 1996 I met, through book reviewer Michael Silverblatt, Ronald Tavel, the subject of one of Brecht's essays. Tavel had been living in Thailand, and that year was invited to return for a short teaching gig in Los Angeles, during which time several of the Andy Warhol films, for which he'd writ-ten screenplays, were shown in Pasadena and elsewhere.*

In May of that year, I invited Ronald to a garden party, thrown in my honor, at the home of Marjorie and Joe Perloff, and over the next couple of years, we kept in close touch as I attempted to put together a collection of his Warhol screenplays and hoped, in the future, to publish several of Tavel's other dramas.

The process was a slow one since all of the copies of films he sent me were typescripts from the period in which they'd been written, nearly impossible to scan and quite clearly unedited, without any standard format or spell-ings. With only an editor and a volunteer we attempted to type up several of the film scripts, but it was a slow process.

Finally in 1998 we signed a contract with his agent, Helen Merrill, to publish "The Complete Warhol Screen-

plays," which also included extensive commentary by Tavel about each work, the processes of filming, and discussions of cast members. It would have been a brilliant work, and I tried hard to make it happen. But Tavel had been long out of touch with the difficulties and vagaries of a small publishing house and grew understandably impatient with the slow process.

In 1998, I did publish his 1969 play, Boy on a Straight-Back Chair, in Mac Wellman's and my anthology, From the Other Side of the Century II: A New American Drama 1960-1995, a copy of which I sent to Thailand.

Meanwhile Ronald, generally a quiet man, but, one recognized, an intensely controlled person (one could easily detect a great deal of anger and frustration just beneath that quiet demeanor), lost his patience and angrily lashed out at the difficulties I was having in completing his book. He demanded all materials to be returned, which I did.

However, I kept Xeroxed copies of all the plays and scripts, with the hope that, were he unable to find another publisher, Green Integer (then replacing Sun & Moon Press) might be able to step in and complete the project.

Earlier this year I determined to check on the internet to discover whether the Warhol scripts had ever seen print. I found no evidence of their being published. I was shocked, moreover, to discover that just two weeks before Stefan Brecht's death, Tavel had died on an air flight *from Bangkok to Berlin, apparently of a heart attack.*

Another figure who often appears in both Brecht's writing and in the performances and films of Tavel is actress Mary Woronov, whom I have known for several years as part of the art scene in Los Angeles and, more recently, in conjunction with her writing and teaching in the M.F.A. Literature Program at Otis College of Art + Design.

Mel Andringa, mentioned in Brecht's Queer Theatre *volume, and named as a future subject in his theater chronicles, has been a friend for many years, beginning when*  *I published a book by his companion, F. John Herbert,* The Collected Poems of Winston Churchill. *As an assistant professor at Temple University, I invited both John and Mel to perform in my English Department performance series in Philadelphia. Later these University of Iowa graduates founded a performance and art center, The Drawing Legion, in an old Bohemian Hall in my hometown of Cedar Rapids, Iowa. I have often visited them on my trips home to see my family.*

    On one such occasion, I questioned them what being

gay was like in Cedar Rapids, since I had never experienced living in that city while I was sexually aware. They took me to the island sitting in the midst of the Cedar River, upon which stood the Veterans Memorial Building (wherein existed the Cedar Rapids City Hall), the Police Department, and, apparently, the city's only gay bar. I had driven across this island countless times, of course, but never had actually been on the island itself. In its unpaved roads and scrubby undergrowth, it reminded me a bit of something one might encounter in a drive through Flannery O'Connor's Georgia or Faulkner's Mississippi backwoods.

The bar itself was bustling with activity, filled with, as they described it, every kind of gay and lesbian "type." Since it was the only bar of its kind in Cedar Rapids, it brought together the entire openly gay community. Everyone seemed to know one another, and I felt strangely displaced. That entire island was severely flooded during the great flood of 2008, and today little remains but the shell of those buildings.

Afterwards, I believe, we drove on to what they described as one of the few "real" restaurants in the city, since almost all other eateries in Cedar Rapids today consist of chain restaurants or bars. It may have been called the Bistro on First, but I truly can't remember. In any event, over dinner we discussed theater and many other topics, including the Brucemore Mansion near where author Carl

Van Vechten had been born and raised. Built originally by Thomas Sinclair in 1886, the mansion eventually was exchanged by his widow with the home of George Bruce and Irene Douglas, who, in turn, came to live in that grand house.

Bruce was a partner in the business Douglas' father founded, Quaker Oats. 14 years after George Bruce's death, Irene died in the house, bequeathing it to her daughter, Margaret Douglas, married to Howard Hall, founder of the Iowa Steel and Iron Works and the Iowa Manufacturing Company.

During their occupancy, the sociable couple redecorated the basement rooms as a Tahitian Room and a room they called the Grizzly Bar. They also kept a pet lion, Leo—relative, so we are told, of the famous MGM lion—along with an aviary and two German Shepherds. When Margaret Douglas Hall died she willed the mansion to The National Trust for Historic Preservation, who continues to operate the house as a tourist site today.

Mel had apparently been in contact with the Trust regarding a long-held suspicion that under the jungle motif images of the Grizzly Bar lay an original mural painted by a friend of the Halls, Grant Wood. Mel suggested some tests to determine if the painting was indeed behind the current mural, but the Trust showed little willingness to consider such a possible desecration of the decor.

By coincidence, an elderly woman sitting next to us, overhearing part of our conversation, asked if we were writers and struck up a discussion of Brucemore. As she described herself, she had been socially involved with the Halls and their circle of artist and author friends. "Yes," she proclaimed, "there had been, at one time, a painting where the Grizzly Bar now stood. Those were wonderful days," she reminisced, "days I had nearly forgotten until I heard the three of you speak."

Andringa's and Herbert's Drawing Legion was also heavily destroyed by the floods of 2008, but evidently they were able to save their building and are actively operating today.

In 2005, on another visit home, I took poet and

translator Cole Swensen, who was then teaching at the University of Iowa, on a tour of Cedar Rapids, stopping by Brucemore and later The Drawing Legion, where she met Mel and John.

LOS ANGELES, OCTOBER 4, 2009

Out of the Rain

IN THE *LOS ANGELES TIMES* obituaries of January 28, I read of the death, on January 16, of collector, curator, and publisher Judith Hoffberg. She died, at the age of 74, of lymphoma.

I was startled by the news since we had seen her quite recently at a party in the home of an art collector in Malibu, and I had talked to her briefly about my recently having had cancer. She made no mention of her own disease.

I can't remember when I first met Judith. It seems like Howard and I have known her forever, certainly as far back as Washington, D.C. In some ways she reminded me of an aunt who was never introduced, but had known you all your life.

Hoffberg had been a major force in collecting and

exhibiting the seemingly ephemeral work of the art world: artists books, mail art, and hundreds of other objects produced by artists that did not quite fit into the standard notion of art, focusing, in particular, on the work of early Feminists and Fluxus artists.

Since Howard had shown early on work by Eleanor Antin and others who dominated the field of art mail and artists books (and I published Eleanor's *Eleanora Antinova Plays* on Sun & Moon Press and part of her "Recollections of My Life with Diagaliev" in my *Sun & Moon* journal, as well as having planned to publish her art mail masterwork *100 Boots*), Judith appeared at numerous events we attended. Indeed, over the years, she appeared to be everywhere, expressing her joy of participating in the art scene while collecting essays and other information for her long-lived magazine, *Umbrella*.

People clearly loved Judith, inviting her to casual Sunday brunches, openings, special dinners, etc., and Judith reciprocated by joyfully flashing her open smile while gossiping about recent events and the people involved.

That she also found time to work as at art librarian at various universities (Johns Hopkins University, The University of Pennsylvania, University of California, San Diego) and institutions (the Bologna Center in Italy and the Library of Congress), as well as curating shows such as *Freedom: The International Mail Art Exhibition*, is a testament to her energy and love of the artistic life—which meant, for her, nearly anything the artist touched.

LOS ANGELES, FEBRUARY 6, 2009
Reprinted from *Green Integer Blog* (February 2009).

The Walls Come Tumbling Down

HEIMITO VON DODERER **DIVERTIMENTI AND VARI-ATIONS**, TRANSLATED FROM THE GERMAN BY VINCENT KLING (DENVER: COUNTERPATH PRESS, 2008)

IN HIS INFORMATIVE introduction to this collection of short tales by the great Austrian fiction-writer, Heimito von Doderer, translator Vincent Kling explains the psychological structures behind so many of von Doderer's works. For von Doderer, who briefly joined the Nazi party  before abandoning and renouncing it, what most interested him about humans was their failures, how an individual could be emotionally crippled by seemingly unimportant childhood traumas or humiliations that in adult life create what he described as *Apperzeptions-verweigerung*, a calculated refusal to perceive and a refusal of perception of a secondary reality the individual has created around him. Only when that person experiences *Menschwerdung*, a sudden recognition often triggered by a violent experience and societal shock, can that individual break through to his humanity.

It would be fruitless to reduce von Doderer's great writings to this simple pattern, but it is nonetheless helpful in understanding the motivations of a great many of his characters, not only in the novels *The Demons*, *Every Man a Murderer*, and *The Strudhof Steps*, but in *Divertimenti and Variations*, now translated and published in English for the first time.

The very first "Divertimento" seems to come almost directly out of *The Demons*, as a mob of workers rebel in Vienna, sweeping up along with them a purposeless young Technical Institute student, Adrian, and a young woman, Rufina Seifert, who works as a cashier in a store which has been among those trashed by the angry crowd. Finding themselves deposited at the edges of the skirmish and bloodied by the flying glass, they escape together, resulting in a relationship that seems more a dependency upon one another than a true passionate affair.

While Adrian has been ignorant of all about him, including the possibility of such violence, Rufina sees herself as the cause of it, as if she herself had willed the crowd into being. Yet strangely they are drawn together and begin an affair that suddenly ends as Adrian realizes how unsophisticated and desperate Rufina has been. Rufina breaks down, ridiculously admitting to crimes of "human degradation" and being the cause of "everything that's happened to all those people," before rushing madly into the streets.

Adrian desperately strives to find her, and discovers her in the hospital, where the professor explains to him that she is "incurable," and will be sent to an asylum. For some patients, he explains, "the world simply won't fit into any conventional framework; they no longer possess the ability to put most things to functional use as 'ready-made' objects—predominantly abstract concepts with all their concatenations—which is one of the signs that they're confronting the abyss."

Confronted with these statements, Adrian is forced to leave her in the hospital, and he reenters the outside world, where a violent rain and thunderstorm erupt. While Rufina has been lost, Adrian has been saved, come back to himself, so to speak. The story ends at a concert, with "the sky, high and deep in its midnight blue...standing above the many covered tables out on the terrace, above the colorful lights and the flowers." That night, Sofia Mitrofanov falls "all-out in love with Adrian, head over heels." In short, Adrian has been returned to everyday human life.

In "Divertimento No. 5," a young Viennese gentleman, Georg, awakens to find all sorts of trials and tribulations facing him. He has promised friends, the Tangls, that he will take Frau Tangl's pearls to be reset, but has somehow lost them along the way. Meanwhile, he has promised their previously divorced daughter Fanny that he will intercede with her parents about a another, equally undesirable young man she now wants to marry. Georg is tortured by the look and smells of his apartment, and is desperate to move to the suburbs; he may be able to make an exchange with Doctor Polt, but is skeptical about the meeting. Besides that, his toe is swollen and, although he should see a doctor, he has to get to work!

Jumbling these complaints together and intertwining them, he seems to face a vast array of disasters, which von Doderer comically has him list:

1. Toe (ought to go see the doctors!);
2. Pearls;
3. Hot-water heater (under this point he meant everything about his apartment);
4. Marriage negotiations;
5. Building falling apart.

Running between his job and the classified-ad office, he

waits to escape the notice of Fanny passing by, then juts out into the street where he is hit by a bus.

After being hospitalized for a few days and finding himself able to escape into a blissful world of peace, Georg is determined to spend one more day at home in the protection of his bed.

Word suddenly comes from Frau Tangl that she has changed her mind about the pearls being reset; Doctor Polt, having visited Georg's apartment, is quite ready to exchange, even offering to pay more money for his furniture (which Georg abhors); Fanny has found another young man and writes him, that if it's not too late, not to talk to her parents; and Georg's maid has discovered the pearls in one of the pockets of his coat!

Ensconced, at tale's end, in the peaceful green pathways of the suburbs, Georg has returned to normality.

In the best story of this collection, "Divertimento No. 7: The Trumpets of Jericho," we follow the dissipation of a seemingly well-adjusted Viennese doctor who, after witnessing what appears to have been an attack by an obnoxious-looking neighbor, Rambausek, upon an eight- or nine-year-old girl, temporarily stops the perpetuator, who is afraid the doctor may turn him in to the police. The neighbor is willing to pay the doctor to keep quiet (he has already paid the girl's parents), but the doctor devises a seemingly ridiculous alternative, that Rambausek go to a certain street near the Café

Greilinger and make "three deep knee bends with [his] arms held straight out in front of [him]."

The strange punishment accomplished, the doctor slowly begins to fall, himself, into more and more deviant behavior, drinking heavily and allowing his apartment to be the scene of rowdy, all-night, male parties. An accidental encounter with the young girl, Rambausek, and his wife, seems to further trigger his decay, as he seeks out sex with the mother of the girl Rambausek has raped, Frau Jurak. The only humanity left him seems to be his fondness for his next-door neighbor, Frau Ida.

On one particular evening, a young man attending a party and another doctor friend suggest that they play a trick on the friendly elderly neighbor, involving what they describe as "the trumpets of Jericho." Hiring several trumpeters to lock themselves in playing the triumphal march from Verdi's *Aida*, the partygoers enter the hall and pound on the door of the "little mousie" next door while shooting off pistols. Entering Frau Ida's apartment, they discover it empty, but riot police soon arrive and the merry-makers are taken away.

Realizing his spin into dereliction, the doctor offers to care for an artist-friend's studio in the suburbs for a lengthy period of time, at first refusing to even return to his old neighborhood. But one evening, walking with Frau Jurak near the river, they discover that her child has nearly drowned, coming upon the scene as Rambausek, having pulled her to safety, is attempting to resuscitate her. The girl regains consciousness and the doctor's hatred for Rambausek abates. The story ends with him on an express train headed west. Like the figures in the other stories I've described, through this violent accident, he has been able to awaken himself from a false world, he has been able to experience the *Menschwerdung* necessary to return him to humanity. The false walls of his irreality have come tumbling down.

Using musical phrasing and patterns, von Doderer has in each of these beautifully crafted stories presented the dilemmas of individuals and the societies in which they live, revealing the need for us all to awaken to new visions of life.

LOS ANGELES, FEBRUARY 8, 2009
Reprinted from *EXPLORING* fictions (March 2009).

As one can see from this essay, I highly admire von Doderer's writing, and, as I have explained, I was proud to have been able to publish him. I was scheduled to publish Vincent Kling's translation described above, as well as Kling's translation of The Strudhof Steps, *but Sun & Moon, in its last days of existence, had significant financial prob-*

lems, and C. H. Beck, the original German publisher, did not feel my offer of a $1,000 advance was sufficient. I was pained not to be able to publish this work, and my inability put a rift—temporary one hopes—between Kling and myself. I am happy that finally his translation has appeared in print.

LOS ANGELES, FEBRUARY 9, 2009

The Blur

HEIMITO VON DODERER **DIE DÄMONEN** (MUNICH: BIEDERSTEIN VERLAG, 1956), TRANSLATED FROM THE GERMAN BY RICHARD AND CLARA WINSTON AS **THE DEMONS** (NEW YORK: ALFRED A. KNOPF, 1961; REPRINTED BY LOS ANGELES: SUN & MOON PRESS, 1993)

PETER ROSEI **WEIN METROPOLIS** (STUTTGART: KLETT-COTTA, 2005), TRANSLATED FROM THE GERMAN BY GEOFFREY C. HOWES AS **METROPOLIS VIENNA** (LOS ANGELES: GREEN INTEGER, 2009)

FRAU MARKBRIETER SITS in a Vienna café with her sister Minna, awaiting the arrival of her daughter and other friends; Imre van Gyurkicz, painter and cartoonist, self-made man with a significant (if false) genealogy, is having an affair with violinist virtuoso Charlotte von Schlaggenberg; Charlotte's brother, the writer Kajetan von Schlaggenberg, is currently engaged in developing his theory of "The Necessity of Fat Females to the Sex Life of the Superior Man Today," a theory which Councillor Georg von Geyrenhoff finds as scandalous and dangerous to contemporary ideologies; the wealthy widow Friederike Ruthmayer, one of the most respectable women of Vienna society, is roused from her bed one night by the wild carousing of a group of men and women known as "Our Crowd," and joins them drinking cognac directly from the bottle; the self-educated factory worker (he teaches himself Latin, for example), Leonhard Kakabsa, falls in love with a widow, Mary K., who has lost her leg in a streetcar accident. If these often slight and somewhat silly incidents and events seem, on first hearing, unimportant, almost meaningless, they are—along with hundreds of others—what make up the epic "story" of Heimito von Doderer's great Austrian novel *The Demons*, a book of 1,329 pages I published in paperback in 1993 (and which I believe is one of three or four of my most notable publications). For few writers have so completely revealed the interconnected fabric of everyday life that results in often shocking and earth-shattering events— in this case the takeover of Austria by the Nazis and its destruction in World War II.

I begin with this great masterwork of fiction because, while reading a translation in manuscript of Peter Rosei's far briefer *Wien Metropolis* (Metropolis Vienna), I was struck by how similar it is to von Doderer's work—at least in method and incident. *Wien Metropolis* begins almost at the moment that *The Demons* clos-

es, at the other end of World War II, as two Austrian Nazi soldiers, Oberkofler and Pandura, wait out the night in a Polish mansion into which they and their compatriots have forced their way, presumably to drink up the remaining wine. That evening, as the Russians advance toward the town, these two strike up a conversation, beginning a strangely close friendship, which ends in their sharing an apartment on Josefstädterstrasse after the war.

I describe this relationship as "strange" only because, although the two are outwardly heterosexual—with Pandura described as a "ladies man" and Oberkofler developing a near sado-masochistic relationship with the beautiful Viktoria Strnd—they function as a team, as a kind of semi-comic duo (Laurel and Hardy spring immediately to mind), who run a local dancing and charm school for the entrepreneurial Leitomerizky. One night, moreover, Pandura, screaming out in his sleep, is shaken awake by Oberkofler; Pandura, "still fully stupefied with sleep," flings an arm around his comrade, pulling him forcibly down to him as the two engage in a kiss. Nothing more is made of this exceptional event; however, as the relationship between

Oberkofler and Strnd continues, Pandura threatens to move out; Oberkofler commits suicide by putting his head into an oven filled with gas.

Suddenly the narration shifts to Klagenfurt, the Carinthian capital city, the birthplace of writers Robert Musil and Ingeborg Bachmann (whose own father became a Nazi six years before Hitler's invasion), where we encounter another male couple, two young boys, Alfred and Georg, both natural-born leaders, whose stories make up the heart of Rosei's fiction.

Like Oberkofler and Pandura, these boys grow up—Alfred, short and broad-shouldered, and Georg, talk and lanky (in the Laurel and Hardy mold)—to develop a deep friendship as they attend the university in Vienna, a friendship which one day results in Alfred kissing his friend Georg upon the lips. Again, nothing is made about this event, and the narrative of their lives continues as if it has been of no importance. Alfred, we discover, is the child of Viktoria Strnd; the backer of Oberkofler and Pandura's dance school, Leitomerizky (now a successful automobile dealer, with outlets eventually throughout the country) is, so he announces in Strnd's prensence, Alfred's father. The Jewish Leitomerizky and the Catholic Strnd had been deeply in love before the war, we are told, and for some time after the Nazi *Putsch* Leitomerizky successfully avoided capture; ultimately, however, he was sent to the camps, returning to Vienna as a survivor. Strnd has, we discern, created a real estate business which has sold Jewish property to numerous Nazis and continues in these nefarious connections after the war. Later, Strnd denies Leitomerizky's paternity.

I won't describe all of the various interlinking stories and events this fiction conveys; as the narrator admits, in Vienna everyone knows everyone, and, as in von Doderer's fiction, *Wein Metropolis* weaves numerous lives together in a way that, while describing everyday events, reveals something far deeper. For we soon perceive that nearly all the figures in this book—all in some sense "survivors"—seek other kinds of love that are not always as sexual as they are based on interdependence. Both Alfred and Georg, at various times in the book, romance the wealthy, young, sophisticated Klara Wohlbrück; neither of these young men seem actually to *love* her—each are slightly disgusted by her endless laughter and chatter—yet each develops a near-desperate need to have her near them. As Alfred breaks with Georg to travel abroad, Georg takes up with another young man, Stepanik, with whom he develops a successful advertising business. As that relationship, in turn, begins to wane, Stepanik turns to gambling each night with a new friend, the elder Leitomerizky. Numerous other pairings appear and disappear, almost as in Schnitzler's *Hands Around* or as in a grand Strauss waltz. The dance, for these alternating couples, is just that, a patterned performance that has little to do with emotional or sexual fulfillment.

It quickly becomes apparent that each of the characters living in this post-World War II Vienna are seeking some sort of meaning in their lives, grasping at get-rich quick schemes and attaching themselves to other beings in order to fill their emptiness. As the older generation has already lost its way—Viktoria turning to alcohol, and Leitomerizky to, at first, women, then to late-night partying, and finally to the Bible—the younger figures desperately try to carve out meaningful lives through vague political alliances (Alfred is fascinated by the German Baader-Meinhof Group, and, on his own, plots the death of a wealthy lawyer whose villa reminds him of the Wohlbrük villa back in Vienna—which, if he actually had joined the political left, could be the subject of an entirely different essay) or social connections (Georg marries Klara, moving to a reconstructed villa with her and his mother); yet these couplings with individuals or organizations provide only ephemeral happiness. Like her mother, who later in her life retreats from her family by seeking out sexual partners each night on the Vienna boulevards, Klara retreats from Georg into her sick bed, finding a sexual outlet with her new friend and confidant, Professor Frodl. In the end, nearly all the active players in

Wien Metropolis are left alone in a kind of hazy vision of reality that Rossei describes effectively throughout the fiction in the pattern of Viennese sunlight dappling the trees, a pattern that blurs perception.

Rosei's Vienna is not at all the black-and-white Expressionist-like world of Carol Reed's film, *The Third Man*, a world reminding everyone—characters and viewers both—of that great city's monstrous acts and the culture's fall from grace. Instead, Rosei's figures—caught up in a society of avoidance—pick up existence as if the war had not occurred, attempting to ignore or outrun their terrible past in a rush for money and success. Even in their achievements, however, they discover they have no lives, that their beautifully reconstructed city—as the novelist who drunkenly intrudes upon one of Klara's salons argues—is "nothing but a playground of stupidity and beastliness, of beastliness and stupidity, where nothing but baseness ever prevails, or at best the ridiculous." Too often, as in the murder by Alfred's father (the only father he knew as a child) of a nearby neighbor and in Pandura's violence against nonviolent protesters, that beast they attempt to hide terrifyingly reveals itself.

By fiction's end, the reader comes to recognize that the two incidents of kissing I described at the beginning of this essay are emblems of an impossible search for innocent love, a child-like love, perhaps even a kind of narcissistic self-love that is not permitted for these Viennese survivors. Even the healthy working class passion between Johann and Maria Oberth ends in a cancerous-induced fog of forgetfulness.

Metropolitan Vienna is a culture doomed to death by the past and its refusal to accept responsibility for its acts. Like the frieze on the corner of Oberkofler and Pandura's apartment, depicting "an oversized male head with the flowing beard of a prophet," lips sealed, eyes wide-open in a blind stare, these figures of postwar Vienna are souls that have lost track of themselves in their "joy-crazed adaptation to existence."

Rosei has brilliantly picked up were von Doderer's fiction ended, only to reveal that nothing much has changed, except what once was a world of self-made men is now a society of men and women who create identity, like drowning beings, by grabbing onto anything or anyone they can.

For all that, we still feel for Rosei's drowning damned, allow them to grab onto us through our distant imaginations, suffering some sorrow (in the cases of Oberkofler, Strnd, Leitomerizky, Frau Wohlbrück, and Alfred) for their deaths and disappearances, and sympathizing for (in the examples of Klara, Maria, and Georg) their meaningless lives—even as we fear the tenacity of their empty aspirations. If, as one of Rosei's character's argues, the Holocaust is the most important event of the 20th century, what might we fear and imagine for the century in which we now live?

LOS ANGELES, JANUARY 16, 2007
Reprinted from *The New Review of Literature*, V, no. 2 (Spring 2008).

Changing Hands

DAVID BROMIGE **THREADS** (LOS ANGELES: BLACK
SPARROW PRESS, 1971)
   DAVID BROMIGE **MY POETRY** (BERKELEY: THE
FIGURES, 1980)
   DAVID BROMIGE **DESIRE: SELECTED POEMS 1963-
1987** (SANTA BARBARA: BLACK SPARROW PRESS, 1988)
   DAVID BROMIGE **THE HARBORMASTER OF HONG
KONG** (LOS ANGELES: SUN & MOON PRESS, 1993)

ON JUNE 3 of this year, poet David Bromige died at his
home in Sebastopol, California, of complications from
diabetes, a stroke, and a heart attack. During his last
years, according to friends such as D. A. Powell, Bromige suffered from "dementia."

How different was the David Bromige I knew in
the 1990s, the time when I first met him—if I remember correctly, at a reading of his in New York City—
publishing his book *The Harbormaster of Hong Kong*
(the title poem is still one of my favorites of his works)

in 1993. The following year, David appeared at a literary salon in the Sun & Moon offices on September 22, and read, I believe, that same weekend at Beyond Baroque in Venice. In those days he was the very image of a clever, stunningly quick-witted punster, creating his famed maxims and dicta, many of which dotted his poems, seemingly out of clear air: "There is no revision in the grave," "Lambs live a long time in our recipes," "Every endless summer hurries in a fall." Many of these were presented in the form of "pairings" of lines which in their oppositional syntax nonetheless paralleled and defined the other:

infatuation

———————

break break break
on thy cold gray stones o shore

kiss me quick

———————

too late

Bromige was what at one time would be described as a wit, and his poetry literally shimmered with his quick connections, or, at the other extreme (as in "You"), revealed a slow, "deliberate" process, where the reader moved through the matter of the poem, "changing hands," so to speak, with the author. But these are only two aspects of a body of writing that was constantly in shift, moving between narrative and lyricism, rhyme and radical disassociation at the drop of a hat; sometimes, as in "In an Orchard, in America, In August," focusing on the lush surfaces of things in order to reveal their inner core:

> Let this be
> the story of the core.
> The part that's thrown away,
> that can't be used.
> That can't speak for itself,

Bromige's quick shifts in syntax and genre clearly irritated some, particularly poets and readers who demanded a signature style from a writer. I remember attending Bromige's reading at Beyond Baroque where I sat next to the usually fair-minded poet-editor Lee Hickman, with Hickman hissing into my ear, "I just can't stand this kind of writing." Hickman was an often obstinate critic, but here I suspect it was just Bromige's wide poetic range and abilities that irritated him—and so delighted me.

Born in London in 1933, Bromige grew up with signs of becoming tubercular, and was sent to an iso-

lation hospital for four months as a child. His second childhood "trauma" was being in London during the Blitz, when, on one particular night, a series of bombs seemed likely to destroy his family home. After the war Bromige won a scholarship to Haberdashers' Aske's Hampstead School, but after completing his certificate he took a job on a dairy farm in southern Sweden. Soon after, he emigrated to Canada, living for a while in Saskatchewan, Ontario, and Alberta, before moving to Vancouver to be near to his sister, and where he attended the University of British Columbia, meeting poets such as George Bowering, Frank Davey, Robert Creeley, Charles Olson, Denise Levertov, and Robert Duncan, who might be described as Bromige's mentor.

In 1962 Bromige won a Woodrow Wilson Scholarship, which required he do his graduate work in a different university. Accordingly, Bromige chose the University of California at Berkeley, moving to the Bay Area. From 1970 on he became a Professor of Literature at Sonoma State University. His poetry collection of 1988, *Desire: Selected Poems 1963-1987,* won the Western States Book Award.

Many of his students have described David as a caring and giving teacher. As D. A. Powell wrote soon after his death:

> Our classroom was in the theatre department, and it was furnished with ungodly dilapidated sofas.... So each week we'd sprawl on the sagging couches, reading poems reproduced in purple ink on a ditto machine, and David would sit cross-legged in the center of the room, sigh deeply, smile, and praise even the most sickly poems, though he often seemed to pass first through a period of deep physical pain before he'd bless us with that smile and praise.

I did not know David Bromige well; apart from working with him on the one book we published, attending three readings, and working with him on his selection of poems for *From the Other Side of the Century: A New American Poetry 1960-1990,* we seldom communicated over the years. Yet I sensed in David a similar openness and a complete commitment to living.

As we left my offices to take him to the airport, David called out to my companion Howard, "Please, you have to get a photograph of the two of us in front of Sun & Moon. Here, Douglas, let us hold hands."

We did, the camera catching us in the act of "changing hands."

LOS ANGELES, NOVEMBER 20, 2009
Reprinted from *PIP (Project for Innovative Poetry)* (November 2009) and *Shearsman* [England], No. 83/84 (April 2010).

Holding In, Holding On

MARIO BENEDETTI **THE TRUCE: THE DIARY OF MARTIN SANTOMÉ**, TRANSLATED FROM THE SPANISH BY HARRY MORALES (NEW YORK AND LONDON: PENGUIN BOOKS, 2015) (READ THIS BOOK IN MANUSCRIPT IN 2009*)

I HAVE JUST finished reading Mario Benedetti's 1960 novel *The Truce* for the third time. I first read Benjamin Graham's translation, published by Harper & Row, sometime in the 1970s. In 1996 translator Harry Morales sent me a new version (which he revised again in 1998), restoring what he described were missing passages in the Graham translation, and retranslating the entire text. I read this new version with great pleasure, and offered to publish the book on Sun & Moon Press. We offered a $1,000 advance to Benedetti through his agent at the time, Thomas Colchie, but Benedetti inexplicably rejected the offer, Colchie responding that he could not dissuade the author from that decision.

Both Morales and I feel it may have had something to do with Benedetti's anti-Americanism. So ended my brief "relationship" with the great Uruguayan author.

Upon hearing of Benedetti's death on May 16th of this year, I momentarily thought of opening my files and contacting Harry Morales again to see if he had ever found a publisher for his version of the book. A few weeks later, Morales called me, soon after providing me with yet another revised version of his translation, which I finally completed reading this week.

Accordingly, I feel I now know this fiction well enough that, whether I end up publishing it or not, I should write something about the book in memory of its renowned creator.

Few major characters are as unassuming, unpretentious, and outright boring as Martin Santomé. When one first meets him in the pages of his private diary, the reader might almost give up a yawn to this bookkeeper's calculations about his retirement and his unimaginative speculations of what he might do when he stops working:

Do I really need leisure so much? I tell myself no, that it's not leisure that I need, but the right to work at what I love. For example? The garden, perhaps. It's good as a restful activity on Sundays, for counteracting sedentary life, and also as a secret defense against my future and guaranteed arthritis. But I'm afraid I couldn't bear it every day. The guitar, perhaps. I think I would like it. But it must be lonely to start studying music at forty-nine. Write? Perhaps I wouldn't be too bad at it, at least people usually enjoy my letters. And so what? I can imagine a short bibliographical note about "the worthy values of this new author who is nearing fifty" and the mere possibility of it is repulsive.

From the first words penned to his journal, we already know Santomé is a man of no special talents, no great imagination, and so equivocal about every aspect of his life that he can make no significant decisions.

Nonetheless, before long we are drawn into his diary as he describes his children, his dead wife, and his office companions, none of whom he knows very well nor has any deep relationships with. Like almost all office workers, Santomé complains of the boredom of his job and his treatment from his superiors, yet, as the head of his department, he is a good worker, and it is, accordingly, hard to imagine what else he is good for.

His relationships between his sons Jaime and Esteban are fractious, Esteban seemingly destined to be an office worker with even less imagination than his father. Jaime, as the story develops, is discovered to be gay, and is virtually disowned by Santomé. Indeed, this son leaves home, never to be seen again. Only Santomé's daughter seems to have serious communication with him, but she has just fallen in love and has little time to devote to her father.

For all of the insignificance of Santomé's life, however, we begin to understand his series of indecisions as being related to his moral character. He is a caring and careful man, however in his equivocation is simply unable to express those feelings to anyone. Given the perversities of his acquaintances, particularly his friend Vignale, who begins an affair with his sister-in-law living in Santomé's house, Santomé is nearly a saint, albeit a saint with few temptations put in his way.

In short, Santomé has given away his life, never challenging himself to live up to his dreams, perhaps never having significant enough dreams in the first place. He can hardly even remember the face of Isobel, his dead wife.

It is wondrous, accordingly, that he gradually falls in love with a new employee, Laura Avellaneda. But even here his relationship begins with timidity. At first she does not appear as a beautiful woman, but slowly he begins to enjoy her company, seeing her as a whole being, suddenly slipping into a friendship which promises something beyond his own expectations. When it dawns upon him that he is truly in love, he is amazed by the possibility.

Here again, however, the two, working together, must meet covertly, must spend much time in cautious hand-holding rather than a sexual relationship. The difference in their ages, Avellaneda being a young woman just beginning her life, forces him to suggest an open relationship, in his reasoning a way to make it possible for her to leave him as he ages. When a friend suggests his lack of commitment to marriage is simply a way to protect himself from possibly being hurt, Santomé recognizes the truth, but having purchased a small apartment for their meetings, it has become too late for him to change, he feels, the nature of their relationship.

In fact, one might argue that each of Santomé's acts is too late. The love between the two actually blossoms into a kind of happiness which the narrator has never known before, but the moment he realizes this new-found joy, the moment he becomes determined to act out of impulse, asking Avellaneda to marry him, she becomes sick and dies. His temporary rebirth withers before his eyes.

Throughout Benedetti's slow accumulation of the details of Santomé and the figures on whom he writes, we grow almost fond of this over-cautious Bartelby, who has suddenly found a way to say "yes" to life. For men like Santomé, however, there is perhaps no possible way out. Their very equivocation in life means that they will not experience life itself.

Benedetti's Montevideo, indeed, seems filled with just such people. One of the saddest episodes in the entire work is when, weeks after his lover's death, Santomé visits her father, a tailor, and her mother, neither of whom have ever met him. Both reveal, privately, their own failures at having been unable to express themselves to their daughter, the father admitting that he had always intended to tell Laura of his love, but continuing to put it off until now he has lost his chance of expressing it. The mother, sensing who the stranger is, tells an even more tragic story: she once had a lover, but had told him to go away. The daughter of that man, Avellaneda was all she had to remember that lost love, the possibility of true joy in her life:

> "Laura was all I had remaining of him. Again, that's why I feel that the heart is an enormous entity which starts in the stomach and ends in the throat. That's why I know what you're going through."
> …She was looking upwards and crying, without passing her hand across her face; she was crying proudly.

Those tears are the closest Benedetti's figures come to outrightly expressing the horror of their empty lives. The fiction ends where it began. No change has been possible in such a world of holding in while holding on. "Starting tomorrow and to the day I die," Santomé says, "time will be at my disposal. After so much waiting, this is retirement. What will I do with it?"

---

*I wrote this essay, after reading it in manuscript, in 2009. *Rain Taxi* will publish this essay, in different form, in 2016.

LOS ANGELES, OCTOBER 10, 2009
Reprinted from *EXPLORING* fictions (October 2009).

It Comes with the Job

GEORGE ABBOTT AND RICHARD BISSELL (BOOK, BASED ON BISSELL'S NOVEL *7½ CENTS*), RICHARD ADLER AND JERRY ROSS (MUSIC AND LYRICS) **THE PAJAMA GAME** / NEW YORK, ST. JAMES THEATRE, MAY 13, 1954

BUDD SCHULBERG (WRITER) (BASED, IN PART, ON ARTICLES BY MALCOLM JOHNSON), ELIA KAZAN (DIRECTOR) **ON THE WATERFRONT** / 1954

GEORGE ABBOTT AND RICHARD BISSELL (BASED ON BISSELL'S NOVEL *7½ CENTS*) (WRITERS), RICHARD ALDER AND JERRY ROSS (MUSIC AND LYRICS), GEORGE ABBOTT AND STANLEY DONEN (DIRECTORS) **THE PAJAMA GAME** / 1957

HARRIET FRANK, JR. AND IRVING RAVETCH (WRITERS), MARTIN RITT (DIRECTOR) **NORMA RAE** / 1979

CONSIDERING THAT BENEDETTI'S novel, and his short story "The Budget" (which I published in translation in *1001 Great Stories, Volume 1*) both take place primarily in the workplace, I thought it might be interesting to explore a few films that focus on workers and,

in particular, the employee relationship with employers, which also involves the issue of labor unions. The three works on which I've decided to focus center on the unions, linking the labor organizations with better pay, better working conditions, and, in the second example, representing them as a corrupt force demanding the employees' blind faith. I might have chosen numerous other films about the workplace, *The Apartment* (a film on which I've already written in *My Year 2003*), *How to Succeed in Business without Really Trying* and *Nine to Five* immediately come to mind. But I chose these particular three films because their focus is on the relationship of workers and unions more than on extracurricular situations involving affairs of the heart.

The Pajama Game, based on Iowa writer Richard Bissell's 1952 novel *7½ Cents,* however, is a none too serious example of a workplace drama, and were there not a real battle between labor and management presented in this work, it might have floated off into a love comedy. The head of the Union Grievance Committee, Babe Williams (Doris Day)—despite her denials

("I'm Not At All in Love")—is clearly attracted to the new superintendent of the Sleep-Tite Pajama Factory, Sid Sorokin (John Raitt). But, as she later explains to him, she is a "Union girl," and resists his attentions precisely because she is afraid of what will come between them. Although it is a comic resistance—one that we immediately know will ultimately be overcome—there remains throughout the play a serious breach between management and labor that ends, temporarily, in their separation.

A more comic series of characters buoy up these more serious issues facing the feuding lovers by mocking all love quarrels: Vernon Hines (Eddie Foy, Jr.), the factory timekeeper, is perpetually jealous of the woman he loves, Gladys Hotchkiss (the great comic dancer Carol Haney), secretary to the head of the factory "Old Man" Hasler. That jealousy, combined with Hines' drinking and "skill" at throwing knives, a skit he is determined to perform at the annual employee picnic, creates its own fireworks, underlying the more serious battles between the superintendent and union representative. One of the best comic moments in the work, indeed, is played out by Sid's secretary, Mabel (the delectable Rita Shaw), and Hines, as she tries to cure him of his jealous behavior ("I'll Never Be Jealous Again"); that "cure," however, is short-lived, and ultimately, hinting at even darker fears in the war between factory employees, culminates in the possibility of murder and death!

As Sid and Babe fall more and more deeply in love (helped along by songs such as "Small Talk" and "There Once Was a Man"), the war between the union and management threatens. Workers demand a raise most other such employees have received throughout the state of 7½ cents, and as Hasler continues to resist, a slow-down is ordered. Outraged by their actions, Sid orders an "honest day's work," and as the slackers again speed up production, Babe jams the machinery. Sid has no choice but to fire his lover. His lonely fate is beautifully spelled out twice in the musical as he sings to himself into a Dictaphone ("Hey There").

Meeting at Babe's house, several rebellious workers plan strategies to embarrass the company: mismatching sizes of pajamas, flimsily sewing on fly-buttons, etc. In order to correct the threatened mayhem, Sorokin becomes determined to see the financial records which the company head keeps carefully locked away from sight. Pretending to court Hasler's secretary Gladys (who has dismissed her dangerous lover Hines), he meets her at the popular city nightclub, Hernando's Hideaway, with the attention of wheedling away the key to the company records she keeps on a chain around her neck.

In fact, that key reveals another kind of "chain" around all the workers' necks. Sid discovers that Hasler had already raised the cost of his products to account for the 7½ cents months before, refusing to grant the raise simply out of greed.

The union rally is in progress as union leaders explain just what that raise of  7½ cents will mean to the underpaid workers over a lifetime. But before the strike is declared, Sorokin arrives with Hasler in hand, having threatened to reveal Hasler's actions to the workers. The old man has no choice but to give in to Union demands. Sid is restored to a hero in Babe's mind. And everyone is suddenly off to celebrate at Hernando's where "All you see are silhouettes. / And all you hear are castanets. / And no one cares how late it gets," clearly a kind of laborers' heaven.

The same year that *The Pajama Game* opened on Broadway, Elia Kazan's *On the Waterfront* premiered in movie houses; the two could not be more different in how they deal with the subject of workers and unions. Whereas in *The Pajama Game* the local union, completely controlled by the local workers, successfully serves their concerns, writer Budd Schulberg's International Longshoreman's Association, run by the mob (in New York by the infamous Genovese family), robs union funds while demanding complete fealty and further financial extortion from the workers.

The film, based on newspaper stories written by Malcolm Johnson in the *New York Sun*, begins with a somewhat dim-witted but gentle tough, Terry Malloy (Marlon Brando), playing lackey to the gangster union boss Johnny Friendly (Lee J. Cobb), who orders him to lure a young dockworker, Joey Doyle, to his apartment rooftop. Doyle has evidently informed on union workers to a new Crime Commission committee, and Johnny wants him killed. The unsuspecting Malloy (who presumes Friendly's henchmen will only rough him up) does what he's told, inviting Doyle, himself a bird lover, to inspect his rooftop pigeons. In shock Terry witnesses Doyle's murder as he is hurled to the street below.

From that moment on, Elia Kazan's film takes its subject by the teeth and refuses to let go. No matter what one thinks about Kazan—most of my older Hollywood friends have refused to speak to or even *of* him since 1952 when he served as a friendly witness before the House Un-American Activities Committee—there is no question that *On the Waterfront* is a powerful and mesmerizing film, with brilliant performances by Brando, Karl Malden, Rod Steiger, and Eva Marie Saint, and an original score by Leonard Bernstein. The film won eight Academy Awards, including the Oscars for Best Picture and Best Director, and is listed on the American Film Institute's list of most memorable movies.

It is useful to realize, however, that no matter how factual Schulberg and Kazan's film is (and there is every reason to believe that they correctly portrayed the brutality of the New York shipping docks), Kazan's intention was to create a kind of allegory for his own position before McCarthy and others. The original screenplay, *The Hook*, was by Arthur Miller (who refused to name names before HUAC), but he was replaced by Schulberg (who, like Kazan, testified as a friendly witness before the committee). Pressure from HUAC wanted the mob villains to also be Communists, but fortunately Schulberg did not defer to their wishes. Nonetheless, Kazan's film, with its emphasis on those who refuse to speak up against the mob, his obvious disdain for those who remain "Deaf and Dumb (D & D)," was clearly a statement against the criticism he had received for speaking out at HUAC. (It's interesting that Miller went on to write two works that told a different story of behavior regarding public testimony: *A View from the Bridge*, about the family loyalty of Italian immigrants, and *The Crucible*, about the Salem witchcraft trials and the related testimony of young girls and others against the so-called witches.)

Most of *On the Waterfront*, accordingly, is devoted to the long struggle by Father Barry (Karl Malden) and Joey Doyle's sister, Edie (Eva Marie Saint), with whom Terry gradually falls in love, to convince Terry to come

clean and report what he has seen to the Crime Commission. When the mob begins to suspect that Terry might squeal, they order him killed, unless Terry's older brother Charley (part of the Union mob) can convince him to remain silent. Through conversations with Edie and Father Barry, Terry gradually begins to understand the difference between survival and hope, as he develops a new set of moral values which reaches back into his own past.

In what is one of the most heart-wrenching scenes in the film, Charley literally takes his brother "on a ride," trying to force Terry to understand the danger of his potential acts. As they discuss Terry's past career as a boxer, Terry admits that he has very little to offer in his current life. But whereas Charley blames his brother's manager ("That skunk we got you for a manager, he brought you along too fast"), Terry suddenly blurts out the truth:

> It wasn't him, Charley! It was you. You remember that night in the Garden, you came down to my dressing room and said: "Kid, this ain't your

night. We're going for the price on Wilson." You remember that? "This ain't your night!" My night! I coulda taken Wilson apart! So what happens? He gets the title shot outdoors in the ball park—and whadda I get? A one-way ticket to Palookaville.

Their final interchange represents Terry's transformation from dim-witted lackey to a man of growing wisdom and moral integrity:

TERRY: You was my brother, Charley. You shoulda looked out for me a little bit. You shoulda taken care of me—just a little—so I wouldn't have to take them dives for the short-end money.

CHARLEY: I had some bets down for you. You saw some money.

TERRY [*yelling and heartbroken*]: You don't understand! I coulda had class. I coulda been a contender. I coulda been somebody, instead of a bum, which is what I am. Let's face it [*pause*].... It was you, Charley.

With such an intense scene between brothers, Kazan needs to say little about the union Charley represents. The relationship between the workers and the union is played out in *On the Waterfront* in terms of sibling rivalry, saving the director from having to focus on the

deeper issues concerning the relationship between the two forces.

Obviously, Terry must die! And in Schulberg's original script that was to have been his fate. But Kazan would then have been without a hero to give evidence to his righteous act of testifying. In the final film Terry battles Friendly directly through a kind of end-all fighting bout; he is nearly killed by the union henchmen, but, once Terry, his supporters in pietà-like formation, is helped to stand, he refuses to give in, weaving and lunging forward, a working man's Christ, into the maw of the ship, Friendly shouting after like some angry schoolyard bully who has temporarily lost his powers. The myth Kazan has created is perhaps more powerful than Schulberg's original political commentary.

Martin Ritt's 1979 film *Norma Rae* is clearly, of the three union films I discuss, the most realistically conceived as well as the most focused of these films on the actual issue of unions. Located in a small Southern US town, a region (as I mention in my discussion in *My Year 2006*) where union leaders and even members were often thought to be Communists, and joining unions, accordingly, was perceived as an un-American act, the film presents the often brave and always strong-willed activities of Norma Rae Webster (Sally Fields, who won an Oscar for her role) and a union organizer from New York, Reuben Warshowsky (Ron Liebman). Based on a real-life figure, Crystal Lee Sutton, who, while earning $2.65 an hour folding towels at the Roanoke Rapids, North Carolina, J. P. Stevens plant, tried to organize her co-workers, the film proceeds in a fairly true-to-life, unspectacular manner to depict the gradual awakening of the workers to their needs and, most importantly, their rights.

Norma Rae's own difficulties with men, her latent attraction to Reuben, and their discomforts with opposing cultures and religions are all gently laid to rest early in the film so that Ritt can focus on the growing union activities and the inevitable repercussions upon her life. The mill itself, more than its unsympathetic owners and managers, is represented as a monstrous Dickensian machine, the air filled with wool dust and the pounding sound of the looms that voids almost any possibility of verbal communication and assures the eventual loss of hearing for employees. The moment in the film where Norma Rae discovers that her mother has become hard of hearing is one of the most memorable in a series of scenes played out in the infernal factory, where employees are carefully watched for even the smallest of infractions.

Refused permission to put up a union sign or even post company policies, arrested, and fired, Norma Rae gradually grows through Reuben's mentoring from a fairly ignorant country girl into a wiser woman, from just another worker into someone, as Crystal Lee Sutton is purported to have asked to be remembered, "who deeply care(s) for the working poor...." Upon being arrested and humiliated, Norma Rae, breaking into tears, is given little sympathy by Reuben, who reports, "It comes with the job."

Her growing sense of determination and righteousness is at the center of Ritt's film, and its trajectory is what makes his film a fulfilling work. By the time that Norma Rae, like Sutton before her, closes down her machine and, standing on her work table while holding a cardboard sign upon which she has scrawled UNION, brings the entire factory to a silent halt, we know that, no matter what the outcome, the workers have won and their relationship to the monstrous mechanic in which they toil has been changed forever.

In reality it took a year before the Amalgamated Clothing and Textile Workers Union won the right to represent the seven plants located in Roanoke Rapids. The court ordered that Sutton be paid back wages and return to work. She returned for two days, quitting to work as a union organizer. On September 11th of this year, Sutton died of brain cancer at the age of 68.

LOS ANGELES, OCTOBER 14-17, 2009
Reprinted from *World Cinema Review* (October 2009).
Reprinted from *Reading Films: My International Cinema* (Los Angeles: Green Integer, 2012).

Another Job, or The Uncertainty Principle

ETHAN COEN AND JOEL COEN (WRITERS AND DIRECTORS) **A SERIOUS MAN** / 2009

A YIDDISH PEASANT'S cart beaks down when, suddenly, out of nowhere a man in a horsecart appears to help him. Miraculously, he is an acquaintance, so the peasant invites him to dinner. Upon hearing the story, his wife becomes horrified, for the good Samaritan, she has heard, died years before. He must be a dybbuk, a body possessed by a dead spirit. When the "dybbuk" appears at the door, she announces her feelings, which he politely denies: here he stands before them, not dead in the least, but a helpful passerby. Without hesitation she stabs him with a kitchen knife. For a moment he looks utterly surprised, but quickly regains his composure. No, he will not stay for dinner, not remain in a house where he is not wanted. However, as he leaves,

we can see a blood stain slowly growing over his chest where she has stabbed him. Is he a dybbuk surviving the wound or a man about to die? The couple are cursed forever for their possible mistake.

The uncertainty of the situation, the curse of the dead, and the ludicrousness of the system of beliefs underlying this tale set the tone for the Coen brothers' new film, *A Serious Man*, set in St. Paul, Minnesota in the late 1960s, where the brothers grew up.

Larry Gopnik (wonderfully performed by Michael Stuhlbarg) is a physics teacher at a local university who is about to be reviewed for tenure, and who is blessed with a wife, two children, and a nice suburban home. True, he is tormented by a brother living with them, who spends most of his time in their bathroom draining a cyst. But otherwise his life, if uneventful, is what we might describe as ordinary and pleasant.

His children, we soon discover, have little interest in their education or, for that matter, anything of value. The boy, Danny, about to be *bar mitzvahed*, is forced to go to Hebrew classes, during which he secretly listens to music on his headphones. Outside of the classroom his greatest activity is smoking pot. Sarah, the daughter, consistently steals money from her father's billfold and spends most of her time, as Larry later puts it, "washing her hair."

Larry's wife Judith suddenly announces that she wants a divorce; she has fallen in love with another man, Sy Ableman, an oily pragmatist with whom one finds it hard to imagine anyone could fall in love. Not only does she suggest her husband move to a living room cot (Larry's brother inhabits the couch), but she insists upon a *Get*, a Jewish decree that will allow her to remarry.

At school, an Asian graduate student whom Larry has failed tries to bribe him by leaving behind an envelope filled with hundred dollar bills, and when the professor attempts to return the incriminating evidence, threatens to sue him for defamation. A fellow professor reports, moreover, that the tenure committee has been receiving anonymous letters attacking Larry's moral character.

What more could go wrong? In the Coens' world this is only a warm up for a series of painful events as Larry is  forced to move with his brother into the Jolly Roger Motel, discovering through the police that his brother has been gambling. He, in turn, is sexually tortured by the nude sunbathing of the woman next door, is involved in a car accident, and—when his wife's lover Sy is killed in an coincidental accident—is forced to pay for his enemy's funeral! Wait! More is coming. The Coens' great joke in this well-crafted and alternately sad and silly tale is that the sufferings of a schlep like Larry can be worse even than those of the Old Testament's Job.

The subject, the utter unpredictability of life, is a rich one, especially when the hero, like Job, is a believer, a good man. In his search for answers, Larry seeks out three rabbis who, predictably, can offer him nothing accept simple prescriptions ("you have to see things from a different perspective") or meaningless stories (the second rabbi's tale of a dentist who discovers a secret message in the teeth of one of his patients is a gem). The third rabbi (played by an acquaintance of mine, Alan Mandell) can't be bothered to see him. The attorney only complicates Larry's life further by charging him large sums of money.

What happens to faith, to one's sense of being, to an understanding of the universe—a subject at the heart of Larry's love of physics—when faced with such a series of dilemmas and betrayals? Would that the Coens really cared about these issues and at least sought out some possible suggestions to the problem, even if we know there can be no real explanation.

Too often in their films, the Coen brothers present characters that are more like cartoons than actual living folk, and in this film we quickly discover ourselves unable to sympathize with anyone, including the confused Larry; he's so passive and unassertive that, at times, we almost feel he deserves what he gets. And the Coens, in their manipulations of their character types, purposely require us to laugh and cry at situations that often are so bizarre that we feel the directors are simply thumbing their nose at us.

For a few moments in this film, a fog seems to lift: stoned out of his mind, Danny nonetheless gets through his reading of the Torah splendidly: the family is proud, Larry's wife almost seeming to suggest that there might be a way to return to normalcy. Larry even gets tenure.

But the Coens are determined to turn even that possible resurrection of life into a joke. The doctor calls, reporting that there was something in Larry's recent Xrays that they need to discuss. A tornado is pounding down upon Danny's school and the principal cannot seem to open the basement door. The End. Thumbing their nose in complete disrespect of any genuine audience emotion, the Coens throw their work to the dogs. All right, so there is no predictable order in the world! But even Job finally got a break, was ultimately restored to God, awarded a new family and wealth, and allowed to live on for 140 years.

LOS ANGELES, OCTOBER 9, 2009
Reprinted from *World Cinema Review* (October 2009).
Reprinted from *Reading Films: My International Cinema* (Los Angeles: Green Integer, 2012).

The Creepy Stuff I Did

DAVID LETTERMAN **LATE SHOW WITH DAVID LET-
TERMAN** / OCTOBER 1, 2009, CBS

WOODY ALLEN AND MARSHALL BRICKMAN (WRIT-
ERS), WOODY ALLEN (DIRECTOR) **MANHATTAN** / 1979

JOE BINI, P. G. MORGAN, AND MARINA ZENOVICH
(WRITERS), MARINA ZENOVICH (DIRECTOR) **ROMAN PO-
LANSKI: WANTED AND DESIRED** / 2008, THE SHOWING
I WITNESSED WAS AT THE MELNITZ THEATRE, UCLA, ON
OCTOBER 1, 2009

WHILE RECENTLY LISTENING to David Letterman's
"confession" of his sexual encounters on late-night television, I was bemused and more than a little frightened,
once again, by my fellow citizens' sexual prudery and
by the underlying attitudes we Americans seem to have
about sex in general.

Letterman, as most Americans now know, was being blackmailed by CBS producer Robert "Joe" Halder-
man for having had—are you sitting down?—"sex with
a woman who worked with me on this show." Alleg-

edly these sexual encounters all occurred before his marriage to Regina Lasko and the birth of their son, although there are now suggestions that he took one of the women, Stephanie Birkett, on a Caribbean vacation with his wife and son.

However, unless Letterman threatened these women with dismissals from their jobs if they did not have sex with him, it amazes me that anyone might have thought that he could get away with blackmail or that viewers might even imagine this to be of interest except to Letterman, his wife, and the women with whom he had sex. Certainly, these issues can lead (and evidently have) to matrimonial difficulties and may someday end up as an issue in divorce court, but in my estimation those issues have no place at all in the minds of prudish American television viewers, who every day, it seems, are shocked and absolutely amazed that our celebrities and leaders lead lives as sexual beings!

The media, of course, mightily fuels this ridiculous outrage. In France or even Italy, the public and press might hail Letterman as an ordinary man. But here he is forced to describe his noncriminal behavior as "creepy," as if he were some strange deviant, hiding his actions from an innocent American mass. Although the American divorce rate, as some sources show, has decreased in the last few years by 30%, it is still, according to The Marriage Index, two to six times higher than in Canada and European countries. Divorce may occur for numerous reasons, yet infidelity is obviously high among its causes. Accordingly, Letterman may be a *very* ordinary man. Why are we so fascinated by the topic?

If one of these women had been an underage intern, it would be a different matter. And that is what we must consider in the recent arrest of Roman Polanski, to whose side numerous Hollywood figures have recently come, in support of his being freed from Swiss prison and possible US extradition.

At some point I would like to discuss American and current international attitudes (largely in response to American pressure) about sexuality and children. As a society, the rising hysteria about child abuse—and I will assert that it has reached that level of behavior since it has become something that cannot be rationally discussed—is dismaying to the say the least. Our viewpoint is based on a Victorian notion of childhood isolation, a blessèd time of innocence in which children are to be protected from the world at large, and there is a certain wisdom, I am sure, in this vision, even if the reality seems to be pointing to the opposite, that today's children are increasingly behaving, earlier and earlier in their childhood, as adults (with results both good and bad). Those facts, also fueled by the media, in turn fan the flames of further fears which Americans play out.

Nearly everyone save sexual predators themselves, recognizing the power adults have over children's minds and bodies, wants to protect juveniles from the sexual advances of men and women who may psychologically hurt them, physically abuse them, or even kill them; most civilized societies understand those dangers and seek to protect their young. But at what age to draw the line? We have somewhat arbitrarily named the age of 18, even though one can enlist, without parental consent, to go to war at age 17. Evidently, children have permission to die, as long as they do it as virgins.

No matter what age is chosen to be appropriate, on the other hand, there will always appear to be exceptions, children more advanced, physically and sexually, than their peers. And one cannot expect the judge or jury to make such determinations, to pick and choose among the victims. On the other hand, in severe cases of murder and mayhem there seems to be an increasing decision among prosecutors to try some juveniles as adults. Not being a lawyer, I don't know what kind of criteria goes into these determinations, but it does seem somewhat hypocritical when we can pick and choose how we apply life imprisonment or even the death sentence to underage children, while making no allowance for their sexuality.

In his 1979 film *Manhattan*, Woody Allen flirts with this very issue. Recently revisiting this film, I was a little abashed to remember that the girl Allen takes up with, after his second wife (Meryl Streep) has run away with another woman, is a 17-year-old high school girl (Mariel Hemingway). Although the Allen character is clearly uncomfortable with the idea—joking at one point, "I'm older than her father, can you believe that? I'm dating a girl wherein I can beat up her father."—no one else seems appalled by the fact. Indeed all of Allen's friends in the movie seem to be involved, like Letterman, in extramarital affairs (particularly the character Yale, played by Michael Murphy) or, in the case of Diane Keaton's character, easily shift from bed to bed. Only Tracy, Allen's 17-year-old lover, seems to know what she wants—an older lover to "fool around" with. Not until Allen has sent her packing does he realize how much he misses her; but she's now 18 and on her way to a new experience in life, a six-month stay in England, which, incidentally, he had previously recommended to her.

That film received nearly unanimous praise, and no reviewer I've read seemed at all appalled that it was, in some senses, a film about child abuse. Maybe because it was fiction it was saved from public outcry, although one must remember that just two decades earlier *Lolita*, another fiction about this subject, was banned in the US.

Allen, one should recall, has had his own sexual *scandale*, involving himself in an affair with Soon-Yi Previn, the adopted daughter of Allen's lover of the time, Mia Farrow, a romance she discovered by finding nude pictures of her daughter taken by Allen. Frankly, I might describe Allen's actions as far more "creepy" than anything Letterman has done. Ultimately, Allen married Soon-Yi, and they remain married today. It comes as no surprise, accordingly, that Allen is one of the signatories of the petition demanding Polanski's release from jail.

If, in the film-fiction *Manhattan*, Tracy is apparently more mature than all the adults of that film, the girl with whom Polanski had sex in 1977, Samantha Geimer, although a mature-looking girl, was not even close to legal age; she was only 13 at the time. Geimer, moreover, clearly did not want a sexual relationship with her photographer and reported his sexual advances as rape to the police. Whether Polanski had set out to rape her or whether his sex with her seemingly arose from a too-intimate setting, a sauna at Jack Nicholson's house, is not really the issue. Polanski fed her both champagne and part of a Quaalude before engaging in sex. And even imagining that, as a sexual swinger of the international set, he was unaware of how serious Americans took such infractions, he surely couldn't have been so stupid to think his actions would have no consequence.

Although one might find it psychologically fascinating that he committed these infractions just a few years after the brutal slaying by Charles Manson and his dreadful followers of Polanski's beloved wife, Sharon Tate—events all further interwoven, surely, with his childhood memories of the murder of his parents in the death chambers of World War II concentration camps—it can have no direct bearing on his criminal behavior, particularly since he was twice found to be free of serious psychological problems. It may be fascinating to consider those issues when discussing his films, but they cannot be seen, as some have attempted, to be an *excuse* for his actions.

Finally, it seems ridiculous to argue, as some in Hollywood have, that he should be excused from this sexual "slip up" because of his immense talent. When will we learn that great artists, writers, and other geniuses are capable of supporting evil actions and those behind them? I love the writing of Knut Hamsun, but to do so one must also accept the fact that he was a supporter of the Nazi cause and actually met with Hitler. My own thinking about poetry has been very influenced by Ezra

Pound, but I cannot condone his support of the Fascists and his anti-Semitic writings. Great artists can also be bad human beings.

Yet Polanski's acts are even more muddied by the actions of the press, lawyers, and judge overseeing his criminal case. As Marina Zenovich's 2008 film *Roman Polanski: Wanted and Desired* (screened at UCLA soon after Polanski's Swiss arrest) reveals, from the moment of Polanski's act he was hounded by the news media, who cast him as the perfect target for Americans who hated the intelligentsia, were xenophobic, and who feared the sexuality he exuded.

The appointed judge for the case, Laurence J. Rittenband, was noted for his relationships with celebrities, and sought out the case, purposely generating news coverage of the hearings. The opposing lawyers, Douglas Dalton (Polanski's lawyer) and Roger Gunson (for the accuser), were intelligent and dedicated lawyers forced to play charades by the judge's shifting impositions of law. Even when the parties agreed to drop all charges except rape and that Polanski would undergo psychological observation, Rittenband further played to the

grandstand, demanding a series of new tests in Chino State Prison. Once again all parties agreed to his demands, yet Rittenband audaciously made them perform his decision out in court, each lawyer playing out the case that had been already previously decided.

Even after serving his time in the Chino prison, Polanski and his lawyer were further threatened by the judge, and after flying to Europe, where the filmmaker was captured in pictures at the Munich Oktoberfest surrounded by young women (an event Polanski had not even wanted to attend, but was encouraged to by a German friend), Rittenband threatened to sentence Polanski to more time in Chino and demanded, *illegally*, that Polanski give up his rights for deportation. Dalton and Polanski refused. Even the blue-eyed upstanding Mormon prosecutor Gunson admits, had he been asked to do what Rittenband had demanded, he too might have left the country. In 1978, after almost a year of such public torture, Polanski illegally fled the US.

That the California enforcers are still vigilantly attempting to return Polanski to the US for sentencing—a sentencing which clearly threatens, as *The New York Times* recently pointed out (Sunday, October 11, 2009), to be a less forgiving prison time for his acts—seems unfair at best.

Although there is little question that Polanski "got off" the first time around, with a very short time in jail, in the end one must ask what is justice, what is imprisonment about? Certainly, justice did not win out in 1978, either for the accuser or accused. Why do we imprison people? Obviously, in part, we incarcerate the guilty as punishment for their crimes. But we seem to have forgotten that we also jail individuals with the hope of reformation, with the desire of somehow redeeming their lives. Today, it appears, particularly when it comes to sex crimes, that we no longer believe in that possibility. And we all know that some sexual abusers, particularly when it comes to children, have committed crimes over and over again. I do think, however, that we should not presume by such recidivism that all such criminals are unable to be reformed. Clearly, Polanski has led, in the 31 years since his escape from America, a productive and seemingly governed life. What can be the use of trotting a 76-year-old man off to prison for a crime he committed at age 44? It seems to me that Polanski has been more than punished for his acts, unless, as I suspect, we are a terrifyingly vengeful society when it comes to sex.

LOS ANGELES, OCTOBER 12-13, 2009
Reprinted from *N^th Position* [England] (November 2009).

When I shared some of the above comments with my M.F.A. students at Otis College of Art + Design, in conjunction with our reading a book that involved issues of sexuality, I found their reactions very similar to what I feared were those of the general American public.

Several of my students insisted that Polanski had to be returned if only to be made a symbol of the fact you cannot simply escape our justice system and "get away with it."

I suggested that I had never been much interested in converting human beings into symbols. But even more importantly, one has to ask what is a symbol?

No one in my class could say, although one ventured, "Something or someone that means something else."

"Perhaps," I replied, "but such a trope could also be an allegory, where every time you see a figure or an image it also stands for another thing throughout the entire text. A symbol, on the other hand, is not one *other person or thing but represents a whole group of possibilities.*

"In Eudora Welty's The Golden Apples, *for example,*

particularly in the first story titled 'Shower of Gold,' we are presented with a character, Miss Snowdie MacLain, a woman who is nearly an albino, who from time to time is visited by her itinerant husband, King MacLain, who upon these occasions impregnates her, only to leave again for more than a year at a spell. The MacLains are characters, a couple in Welty's fiction, who have a very strange relationship, but remain credible characters nonetheless.

"*Surrounding this couple, however, are a series of associations, the 'shower of gold' hinted at in the title, and the fact that she is an albino, unable, at some points, to explain her pregnancies, information we get from the narrator of this story, Mrs. Rainey. When Snowdie announces she is going to have a baby, for example, the narrator notes:*

> *She [Snowdie MacLain] looked like more than only the news had come over her. It was like a shower of something had struck her, like she'd been caught out in something bright. It was more than the day. There with her all crinkled up with always fighting the light, yet she looking out bold as a lion that day under her brim, and gazing into my bucket and into my stall like a visiting somebody.*

"*Now that's good descriptive writing. We feel almost as if we can see Snowdie MacLain, a woman who is a bit* confused about the facts but nonetheless proud of knowing that she is soon to give birth. The story remains just that, a story. But for the knowledgeable reader, the way this story is told suggests other things, stories, images, etc. Do any of you recognize what that 'something else' is?"

None of them spoke.

"In Greek legend we have many stories about Zeus: his rape of Leda as he transformed himself into a swan, his abduction of Europa while disguised as a bull, his love of the Trojan prince Ganymede who was stolen by an eagle sent by Zeus. In short, Zeus, King of the gods, was a serial rapist.

"Another such tale concerns Danaë, the daughter of King Acrisius and Eurydice. When the oracle reported to her father that he would be killed by his daughter's son, Acrisius locked Danaë up in a cave to keep her childless. But Zeus appeared this time as a golden rain, a 'golden shower' that impregnated her with a child, Perseus, who would later kill Medusa, the female monster whose gaze turned people to stone. Perseus later participated in the athletic games in Larissa, throwing a discus which, by accident, hit an attending guest, Acrisius, in the head, killing him and fulfilling, of course, the oracle's prediction.

"Welty's character Snowdie shares a great deal with Danaë, and reading about her reminds one of that myth and other such myths Welty weaves throughout the stories of The Golden Apples. Snowdie is not Danaë, but shares things in common with her and the events surrounding that Greek myth, and Welty's story is enriched by this combination of associations.

"That is a symbolic relationship. But it works only if the reader knows the Greek myth. None of you knew it, which is why, I would suggest, most writers don't use symbolism these days. In our society in which fewer books are read and we have forgotten much of our literary history, we have lost sight of many of the associations that allow for symbols to properly function."

As I told this story, I privately wondered how Welty's brilliant collection—filled with tales of abduction and rape—might be received today. Would today's readers find the genteel Miss Welty an immoral writer advocating child sexuality since, at one point, two young twin boys rape a girl their age?

"Perhaps you mean that Polanski should be made an 'example,'" I suggested. "But, I might ask, in my role as Devil's Advocate, what would his being sent back to jail be an example of, to whom would that example be conveyed?"

"An example of our justice system," one student nearly shouted. "An example to others that you can't just expect to run away from your criminal actions and live happily ever after just because you're rich and famous."

"I have my doubts," I answered, "about punishment actually preventing crimes. I think most people who commit such acts as Polanski did are either convinced that they are somehow above the law, that it doesn't apply to them, or that they probably won't get caught. I suppose there are some potential child molesters out there who might think twice about actually acting on their thoughts; perhaps there are more than I can imagine, and the punishments meted out by the system prevent these men and women from acting. I hope that's true.

"Yet it seems to me that criminals will continue to proliferate, with or without examples of how our system operates. Just look at the overcrowded prisons we find throughout our country. Never before have our prisons been so full of men and women who have broken our laws; in 2008 almost 4 million people were incarcerated at year's end."

(While I was editing this, CNN reported that this year to date there have been 90,000 rapes! Could that be true, I wondered to myself? Upon checking the statistics elsewhere I discovered that over the past two years 787,000 US women were the victims of sexual assault! What can that say about our society, when even rape becomes, in some perverse way, ordinary? Imagine every man and woman and child in the state of South Dakota, population 804,000, involved in such acts! I can only ask myself, "What is wrong with this picture? Could it be that there is a correlation between our fears about and lurid fascination with all things sexual and the brutal behavior behind these acts?")

"When I hear, we have to make an 'example' of someone, I think of something like a frontier posse angrily gathering to track down their man, an event that usually ends in a hanging or a shoot-out. Even if this posse were to catch their man and bring him safely back to justice I suspect any example it might convey would be to the law-abiding society itself, which implies that the example works something like a pat on the back: 'Good for us! Hooray! We've got a great system of laws.'

"I don't think I like the idea of turning human beings into examples either."

"Justice has to be served!" proclaimed another student.

"That may be true," I argued, "but in this case it wasn't served. Judge Rittenband, as I told you, twisted the system for his own purposes. Were Polanski to have stayed for his sentencing, I should imagine his case might easily have been overturned given all the illegal maneuvers the lawyers from both sides describe. What that would have meant for Polanski is probably numerous other courtroom battles. Whose justice is it, finally, to try a man over and over from the same crime? In a sense, by fleeing the country, Polanski gave Rittenband just what he had illegally demanded. Polanski deported himself, and for all these years has never been able to return to the US."

Two of my women students stridently spoke up: "I

think he should be locked up and they should throw away the key."

"Precisely my point," I responded. "With regard to sex we are a vengeful folk."

At that instant I don't think my students much liked me.

Evidently, the seemingly non-judgmental Swiss also felt that the American attitudes towards sex were slightly perverse, and let Polanski out of prison so that he might return to his home in France.

LOS ANGELES, OCTOBER 13-14, 2009

A Desperate Foolishness

GLENN FICARRA AND JOHN REQUA (WRITERS AND
DIRECTORS, BASED ON A BOOK BY STEVEN MCVICKER) I
LOVE YOU PHILLIP MORRIS / 2009, USA 2010

GLENN FICARRA and John Requa's comic-drama, *I Love You Phillip Morris*, is hardly a great film, but in its mix of *Catch Me If You Can*  and *Dog Day Afternoon* (with perhaps a little of *Raising Arizona* tossed in) it's a kind of delightful mulligan stew about gay love.

Like *Catch Me If You Can* and *Dog Day Afternoon*, this film was based, for the most part, on true events. A former policeman, church choir director, and married father of a young girl, Steven Jay Russell (a less frantic than usual Jim Carrey) apparently lives out a desperately closeted life in Virginia and later in Texas, enjoying a close, if sexually unsatisfying, relationship with his wife and good social relationships with his neighbors—until one day, after a car crash, he comes to an epiphany that he is dissatisfied with his life. He leaves his wife and child and moves to Miami, finds a boyfriend (Rodrigo Santoro), and begins living an openly gay life. Unfortunately, as he explains, the gay lifestyle is quite expensive, so Russell begins the life of a con-man, but is soon discovered and sent to prison.

Russell quickly develops in prison the same kind of skills to manipulate the system as he did on the outside. When he meets a young, innocent, fellow prisoner, Phillip Morris (Ewan McGregor), he immediately falls in love. Although Morris is being relocated to another part of the prison, Russell finds secret ways to keep in communication, and before long has been transferred to Morris' cell, where their love is quickly consummated and they enter a deep-committed relationship, Russell promising to protect the younger Morris.

After Russell pays for others to beat a screaming inmate next to their cell ("That is the most romantic thing anyone ever did for me. I love you so much," gushes Morris) and Morris arranges to have romantic music played late at night so the two can dance, authorities separate the couple, sending Russell to another prison. The breakup is devastating as Morris rushes into the

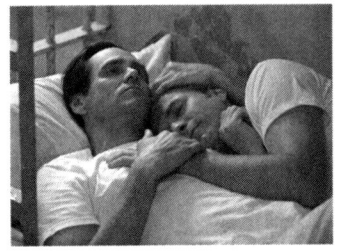

prison yard—which he has previously been terrified to enter—to scream out his love for Russell, Russell responding with the film's title: "I love you, Philip Morris."

It is only here that the movie really begins, with Russell conning his way through system after system, becoming a lawyer so that he can free his lover, accomplishing small check frauds and false bodily injury claims, and, finally, finagling a job as a CFO for a large corporation, where he embezzles millions of dollars just to support Morris in a lifestyle he "deserves." Indeed there is a sense throughout the film of Morris' belief in entitlement, perhaps because he has been previously so closeted, but also out of a righteous sense that the two deserve to live their lives in joyful celebration of their love. And to be fair, his cons actually make his company millions of dollars as well; he simply takes half of what he illegally raises by investing temporary payments into short-term accounts. His theft is petty when compared, one imagines, to the real CFOs and Wall Street business sharks. Yet time and again, Russell is caught and returned to prison. Through various clever ploys he escapes time after time (in real life Russell was described as the Houdini of prisoners), using the telephone with his skillful ability to convince unwitting authorities, several attempts at suicide, costumes, and other manipulations of the system to free himself and return to Morris.

When Russell is arrested after his business fraud, however, Morris is furious with the lies and deceit of his friend:

> From the moment we met, you did nothing but lie. Our whole relationship, just lies. I'm such an asshole. You took advantage of me, just like all the others. You were supposed to protect me. But you did nothing but make a fool out of me. And you expect me to love you? How can I love you. I don't even know who you are. You know what's sad? I don't even think you know who you are. So how am I supposed to love someone that don't even exist, you tell me.

The two, however, remain in love, Morris ultimately returned to prison as an accomplice with Russell. While recognizing the truth of Morris' comments, Russell plots yet one more large con so that he can free himself and work to free Morris. Losing vast amounts of weight and forging prison hospital records, he is de-

clared to have AIDS and, as he grows more and more ill (largely acted), he is sent to hospice to die. Morris hears of his near death, and by telephone reaffirms his love, recognizing that all the crazy things Russell has done have been, at heart, for him and their relationship. They are, as they agree, fools for love.

The final irony is that the man who does "not exist" dies—so Morris is told. But when Russell shows up as a lawyer to visit Morris in prison, his lover punches him in the face. Russell again pleas:

> Wait, listen. I just came here to tell you one thing, and that's it. You don't have to take me back. I just want to say one thing. I know you think that we were nothing but a lie, but underneath all those lies, there was always something that was real. I thought about what you said to me. You said you don't know who I am, but I know now. I know who I am. I'm not a lawyer, I'm not a CFO, I'm not a cop, I'm not an escape artist. Those Steven Russells are dead. Now all that's important is the man that loves you. And if you could see that, believe it, I promise I'll never be anything else ever again.

Morris' response: "How do I know you're not bullshitting me again?" is answered with the inevitable: "You don't."

In fact Russell does try, as a lawyer, to free his friend once again, but in the process is recognized. This time he is returned to prison for 140 years, and the real Steven Jay Russell remains in prison, in complete isolation, today.

Morris was released. But in the last scene Russell is still dreaming of his friend, imagining himself running from the guards in a final race toward love.

What began as a comedy has ended in a kind tragedy, for the man who sought so much out of his life has ended up with absolutely nothing. Whether or not he "deserves" better, the American justice system will not forgive such desperate foolishness.

LOS ANGELES, JANUARY 7, 2011
Reprinted from *World Cinema Review* (January 2012).

Voyage to the Future, Voyage to the Past

JAKUB GOLDBERG, ROMAN POLANSKI, AND JERZY SKOLIMOWSKI (WRITERS), ROMAN POLANSKI (DIRECTOR) **NÓZ W WODZIE (KNIFE IN THE WATER)** / 1962

TENSION IS PERHAPS the operative word in describing Roman Polanski's 1962 amazing debut film, *Knife in the Water*. From the first scene in the film, where Andrzej and Krystyna are driving down an unpaved lane on their way to a boating trip, to the last image of the car at a crossroad, Andrzej undecided about which direction to take, the movie projects a sense of dread, sexual anxiety, and fear of death.

In that first scene, with Krystyna at the wheel of their car, Andrzej criticizes her driving; she stops the car as they silently exchange positions. We know already, accordingly, that this married couple is inured to each other's assaults, and we recognize that their relationship will be a subject of the narrative.

Soon after, the couple encounters a young boy (the only name he is given in the credits) standing in the middle of the road, refusing to budge in his attempt to catch a ride. In anger at the boy's position, Andrzej swears and drives unnecessarily close to the hitchhiker before stopping the car. In a pattern that will be repeated throughout the film, he chastises and dismisses the young man before taking him into the back seat, a situation, obviously, similar to the abusive relationship between him and his wife.

They arrive at the harbor that holds their small skiff, seemingly happy to rid themselves of their unwanted guest. But when the young boy begins to leave them, Andrzej calls him back, inviting him to join their overnight excursion. The young man demurs; he is a hiker, a man of the woods (he later declares he cannot swim). But the older man challenges him further, and the dare is taken up. We know now that the film will center upon the tension between the two, upon Andrzej's attempts to outperform the younger man, the young boy's fearless actions wrapped up in his youthful good looks.

Of course Andrzej has taken in the younger man precisely to prove that, despite his age, he is still a virile being, worthy of his younger, attractive wife. And a great deal of the movie is taken up in the intense detail of the couple's actions as they take the boat out of

harbor, prepare lunch and dinner, raise the sails and lower them, etc. They are a team, like a well-oiled machine, who work perfectly together. And their actions are clearly meant to educate (for Andrzej at least) the young innocent in their midst.

However, what doesn't get discussed in the reviews and essays I have read is that not only is Andrzej attempting to prove his marital rights, he is also sexually attracted to the young boy, and many of the dares they toss to one another are homoerotic flirtations. The fixation of the young man upon his hunting knife and his skill in using it is clearly symbolic of male virility. There is something almost pathetic about Andrzej's attempt to imitate the young man's game of quickly maneuvering the knife between his fingers in stabs against the wooden floor of the boat. Compared to the young man, he is slow and awkward. When the boy easily scampers up to the top of the mainsail it is as if he were putting on display, his lithe, muscled body like some sort of wild beast.

Andrzej, on the other hand, perfectly at home in the boat, relishes the discomfort of the younger man

who has found himself on a voyage that seems anything but a pleasurable day trip. Throughout the movie, the trio is forced to pull the boat—almost like a scene out of *The African Queen*—through swampy rush-covered spots, float it in a frozen barren of windless space, and rudder the craft under storm-laden skies. When, in a sudden squall, they pull the boat into a small haven for the night, retreating to the cramped quarters below deck, we are certain that the psychological battles in which the males have been engaged will spill over into literal violence. A pesky mosquito attacking the young man's face reinforces that sensation.

But Polanski takes the sexual attractions of the trio even further as they play a game of pick-up sticks in which the loser of each round must surrender an item upon his body. Andrzej, a master of this entertainment, loses nothing, while Krystyna loses a shoe, and the young boy temporarily loses his shirt and his beloved knife.

At sunrise, as the young man and Krystyna sit upon the deck, the predicted violence erupts. Andrzej, having pocketed the young man's knife and desperate to reclaim his sexual virility, reveals that he has the taken the weapon, daring the young man to come forward and "get" it. When the handsome boy—standing in frieze as if he himself were the "knife in the water"—attempts to do so, the knife falls into the lake, Andrzej pushing the young man onto a rig that juts over the water, as the boy follows the path of his treasured "tool."

Before they can even take stock, they have lost sight of the man, Krystyna declaring that Andrzej has killed him! Both Krystyna and Andrzej attempt to discover his body, but are unable to do so: the young man hangs on a nearby buoy, diving beneath it as they search all sides of the object.

It is Krystyna now who expresses her anger and frustration. Both men are boys, she declares, playing some absurd game for her affections. Disgusted—and fearful—for the consequences of their sport she vents her rage against her husband. Furiously, Andrzej swims away, also disappearing from sight, and she is left alone, the only stable being, and the only one able to soberly return their boat to port.

The young man, who evidently can swim, if somewhat awkwardly, returns to the boat, as Krystyna now berates him for his own version of swagger, clearly emanating from his bitterness at his poverty-stricken youth, and challenging what, for him, appears as a class difference (few Polish people in those days owned cars, let alone boats; Andrzej is a university professor). Krystyna, however, sets him straight: that, in truth, he is no different from them, that they have had to endure the same difficulties, privations which she straight-forwardly lists. In short, the young man is himself a future Andrzej. The skiff that has circled in its movements throughout the day has been a journey for Andrzej into the past, for the boy into the hidden world that lies ahead.

At the moment, however, the young man (played by Zygmunt Malanowicz, who later appeared in over 30 films) is so stunningly beautiful that her attraction to him is nearly uncontrollable. The two release that tension through sex.

Entering the harbor, the boy escaping to shore before she docks, Krystyna greets Andrzej. Immediately they return to their patterned ways of life as they close up the boat and return to their car, he insisting that he will go to the police. When she finally admits that the boy swam back to the boat, he refuses to believe her, suggesting that it is she who is terrified of facing the truth. Denying this, she admits that she has had sex with the boy. Andrzej rejects her statements as a cover. Yet as their car reaches the fork in the road where they will turn either to the police station or home, Andrzej stops the automobile, clearly unable to make a decision. The camera pans away from them, their car remaining in place as the screen blackens. Either he must face his own criminal behavior or the new future with which she has presented him.

LOS ANGELES, JULY 26, 2009
Reprinted from *World Cinema Review* (July 2009).
Reprinted from *Reading Films: My International Cinema* (Los Angeles: Green Integer, 2012).

20 Days in the City of Angels: The 19th Day (Interviewing the Interviewer)

THE CONDOMINIUM in which I live lies directly across the street from a high-rise building in which are currently located the offices of *Variety*, an entertainment daily magazine to which I do *not* subscribe, but which, as a child—on those rare occasions when I came across a copy in Marion, Iowa—utterly fascinated me since it was an entire newspaper devoted to theater, film, and others of my favorite cultural activities. Even today, I can't imagine who in my small city might have been subscribing to it and how I might have encountered copies, but—as any regular reader of the *My Year* volumes knows—stranger things have happened to me.

Recently I read of the death of one of *Variety's* most noted columnists, Armand "Army" Archerd, on September 8th of this year, and that in turn reminded me of the February 7th, 2008 press opening of the Los Angeles

County Museum of Art's new Broad Museum, when I had lunch with him.

It was not a true interview, of either him or me, but a happenstance of open seating of which I took advantage to introduce myself and to question him on his long career.

I had known a little about him, simply through celebrations in print of his life. Archerd replaced columnist Sheilah Graham (the noted girlfriend of F. Scott Fitzgerald) in 1953, and worked at *Variety* for the rest of his life, most notably covering Hollywood news and gossip in his "Just for Variety" column. Close acquaintances describe him as a handsome, always nattily dressed man; he was both on the day I encountered him as well, although when I met him he had just recently reached the grand age of 86.

Unlike some gossip columnists, who cattily seemed to spy on Hollywood performers, Archerd interviewed them, often reporting their own corrections to tabloid gossip and sharing information the stars themselves wanted to be made public. Accordingly, he was beloved by many in the Hollywood community, and was highly celebrated in a 40th anniversary event thrown for him by his own paper at the Beverly Hilton Hotel in 1993.

Among his hundreds of famous pithy observations were Hitchcock's comments from Army's column in 1966:

> He [Hitchcock] also regrets too many film writers today believe plot is out of fashion. "Plot in a short story and a movie is the most important thing. The motion picture is like a short story—it's the only medium you expect to see in continuity without a break. You have to consider the endurance of the human bladder."

Or the wonderful quip from Cary Grant in Archerd's 1975 column:

> Cary Grant *has his attorneys investigating suits* vs. *People* mag and Associated Press, the former for printing he has false teeth. "I want to get into court and open my mouth," said Grant. And the AP suit involves their quotes from a *Redbook* yarn (which Grant claims doesn't exist), saying he never loved any of his wives.

and Archerd's 1960 news item:

> The "mystery malady" which laid low Marilyn Monroe is an allergy to medication, she says. "At one time I was out cold," she admits. "Now the

only thing I'll take is aspirin." MM mystified guests at her cocktail party launching "Let's Make Love," Friday, by showing up on time.

I asked him what he was presently working on, and he replied without an instant of thought: "A memoir."

"Wonderful," I responded. "It will have to include everyone! I'll read it."

"Except Greta Garbo. I never got to interview her," he admitted.

I briefly explained my work on my own "cultural" memoir, in which he seemed interested. I wish I'd been able to send him a volume or two.

I asked which piece of his reporting he felt had been his most important.

"Oh, definitely my piece on Rock Hudson announcing that he was sick with AIDS."

That 1985 item began:

The whispering campaign on Rock Hudson can— and should stop. He has flown to Paris for further help. The Institute Pasteur has been very active in research on Acquired Immune Deficiency Syndrome. Hudson's dramatic weight loss was made evident to the national press last week when he winged to Carmel to help longtime friend Doris Day launch her new pet series. His illness was no secret to close Hollywood friends, but its true nature was divulged to very, very few. He left for France and possible aid from scientists there over the weekend. Doctors warn that the dread disease (AIDS) is going to reach catastrophic proportions in all communities if a cure is not soon found....

"Of course many Hollywood columnists had long hinted about Hudson's gay sexuality," I added. "I recall reading one such column in the 1950s in which the writer warned that if a well-known actor showed up once again on Santa Monica Boulevard, trying to pick up a trick, there would be no way she could any longer hide his identity."

"I never did that kind of writing," he protested.

"I know. But Hudson was pretty obvious," I admitted. "I once saw him with Rod McKuen on an interview show with Dinah Shore. I guess they were doing some kind of record together. It was quite embarrassing, each of them almost swooning over the other, hardly able to keep their hands to themselves."

"Today, I think there would be no way to cover up such behavior. But we—others and I—kept some respect for the stars' privacy. It was the only way I knew how to write about the men and women on whom I depended for my career."

We ceased chatting and dug into Chef Joachim Splichal's delicious beef short ribs.

LOS ANGELES, SEPTEMBER 30, 2009
Reprinted from *Green Integer Blog* (October 2009).

A New Beginning

KIYOSHI KUROSAWA, MAX MANNIX, SACHIKO
TANAKA (SCREENPLAY), KIYOSHI KUROSAWA (DIREC-
TOR) **TOKYO SONATA** / 2008, RELEASED IN THE USA IN
MARCH 2009

EARLY IN *TOKYO SONATA* we witness a rainstorm, the
breeze blowing the raindrops into the modest Tokyo
home of Megumi and Ryuhei Sasaki. Megumi rushes to
close the sliding glass door and wipe up the water that
has fallen to her floor, but in the very midst of the act,
she pauses, momentarily opening the door once more.
We recognize her immediately as a woman pondering
the dangers that lie outside her seemingly tranquil life.

Ryuhei works as an executive director of a department that suddenly has hired a new Chinese woman—
willing to work for considerably less than most of the
other employees—and before the day is done, Ryuhei
is fired. Startled by his new situation, and completely
unprepared for it, he briefly wanders the streets before

returning home.

Communication between family members is failing. The oldest son, Takashi, a college student, rarely returns home, and when he does he says little; Ryuhei describes him as "hopeless." Kenji, the youngest, increasingly realizes that communication with all adults is a dangerous business. Caught in the classroom passing on a book of sexually explicit manga drawings, he is punished by the teacher. Feeling the punishment to be unfair, he reports in front of the class that he has seen the teacher viewing anime on his way to school, challenging the man's authority. Accordingly, at home he eats silently, while his father broods. When Kenji surprisingly asks if he might take piano lessons, Ryuhei explodes, adamantly refusing to even consider it. Only Megumi seems to be able to speak civilly to her husband and children.

Pretending to leave for work the next morning, Ryuhei spends the day on a park bench, lunching on free food set up for the unemployed and poor. After facing long lines to the unemployment office, he has been told that he might be able to obtain a job as a manager of a food store, but rejects it as too menial. Discovering an old college friend in the same food line, Ryuhei learns how to make use of the local library and other places where the two can wait out their imaginary work day.

Having given up on trying to communicate his desires, Kenji secretly signs on for piano lessons in a near-by home, using the money given to him by his mother for the month's lunches at school. We see an increasingly frustrated Takashi, unable to find any suitable career. Ryuhei, meanwhile, begins a long descent into a world of secrets and lies. Indeed this very normal-seeming family has nearly fallen silent, terrifying Megumi and creating a tension between them that is ominous to say the least. As the overly-wise daughter of Ryuhei's friend observes of Sasaki, "You've got it bad, haven't you?"

Takashi's decision to join the American military as an alien worker further plunges the Sasaki family into anger, as the father refuses to sign the permission, and Takashi leaves their home permanently. Although Takashi survives Iraq, he determines to stay in the USA as a potential terrorist in response to the acts he has witnessed.

Kenji, meanwhile, has discovered that he has a natural gift for music and is told that his playing shows signs of genius. When his mother discovers a small broken keyboard in his room and receives a letter inviting their son to apply to music school, she is both troubled by his deceit and delighted by his talent. But Ryuhei, once again, grows angry in his inability to control his family and his own life, pushing the son from the staircase to the floor below. Fortunately, Kenji survives the slight concussion.

The vortex of fear and anger spirals even further out of control as Ryuhei hears that his friend and wife have committed suicide, and, determining to take any job available, secretly begins work as a janitor in a local shopping center. If thus far *Toyko Sonata* seems best understood as a kind of psychological soap-opera of events which are easily recognizable in the context of today's global economy, Kurosawa pushes his film into another dimension as Megumi encounters her husband working in the red garb of a cleaning man in a shopping center.

Suddenly, the movie shifts from its realist perspective, skipping back into a time a few hours earlier, where we witness Megumi being taped and bound in her home by a would-be thief. Discovering that she has no money, the thief prepares to leave, removing the covering that has hidden his face. The sound of a police siren, sends him back into the house, and, too late, he realizes he will now be recognized by his victim. He forces her into a stolen car, and the two race away to...well, that is the problem: both the incompetent thief and victim have nowhere to go.

From here on the movie pitches into a kind of tragicomic opera, as Megumi demands they stop by the local shopping mall for the toilet and to pick up a few provisions for her new journey. There she repeats the encounter with her husband we have witnessed earlier. Ryuhei rushes away, declaring, "It's not what it seems."

Meanwhile, Megumi surprisingly returns to the car and the astonished thief. Without a destination the two drive to the ocean, where they camp out in a small shed and share with each another tales of their failed lives. The sexual encounter that follows lies somewhere between an act of passion and rape. Megumi determines she cannot go home, and lies upon the beach preparing to wait out her fate. As Megumi has told the thief in their conversation, she feels that she is trapped with no options for a future, but wishes that there could be a way to simply "start over," to be born again. Yet we know Megumi has too much sense of purpose to completely give up her present life, and when she awakens

we discover her back in the shed, the thief having apparently driven the car into his watery grave.

Ryuhei has attempted to run so far from the reality of his life that he is now seen stumbling and falling upon the rubble of Tokyo overpasses and streets. At this point, he is so delirious that he races out in front of a car and, so it seems, is hit. The driver pulls him away from the car's grille and deposits him by the roadside, apparently leaving him for dead.

Kenji attempts to sneak a ride in the baggage section of a bus on its way to another city, and after being caught by the driver, is arrested and imprisoned for the night, refusing to answer any of the police's questions.

With the rising of the sun and the disappearance of her captor, Megumi has little choice but to return home. But this time, unlike all the comings and goings we have seen before, the house lies empty. Without her presence, it is as if none of the others can return either. The increasing silences of the household members has transformed this into a house of death. However, in that reality, and through each of their symbolic deaths, they are now freed. Kenji's cell is opened; the case has been dropped. Miraculously Ryuhei awakens, slightly battered but able to walk. As, one by one, they slowly come through the door, there is a sense that life may "start over" after all.

The final scene depicts Kenji's piano audition, to which Ryuhei and Megumi arrive just before their son plays. Kurosawa ends his meditation on family life with a complete performance, brilliantly played by Kenji, of "Claire de Lune," Claude Debussy's setting of Paul Verlaine's poem in which dead dancers perform in the moonlight, an appropriate piece since it signals the family's recovery from lunacy and death.

At times a bit lugubrious and lacking in believability, *Tokyo Sonata* nonetheless is an engaging portrait of the dilemmas and strengths faced by contemporary families.

LOS ANGELES, APRIL 6, 2009
Reprinted from *N^{th} Position* [England] (April 2009).
Reprinted from *Reading Films: My International Cinema* (Los Angeles: Green Integer, 2012).

Turning Back

ROBIN SWICORD (SCREENPLAY, BASED ON A
SCREENPLAY STORY BY ERIC ROTH AND ROBIN SWICORD
SUGGESTED BY THE STORY BY F. SCOTT FITZGERALD),
DAVID FINCHER (DIRECTOR) **THE CURIOUS CASE OF
BENJAMIN BUTTON** / 2008

AS PERCEPTIVE critics have noted (as opposed to those, such as *Los Angeles Times* critic Kenneth Turan, who dismissed this film), *The Curious Case of Benjamin Button*, very loosely based on a story by F. Scott Fitzgerald, is a love tale, a fable of love moving in opposite directions. The hero, Benjamin Button (Brad Pitt), is born as a man of 80 years old. He falls in love with a young girl named Daisy (Cate Blanchett), who, as she grows to a young teenager and, later, a young woman, continues to reenter and leave Benjamin's life until the moment when they are both nearly the same age and for a few precious years have an intense relationship, conceiving a child.

The tragedy of this tale, however, is that before long Benjamin is doomed to grow too young to care for the child at the very moment when Daisy is becoming too old to care for them both. Accordingly, he leaves her, and she marries another man who is a good father to her young daughter. Benjamin disappears into youth, meeting Daisy only once for a brief sexual encounter, and reenters her life again as a young boy over whom she watches as he descends into infancy and, finally, dies.

If this had been the entire focus of the film, and if Swicord and Roth had let the piece remain, as it is in Fitzgerald's original, as more of a fable than a veristic story, the film might have had a sort of bittersweet charm that could have swept audiences up in its myth. But the authors and director David Fincher have added numerous unrelated adventures, setting the story in a New Orleans about to undergo Hurricane Katrina and propelling Button and other characters into the bitter cold of Minsk and into heroic adventures of World War II, all the while alternating these highly realistically-portrayed events with a kind of moralistic essay on the superior humanity of the film's black figures and the gentle wisdom of its old. Although the movie skirts general sentimentality, it toys with it in its simplistic messages centered around *carpe diem*.

Fortunately, this film is saved by another, more subtle theme, which I believe gives it an epic weight that justifies its length. While Benjamin moves solidly through the film backwards in time, the other characters moving forwards are forced in their encounters with him to rethink their lives and face up to their failures in the past. This results in a kind of "turning back," a decision to change the errors of their past, and, in that sense, leads to a kind of redeeming of life for each of them.

Benjamin's father, Thomas, faced with the horrific specter of an 80-year-old infant, a child moreover that has caused his wife's death, has cruelly abandoned the child on the steps of a boarding house over which a black woman, Queenie, presides. Upon discovering the child, Queenie readily adopts it, allowing it to grow up old in a house of old people. Yet Thomas, upon encountering the child years later, at a time when Benjamin is closer to 50, invites him to dinner and further meet-

ings, ending, as the father grows old, in his revelation
to Benjamin that he is his father. At first, Benjamin is
outraged by the fact of the abandonment as opposed to
the continued kindnesses of his black mother. But Benjamin, in some senses, is presented as a blank slate, and
ultimately a reunion between the two, however shaky,
is accomplished, and he nurses his father into death.

Similarly, the older woman, Elizabeth Abbott
(wonderfully played by Tilda Swinton), with whom
Benjamin has an affair in Minsk, is encouraged by his
gentle love to look back upon her failed marriage and
her own lack of initiative. Once a great swimmer who
attempted, unsuccessfully, to swim the English Chan-
nel, she has done little since except suffer the empty
relationship of her marriage. By film's end, and at the
unlikely age of 62, she successfully achieves the goal she
had previously abandoned.

So too does the heavy-drinking captain Mike of a
New Orleans-based tugboat shift, upon encountering

Benjamin, from braggadocio and whoring to heroic accomplishments as his small craft rams a German U-boat that has destroyed a large Allied warship.

Daisy, intrigued throughout the story by Benjamin, rejects his proffered love simply because he will not go to bed with her the one night she is in town. Later, upon his visit to her in New York, she resists his love because of an affair with another dancer; and finally, suffering from an automobile accident that has robbed her of the possibility of ever again being able to dance, she demands he leave her bedside. Months later, however, she too "turns back," returning to him in New Orleans where they have their intense if brief love affair.

Despite her anger over Benjamin's decision to leave her and their daughter, she gradually recognizes that it has been for the better, and as he descends into boyhood and, ultimately, infancy, she takes over the role of his mother, nursing him back into the metaphorical womb.

Their daughter, Caroline, has clearly been distanced from her mother, but, in the framework of the narrative, has returned to New Orleans to her mother's hospital deathbed during the advance of Hurricane Katrina. She too, accordingly, has turned back, coming to the aide of her mother, as her mother, turning back one more time, insists Caroline read the autobiography of Benjamin Button which reveals the girl's own parentage.

In short, each of the major figures, moving in the opposite direction of the flow of life, is encouraged to reexamine their own forward rush into death. The result is a redemption far deeper than the easy lessons on the surface of Fincher's interesting but deeply flawed film.

LOS ANGELES, JANUARY 5, 2009
Reprinted from *Nth Position* [England] (January 2009).

Letting Go

RONAN BENNETT, MICHAEL MANN, AND ANN
BIDERMAN (WRITERS, BASED ON A BOOK BY BRYAN BUR-
ROUGH), MICHAEL MANN (DIRECTOR) **PUBLIC ENEMIES**
/ 2009

MICHAEL MANN'S *Public Enemies* begins with an intricately-planned and violent prison escape filmed with a hand-held digital camera presenting the up-close, wildly shifting movements of John Dillinger and several fellow prisoners (who later become his "gang"). They break out from the dark confines of the prison into the bright sunlight, a pattern repeated throughout the work as Dillinger moves from dark restaurants, bank lobbies, and hotel rooms to sunny streets and race tracks in his numerous swings between imprisonment and escape. While Dillinger (excellently acted by Johnny Depp) often argues for a life in the sun, symbolized by South America where he plans to escape after a daring train robbery, it is clear that he is almost addicted to the dark.

Even his beautiful girlfriend, Billie Frechette (played by French actor Marion Cotillard), is described as a "blackbird," since she is, she declares, part American Indian (a ridiculous proposition given Cotillard's appearance). Like the heists he hauls from bank vaults, Dillinger steals her love simply by declaring she's the girl for him; she has, evidently, little choice in the matter, and winds up in prison for a two-year term for lying to the police about Dillinger's whereabouts.

Indeed all those who surround Dillinger are doomed, in part because of the ridiculous obsession of the then young Director of the FBI, J. Edgar Hoover (somewhat tongue-in-cheekly played here by Billy Crudup). Through his stand-in, Chicago agent Melvin Purvis (Christian Bale), Hoover is determined to put the Bureau on the map, resulting in greater respect and Congressional funding, which means, in his own terms, that it is "time to take the gloves off." It is almost as if Dillinger and his crime sprees were perfectly timed with the changes in the FBI to make it a national institution.

Just as Dillinger, who brutally kills while seeming, in the public consciousness, to be a kind of Robin Hood—in part for stealing what he calls "bank money" as opposed to the money of everyday investors—so the FBI (and, by extension, Hoover)  demands both blind obedience and love. One of Mann's major themes concerns the growing violence of the FBI, as men dedicated to scientific methods increasingly find themselves on the streets armed with machine-guns. Torture follows, as the agents round up anyone even vaguely connected to Dillinger, demanding information that the detainees often do not have. And one of the most painful scenes in the film is the brutal facial beating of Billie by an FBI interrogator who, when he discovers she has lied to him, is almost ready to kill her until Purvis arrives in time to stop him.

Dillinger, it is clear, is a man on the "go," a man who wants "Everything. Right Now." But like so many American would-be adventurers, unfortunately he does not truly know what he wants and has nowhere to go. He can hardly imagine the life he promises in Buenos

Aires or Caracas. Indeed, as Depp plays him, Dillinger is a man with few deep thoughts, and is forced by the very speed of his living to deliver any ideas up in one-line quips. In a conversation with Purvis, in which Dillinger describes the horrible vision of a dying man, suggesting that the memory will keep Purvis awake nights, Purvis asks: "What keeps you up nights, Mr. Dillinger?" Dillinger replies, "Coffee." In another instance, when Billie complains that she knows nothing about him, Dillinger answers: "I like baseball, movies, good clothes, fast cars...and you. What else you need to know?"

Accordingly, while the movie is spell-bindingly watchable in its dark moments—from the interiors of the banks, hotel halls, and the inky shoot-out at the Little Bohemia Lodge in Northern Wisconsin (where it is almost impossible to tell the difference between Dillinger's gang members and the FBI agents) to Dillinger's final moments in a movie theater—Mann's fable falls apart every time it attempts to establish any aspect of character or explore its simple ideas in any depth. In fact, one might almost argue that, although *Public Enemies* is often lovely and exciting to watch (Depp plays Dillinger, at times, with a balletic beauty), there is little story, and even less substance, to ponder. In short, one might describe *Public Enemies* as a film without a script. And, in that sense, it might as well have been a

silent film instead of one with three listed writers! Like Dillinger, Mann is so determined to get *there* fast that when, at the end, one of the agents visits Billie in her prison cell, determined to tell her that Dillinger's last words were "Bye, Bye Blackbird" (in fact, Dillinger, like the victims he describes in the film, simply slipped away without saying anything), the myth falls apart, and we find no meaning in the act, particularly because the agent has reported to Purvis that he couldn't hear what Dillinger said. Is that last sentimental gesture meant to show there is a heart beating in this empty kettle?

At several times in *Public Enemies* John Dillinger is told that he has to learn how "to let go," to let go of his girlfriend, his actions, and, at some point, his very life. Mann has grabbed on to the Dillinger fable as if it were a bucking bull and rides it for its two hours and 23 minutes as if that achievement might create something of great significance; but in the end, all we have witnessed is a mighty blur of legs and hide. If only for an instant he had let go and fallen off we might have witnessed a bruised human being upon the screen.

LOS ANGELES, JULY 7, 2009
Reprinted from *World Cinema Review* (July 2009).
Reprinted from *Reading Films: My International Cinema* (Los
    Angeles: Green Integer, 2012).

THREE BY HORTON FOOTE

As I mention below, the death of Horton Foote on March 4, 2009 sent me back to three screenplays he had written: To Kill a Mockingbird, *based on a novel by Harper Lee,* The Trip to Bountiful, *and* Tender Mercies, *the latter two emanating from his own pen.*

Foote is the kind of man who, as one of my favorite film guides, Time Out, *describes him, is seen as "admirable." Harper Lee reportedly said of his face something to the effect of: "He looks the way God should, only he's clean shaven." The films I selected to write about are immensely popular, most of them winning awards, two of them being mentioned recently in the* Los Angeles Times *in their list of 10 best "Comfort Films," films they claim to be as appealing in our economically hard times as comfort food.*

Finally, I had enjoyed all three films on which I have chosen to write, having seen the first two of them several times.

How to explain, then, the essays that follow, in which I basically dismiss these films for representing the status quo or, at least, a diminishment of life? Chalk it up, perhaps, to my curmudgeonly shift into older age. Or, perhaps, as I have aged, I simply do not have as simple-minded notions about life and happiness as I did in my youth.

As I wrote early on in this series of My Year *volumes: "I seek no agreement with what I put forth and often have skewed my own perceptions of things in order to explore issues that most interest me."*

Looking at that kindly face—he does sort of look like a god, if you believe in a white god—I am sure that Horton Foote was admirable, kind even, caring, loving, well meaning. But I still don't think I could live in a world created by him.

When Jem Waked Up

HARPER LEE **TO KILL A MOCKINGBIRD** (PHILADEL-
PHIA: J. B. LIPPINCOTT & CO., 1960)

HORTON FOOTE (SCREENPLAY, BASED ON THE
NOVEL BY HARPER LEE), ROBERT MULLIGAN (DIRECTOR)
TO KILL A MOCKINGBIRD / 1962

ALMOST EVERY AMERICAN school child and millions of adults know Harper Lee's classic novel and the
film, scripted by Horton Foote. As Joseph Crespino
wrote in an essay in 2000: "In the 20th century, *To Kill
a Mockingbird* is probably the most widely read book
dealing with race in America, and its protagonist, Atticus Finch, the most enduring fictional image of racial
heroism." Lee's novel and the film, moreover, are etched
in American consciousness; the racial violence of 1936
in the small-town Alabama it recounts dovetailed perfectly with the changes occurring in American minds
and the radical challenges of Southern prejudice which
became a major issue of the 1960s. And in this sense the

book, perhaps, affected more middle-class Americans than any other of its time. Even at a personal level, I remember being impressed when my mother, who read primarily Romances, hosted a book club during this period; my father, brother, sister, and I were consigned to the basement, but I recall creeping up to the doorway, listening in as one book club member dramatically read the scene in which lawyer Atticus Finch is spat upon by the evil Bob Ewell on a downtown Maycomb, Alabama street. When the movie premiered, I was in attendance.

I believe I first read the book a few years later, in 1964, while living in Norway. I recall devouring it in a single afternoon, wiping away the tears as I completed its last pages. There was no question in my mind that it was extremely sentimental—for most of that year I had been reading the works of Thomas Hardy and Henrik Ibsen—but I recognized it for its high moral tone and its gentle nostalgia nonetheless.

With the news of the screenplay writer Horton Foote's death on March 4th, I decided to revisit both the novel and picture. For the most part, Foote's adaptation of Lee's book is successful, if far moodier and grittier than the more comedic original. Indeed Harper Lee was said to have been pleased with Foote's version. But that is not to say there are no crucial differences between film and novel.

Mulligan's black-and-white images, helped by Elmer Bernstein's brooding but lyrical score, create a darker tone than the novel evokes. And Foote's decision to focus the action on the Finch house, the courtroom, and the back country lanes where the Ewells and Robinsons live, along with his  deletion of characters such as Aunt Alexandra and the larger role in the novel played by their childhood friend Dill (based on Truman Capote), further isolates the Finch and Radley families from what is clearly a highly bigoted community. It is almost as if, in Foote's version, Atticus and the children are not given leave to walk the streets of Maycomb. The children's two outings are a nighttime scramble to protect their father from a lynching mob and a hidden attendance in the black-only upstairs gallery of the courthouse proceedings. Even Ewell's open act of hatred, his spitting upon Atticus' face on a downtown street, now occurs in front of the Robinsons' shack. Given Atticus' moral separation and their neighbor Boo Radley's secretive ways, there is almost a claustrophobic quality to Jem and Scout's life in Foote's rewriting of the work.

That sense of isolation, moreover, changes ev-

erything by pitting the people on the Finchs' street against the entire community (epitomized by Scout's several school yard scuffles), a fact emblematized in the appearance of a rabid dog, clearly wandering into their cul de sac from some other part of town. To the children's surprise, their father—who notably refuses to play baseball with the other city fathers—shoots the animal dead, amazingly protecting his loved ones.

Similarly, when Ewell attacks the Finch children (Ewell's attacks in the novel also include Tom Robinson's wife), their neighbor Boo comes to their rescue. It is notable that the sheriff of this hateful town argues against his lawful duty, proclaiming that the truth—the fact that Boo Radley has killed Bob Ewell—would harm the mentally retarded man:

> I never heard tell it was against the law for any citizen to do his utmost to prevent a crime from being committed, which is exactly what he did. But maybe you'll tell me it's my duty to tell the town all about it and not to hush it up. Well you know what'll happen then? All the ladies in Maycomb

including my wife will be knocking on his door bringing angel food cakes. To my way of thinking, taking the one man who's done you and this town a big service and dragging him with his shy ways into the limelight—it's a sin. And I'm not about to have it on my head. ...Bob Ewell fell on his knife.

Like the figures of the musical *Oklahoma!* described in *My Year 2003*, the authorities of this southern town decide to bend truth, something very near to what Scout has earlier on defined (mistakenly, so Atticus insists) as a "compromise."

Frankly, given the outcome of Tom Robinson's trial, we may find it hard to imagine that the "good" ladies of Maycomb would reward the murder of Bob Ewell, who has evidently convinced their kind that his daughter was raped by a black man. Is it any wonder then that Tom Robinson, despite Atticus' advice to "not lose faith," runs "like a rabbit" to escape the police? The fact that he is shot and killed, despite the deputy's proclamation that he meant just to wound him, is, perhaps, inevitable.

Given the events of both film and novel, particularly the more enfolded fiction of Foote's script, it is clear that—despite any moral lessons and perceptions gleaned by the Finch children and the audiences of this film—the world to which Jem will awaken in the morning (the familiar last lines of both novel and film being the adult Scout's words about her father: "He turned out the light and went into Jem's room. He would be there all night, and he would be there when Jem waked up in the morning.") is no better than the one in which he was nearly killed that night. Atticus Finch may represent a hero, but his actions in such an isolate world have little effect. And in that respect, the film embraces the status quo; and the moral indignation of the readers of Lee's classic and the viewers of the Mulligan/Foote adaptation can only represent a kind of righteous pat on the liberal back.

While it may be true that there were no real alternatives in 1936, and that both the novel and the film merely reiterate the truth of that reality, it is the imitation of the facts, the bland realism boiled up with heavy doses of nostalgia and romance, that ultimately disturbs me. Perhaps a more passionate response might be a fantasy where one could celebrate change.

LOS ANGELES, MARCH 13, 2009

Home to Houston

HORTON FOOTE (SCREENPLAY, BASED ON HIS PLAY), PETER MASTERSON (DIRECTOR) **THE TRIP TO BOUNTIFUL** / 1985

BASED ON HIS 1953 television play, Horton Foote's film *The Trip to Bountiful* is, as *The New York Times* reviewer Vincent Canby wrote in 1985, "a richly detailed film," "exquisitely performed" by the great actress Geraldine Page, a role for which she won an Academy Award for best actress.

The story, like most of Foote's writings, is a simple one: one day in 1947, Carrie Watts, an elderly woman now living in Houston with her detestable daughter-in-law Jessie Mae and her unimaginative son Ludie, escapes their constant admonitions—Carrie is told time and again by Jessie Mae not to run through her daily chores, to stop singing her "out of style" hymns, and to stop rifling through Jessie Mae's dresser drawers—and their attentive watch over her—more determined during the time of month when Carrie's social security check is due. As Jessie Mae goes about her daily chores, consisting primarily of shopping  and sipping cokes with her friends at the local drug store, Carrie bolts, first to the train station (where she attempts to buy a ticket to the now-nonexistent stop at Bountiful) and then to the bus station, where, with the help of a young woman rider, Thelma, she eludes her guardians and is able to board the bus.

Thelma and Carrie's journey to Harrison, the nearest stop to Bountiful, is the perfect time to establish Carrie's character, and through a mix of garrulous histrionics, shy inquisitiveness, and gentle poetic wonderments, Page displays her dramatic range in the time it takes for the bus to arrive in Harrison, 12 miles from her goal.

Carrie was born and lived most of her life in a farming community, where, it appears, the last of the inhabitants has recently died; a place that Carrie will only briefly visit before her son, in a rented car, arrives to return her to "civilization." Unlike most of the small-town policemen we encounter in film and television, however, the Sheriff of Harrison is a friendly authority

 who agrees to drive her out to Bountiful. Carrie's encounter with the old homestead is a mix of pure joy and total dismay, as she recalls the "bountiful" life she lived there along with memories of the loss of a child and the hard times she and her family faced, all intertwined with her recognition that "when you live longer than your house and your family, then you've lived long enough."

Even the old cannot go home, and when Ludie finally arrives, it is with complete acceptance that Carrie readies herself for her return. Ludie, at first, is resistant to any notion of a nostalgic past, but perhaps because of Carrie's joy in simply having been able to accomplish her trip, he finally is able to admit that he too has some good memories of the place. Afraid of dirtying her shoes, Jessie Mae has remained in the car, and when she does trot out to demand that her husband and mother-in-law return to the city, she has nothing to offer but another litany of do's and don'ts.

With one final scratch of the hard soil, Carrie is ready to return home to Houston. As in many of Foote's works, the status quo is restored. Once again, we have, along with the characters, experienced a mild catharsis in the form of small psychological revelations, but nothing has truly changed—except perhaps for an even more determined imprisonment of Carrie Watts. Her trip to Bountiful will no longer be a dream of possibility, but simply another remnant of a failed past.

LOS ANGELES, MARCH 15, 2009

Mistrusting Happiness

HORTON FOOTE (SCREENPLAY), BRUCE BERESFORD
(DIRECTOR) **TENDER MERCIES** / 1983

TWO YEARS BEFORE *The Trip to Bountiful*, Horton
Foote wrote and directed what was perhaps his most
successful screenplay, which won him an Academy
Award. Like the others of Foote's scripts I describe, the
story of *Tender Mercies* is a simple one, and the actors,
particularly Robert Duvall in the role of country-west-
ern singer Mac Sledge, are so laconic that at moments
there seems to be no story to tell.

Famed country singer Sledge has fallen into an alcoholic chasm, destroying his marriage to fellow country singer Dixie Scott (played by Betty Buckley) and
alienating him from his daughter, Sue Anne, whom he
has not seen in over eight years.

As the film begins, Sledge loses even his drinking
partner, and is left alone in a rural motel without money or means of transportation. The hotel owner, Rosa

Lee (Tess Harper), a widow with a young son, offers
him two days and some food, which he parlays into a
part-time job working in exchange for room, food, and
$2.00 a day.

Sledge befriends Rosa Lee's boy, Sonny, and a romance between the two adults develops—so quickly,
indeed, that we hardly notice it until he announces his
desire to marry Rosa Lee; before we have even assimi-
lated that romance, moreover, the two are described
as being married. Most of the "action" of this film, in
fact, occurs offstage, with the major onstage movements consisting of Rosa Lee ironing and Mac repair-
ing doors, gardening, and traveling into town to pick
up seed.

Little by little, however, we piece together his

tragic past: a successful singing career that ended in his alcoholically-charged near-murder of his former wife. His new relationship with Rosa Lee, however, is a sustaining one that allows him not only to overcome his alcoholism, but to gradually admit that he misses singing and composing, both of which he has continued on the sly. It is clear that without accepting his past, his present identity is in question. As a town local shouts to him: "Hey, mister, were you really Mac Sledge?" His humorous answer reveals his dilemma: "Yes, ma'am, I guess I was."

As word gets out of his whereabouts, journalists and admirers seek him out. While he rejects the former, he accepts the friendship of four local singers, the Slater Mill Boys, to whom he gives permission to perform his song, and with whom he ultimately sings in a local gig. In the offing is a record.

When Dixie performs in nearby Austin, Mac attends the performance, hoping to get a chance to see his estranged daughter, but Dixie furiously sends him away. A few days later, the daughter escapes her mother's guard to visit the father, but the silence between them offers neither much to go on. The next day, the daughter runs away with a singer from her mother's band, and soon after is killed, again "offstage," in an automobile accident triggered by her husband's drinking.

The film ends in two long distant shots of Mac and

Rosa Lee digging in their garden as he discusses what he sees as the unfairness of life. "I don't trust happiness. I never did, I never will," he proclaims. A few minutes later, however, Sonny discovers a football Sledge has bought him, and the film ends with son and father throwing passes, Rosa Lee fondly smiling, basking in the glow of a normal and good future for her family.

If, as I have argued in my discussions of Foote's other two screenplays, they end in the status quo, in *Tender Mercies* we witness a change—a change that the filmmakers apparently perceive as better than the past. Sledge ends up, indeed, as a kind of American Candide, a man who in his grand past suffered in his innocent pride, but who wisely turns to tending his own garden.

I squirm, however, when I think of Sledge basically sacrificing his musical talents and the appreciation that goes with them for the kind of nostalgically evoked America with which Foote rewards him. Although Australian-born Beresford, like the Germans Wim Wenders and Percy Aldon would do in the years following, poetically depicts the American Southwest, it is hard for me to see the barren flats around Palmer and Waxahachie, Texas, where the film was shot, as representing a kind of new Eden. And, although, Rosa Lee's house seems to improve in appearance with every scene, it is still a grubby, unpainted shack in the middle of nowhere. While I know many thousands of viewers will cry their eyes out (I admit it, so did I) at the very thought of father and son bonding in football heaven, I find it a long way from anything I might describe as *my* American Dream. In order to regain his peace of mind, I would argue, Sledge has had to give up nearly everything, including—the near impossible for a songwriter—language itself. Rosa Lee's quiet smile at the end of *Tender Mercies* sends a shiver through my bones, for in order to survive in her world, Sledge has had to abandon the messiness of a creatively meaningful life.

LOS ANGELES, MARCH 17, 2009
All three pieces reprinted from *World Cinema Review* (March 2009).
Reprinted from *Reading Films: My International Cinema* (Los Angeles: Green Integer, 2012).

Happy Happy

LYNN ZELEVANSKY, CHRISTINE STARKMAN, AND
SUN JUNG KIM (CURATORS) **YOUR BRIGHT FUTURE: 12
CONTEMPORARY ARTISTS FROM KOREA** , ON VIEW AT
THE LOS ANGELES COUNTY MUSEUM OF ART FROM JUNE
26–SEPTEMBER 20, 2009

AS AN ADMIRER of contemporary Korean literature (and publisher of major Korean poet Ko Un) and given the large Korean population of my city, I wanted very much to love the new show of Korean artists at the Los Angeles County Museum of Art, located across the street from my home and my nearby office. This show does indeed give some glimmers of excellent art.

While the show was located primarily in the Eli

Broad wing of the museum, the entire Ahmanson
Building across the plaza was festooned in ribbons of
yellow, red, and blue by Choi Jeong-Hwa, an artwork
that, whipped up by the wind, snapped and seemingly
waved out its title, "Welcome," to the neighborhood
even before the opening of the show. And as museum-
goers entered the plaza they were greeted by an equally
festive and joyful piece also by Choi titled "Happy
Happy," a work made up of hanging plastic tubs, bins,
strainers, bowls, funnels, and pitchers, all purchased
from the nearby 99 Cents Only Store. The latter work,
a celebration of consumerism, was particularly beautiful, lit up so that the colors glowed in the night.

The first piece of the show, Do Ho Suh's "Fallen Star 1/5" was a definite knock-out, picturing a replica of his home in Seoul where the artist grew up that has crashed into the Providence, Rhode Island apartment house where Suh lived in the early 1990s while studying at the Rhode Island School of Design. The apartment, split literary in half—apparently by the crash of the Korean home—is filled with miniature furniture, reading materials, clothing, kitchen utensils, etc. with which Suh surrounded himself, and as the viewer goes from window to window to peer into the home and its contents, he witnesses what Suh describes as an "exposure of his life." The collision of the two buildings, Suh argues, signifies less of an outright statement of cultural differences than it does a kind of *Wizard of Oz*-like tale about cultural change:

> I was in the house, making my first fabric architectural piece. All of a sudden, there was a tornado that took the building into the sky. I didn't know where I was going, but then I saw the ocean and a bridge from Seoul to New York, so I knew

that the house was heading to the US.

I realized the house was going down soon, so I finished my fabric piece to use it as a parachute. I got scared when I realized that the house was slowing down and I couldn't see land. I decided to throw things away, but there were so many things I was personally attached to. I made a list of things I possessed and prioritized them. It gave me time to reflect on my entire life in that house. Then I crossed off things on the list. In the end, I decided to throw out pretty much everything except what was essential to survival.

When the building started to descend, I went up on the roof with the parachute. The house started to come down and crash, but it had a semi-soft landing. And that's how I feel. Culture shock didn't come as a shock to me. It took a long time.

(Quoted from an interview with the artist and Suzanne Muchnic of the *Los Angeles Times*)

Accordingly, Shu's work is personalized, and given its great attention to detail, we recognize these houses as being objects of great personal love and beauty. Yet one cannot ignore the fact that not only has Shu had to deal with a kind of "cultural shock," but his home country is itself a house broken in two. A companion piece, made of translucent resin, presents a more idealized version of the specific, a kind of glowing white quartered house, which could presumably be reunited in various forms by rearranging the four carts on which it stands.

Would that all the artists in this show were capable of this multi-complexity. At first, artist KIMsooja's video, "A Needle Woman," projecting images of streets in Patan (Nepal), Havana, Rio de Janeiro, N'Djanema (Chad), San'a (Yemen), and Jerusalem—in front of which the artist herself stands with her back to the viewer—is fascinating to watch as the various walkers in each of these locations move together and apart, evidencing the differences in the ways people interrelate and simply communicate in these very different cultures. But, in the end, since one cannot truly enter these landscapes, we realize that the various differences we have observed are, in fact, superficial. For the videos keep us at bay, and we can never know through the art what truly *being* in those locations means.

Similarly, throughout the rest of the show, the various objects, tapes, videos, and packing materials seem more to stand *in* for experiences than actually create new meaning or participate in the world. Bahc Yiso's "Your Bright Future," for example, consists of 10 flood-

lights, tilting to the sky, surrounded by the electrical wiring necessary to keep the lights bright. The curators suggest that the work mimics a crowd standing before a charismatic leader, demanding a kind of obedience to the "great" or "dear" leader. But the bright future, given that Bahc lived in New York from 1982 to 1994, could be any false promise, including that of the American Dream or desire for celebrity.

Gimhongsok's videos and large stuffed animals, including a Harvey-sized rabbit laid out on a pink sofa, "Bunny's Sofa," suggest yet another take on the crass commercialism of all things "cute," but in the end seems to lack the political bite it wants to suggest.

Haegue Yang, indeed, queries the whole issue of

even attempting to make art by presenting a room full of small and large wooden storage containers filled, we are told, with art he was unable to sell in various venues. Here the all-important question of the artist's ability to pay for the storage of what he creates comes painfully into play. But like so much else in this show, it is a conceptual piece that leaves one with little to hold onto. An essay on the subject might have been as elucidating as the vision of so many wrapped bundles. How I wanted to open those carefully packed cartons and encounter what lay within.

It is not the "conceptual" quality of this show's art, however, of which I am complaining, but the vagueness and, often, emptiness of the concepts themselves. The bright future of happiness which the various artists seem both to desire and satirize is just that, an unresolved contradiction that transforms any possible enjoyment of the art into an empty promise.

LOS ANGELES, JULY 12, 2009
Reprinted from *Green Integer Blog* (July 2009) and *Art Là-bas* (November 2014).

Five Tales from Ischia: The 1ˢᵗ Tale (The Crossing)

ON JUNE 25, 2007, after a day in Dublin with my dear friend Joe Ross, I took the plane to Naples, from where I had been told I could board the ferry at Beverello (the Naples harbor) to Ischia. But just before leaving, I received an email from my friend Marty Nakell, my host in Ischia, that the hotel where I was to stay had arranged that I should be met at the airport and guided to Ischia. Naples, everyone had noted, was a dangerous city, and a bit intimidating upon one's first visit.

As the plane set down at the airport, the other passengers and I were taken by bus to what appeared to be a large hanger, something left over, it seemed to me, from World War II, from the years when my Air Force-serving father had been stationed in that city.

It was beastly hot—an African sirocco was embracing Naples—and except for the languid movements of a large overhead fan high above the hanger, no air moved. At the passport control, an officer collected all American passports, letting the European Union members through before stamping our documents and returning them to us. My bags seemed to take forever.

As I exited, I was met by a driver who took the bags into his van. We drove to another terminal where he temporarily left me alone to roast, soon after coming back to remove my things and signaling me to follow him. In another van, he stashed my suitcases, waving me to trail after him into the new terminal, where he passed me on to a "collega." His "colleague" pointed to a chair, suggesting I sit there to wait as he went forward, sign in hand, evidently to pick up another traveler or travelers from Milan. Clearly they (my first driver and this new "collega") were consolidating their passengers, but as time passed and no one returned, I began to imagine all sorts of other scenarios. I'd hardly gotten a glimpse of my "new" driver. He might have slipped out the door with the crowds, leaving me to guilelessly wait for his return for hours before the truth would become apparent! Was this a new method of robbery? I had no choice but to patiently endure, and eventually he returned with the elderly Milano couple.

They, like the driver, spoke no English, but we smiled at one another, greeting each other as best we could.

After a few more delays—the Milan gentleman evi-

 dently wanted to buy something to eat and his wife had forgotten to purchase film for their camera—we were off, presumably to Beverello. As he came to the Naples turn-off, however, the driver took the direction to Pozzuoli—a somewhat picturesque but dilapidated harbor, heaped with mounds of garbage bags alongside its winding roads from the hills down into the harbor. At points the passage became perilous, and the couple from Milan, clearly commenting on the terrible filth their southern brethren had to endure, snapped photographs of the mountains of local trash.

Finally, we reached the ferries, crawling into a line so close to the water's edge that I was sure we would fall into the dirty harbor. Again the driver stopped the van, turned off the engine, and signaled for us to collect our bags and follow him. We entered the dark bowels of the ferry and were taken to a small iron cage into which he tossed our suitcases. *Familia*, he said, *familia*, pointing at the cage with pride. I presumed he meant that the placement of our bags in that location was not available to all, but was a special perk offered only to family members and friends. Although family, of course, could mean.... I tried to ignore that possibility.

The Milanese couple climbed to the second level, I, after purchasing *bierra*, to the third level to better witness the Pozzuolian landscape. From this distance the fading colored apartment fortresses appeared like a vision of a Mediterranean movie set. But if one looked closely, the glamour quickly faded.

Eventually cars began to edge forward, winding their way from the first line into the boat. I presumed our van would soon follow, but as the hull began to close, I could see that the second line, wherein our driver had placed the van, had not been permitted to enter. And the boat soon backed away without him from the dock.

So, I concluded, we were now on our own. I had been told that there would be two stops previous to Forio, near where our hotel was located. From Forio I'll catch a taxi to the hotel, I determined.

A short while after leaving the harbor and rounding the coastline, the wind picked up and the waves of the Tyrrhenian Sea became more blue-green. And just as suddenly an island appeared on the horizon. Despite the strong sun and my fear of sunburn I couldn't bear to leave my observation post. Soon we were approaching what I presumed was Ischia Porto. The small town had a series of castle-like structures at its point, just as in the postcard picture I had seen of Ischia's largest city with

the castle Argonese at its tip.

But here my eye was even more drawn to the village itself, a town so absolutely enchanting that I could hardly find words to describe it. It was a kind of fantasy scene as if painted by Henri Rosseau. Each building was a different shade of salmon, yellow, light blue, and green—all flat as a stage set. The harbor street was strung up with little pennants and firefly lights. But the most amazing thing about this charming scene was the variation of windows, some half circles planted into the center of the seemingly flat surfaces, others turned on their sides and set with no particular logic halfway between the second and third floors. No building matched any other, which further gave the whole

a sense of its being a movie or stage set. If this was, as the Nakells had described it, the lesser enchanting of the Ischian cities, what might Forio look like?

"Procida, Procida," the ship's communication system announced. No such city had appeared on my Ischia schedule. After a short stop, the boat pulled away from the village and, soon after, the island I later discovered was Procida disappeared. I was confused, if this was not Ischia Porto, where were we?

Three men in company T-shirts stood before me, and I attempted to ask them if Forio was the third stop, but none of them spoke English. I tried again, counting out my three known stops on my fingers: Ischia Porto, Lacco Ameno, Forio. "Si, Ischia Porto," he repeated. I was confused, and began to seek out someone who spoke English. Apparently no one on this boat spoke anything but Italian, and I began to grow a bit concerned about my destination. A short while later, the man with whom I had attempted to communicate reappeared with an English-speaking Italian in tow, who quickly explained to me that this boat did not go to Forio!

Why hadn't Marty simply left me to follow the first plans we made, to catch the taxi from the airport to Naples itself, where many boats traveled each day to Ischia and back? All right, I thought to myself, I'll have to catch a taxi or bus to Forio from Ischia Porto—another 20-minute trip. No problem, I attempted to calm myself.

But just as suddenly new fears arose. Would I be able to communicate to whomever I needed to that my bags had still to be retrieved from that mysterious iron cage?

FORIO, JUNE 26, 2007
Reprinted from *Green Integer Blog* (March 2008).

Five Tales from Ischia: The 2ⁿᵈ Tale (The Arrival)

JUST AS WE were about to arrive in Ischia Porto, I suddenly realized that had I not asked about the stops, I'd have not even thought about leaving the boat. Where I would have ended up, I am not sure—likely I'd simply returned to Pozzuoli, but perhaps—had the boat moved forward—I'd have eventually wound up in Sardinia!

As we began to enter Ischia Porto I went downstairs to see if I could find the iron cage. Many people had already gathered there, and a number sat waiting in their cars. I found the cage and was delighted to see my baggage still in place.

They opened the hull and people begin to pour out. Soon after someone came with a key and opened the cage. I pulled out the two bags and went forward like Vasco Di Gamma to greet my new worlds. Directly in front of me was a lovely young woman holding up a sign that read "Hotel Cappizzo." A bit later the couple from Milan appeared, and we were led, this time round, to a very *small* van which quickly spun off.

I could already see that this island was not at all the same as the fantasy port of Procida. Everything here looked much wealthier, more lush, and somewhat hidden. Indeed it reminded me of the posh Riviera estates I have seen in films. The road from Ischia Porto to the hotel was certainly busy, but I recognized that Paul Vangelisti's insistence, a few days before my arrival, that the island was "filled with cars" was an exaggeration. There was a lot of traffic, but if the autos were on any normal road one wouldn't even notice them. It was simply that the roads were so narrow that one quickly became aware of every car that passed. I kept feeling that we might soon be sent over the cliffs by a passing truck. But the young driver was not at all intimidated.

The drive was quite beautiful, with hotels appearing every few feet along the way. We dropped off the Milanese couple at another inn, and began the drive up the hill (the same cardiovascular-exhausting hill I would walk every day upon my returns from Forio) to Cappizzo. Maria—the owner—magnificently greeted me, and called Rebecca Goodman, Marty's wife, who appeared soon after. Marty had evidently gone into Forio to await my arrival, having not been told that this particular ferry stopped only in Ischia Porto!

I went to my room and showered, returning to the very pleasant lobby, trying to assimilate the place. My room was quite small, but had a fairly large bathroom. Painted entirely in aqua, it led through a shuttered green Mediterranean-style door directly onto the large pool, heated by natural volcanic gasses. Next to the door was a table and chair that, if I brought it closer, allowed me to take the computer (with cord) onto the terrace.

The view beyond the pool, however, was even more spectacular. My room looked out onto a large cliff with the ocean below, with those Aegean blue-green waves striking the shore, that I could watch while sitting at my small desk within my room. Surrounding the hotel, moreover, were carefully kept royal palms and large cacti that climbed into the sky.

The lobby was quite spacious, with a bar, several couches, and chairs, all with the same stunning view. My arrival coincided, evidently, with cocktail time, and a few of the hotel Germans (most of the hotel is filled with Germans—no Americans save Marty and his class) had begun to sip on their drinks. I ordered a Campari and soda. After about two hours, dinner was announced. Each room had its own regular dining table, and the Nakells and their students were assigned a long table in the center of the room. My seat looked— once more—directly upon that ragged, green cliff and

the ocean below it.

That night we had a fish called Dentrice (which had been translated into English as Dentrex—we all wondered if we were to brush our teeth with it), a fennel salad, and vegetable pasta before it. Dessert was simple, fruit (a fresh pear or fig) or gellati.

The most beautiful time of the day, however, came after the meals, when everyone retired to the front terrace beneath the royal palms. As hot as it had been all day, the wind had risen, cool and refreshing. A bartender served drinks as everyone sat under the stars quietly talking and drinking until 10:30 or 11:00. Then all but the students trotted off to bed, the kids speeding off into town or other island destinations, sometimes not

returning—so I was told—until 4:00 a.m. Ah youth!

I slept well, and awoke to write my adventures of the first day.

After a large breakfast, with Italian sliced meats and cheeses, juices, many kinds of bread, jellies, fresh unpeeled kiwis, and cereals—and of course the thick mud of coffee—I decided that despite the heat (the African sirocco was in its third day; I was told that such weather always lasted three days) I would walk into Forio.

Forio is about 20 minutes away, and much of the trip is hilly—although it's much worse on the way back. I was told to take a bus or taxi upon my return. You travel the coast for much of the way, the ocean off on your left. When you come to a fork in the road with a sign pointing to the right saying "centro," you turn. But I could hardly believe that this little path of a road was the major entrance into the village. I took the road

least likely to be traveled, nonetheless, following it at my peril—anytime a car or motorcycle drove by, one had to stand aside for fear of being hit—until I reached the outskirts of Forio. I'd gone just a short ways when the police signaled all cars to stop. I walked forward to encounter a priest in full regalia being led by a young altar boy carrying the cross, a small van with a coffin inside following. As the priest spoke the ritual words, an older man beside them repeated in antiphon. A small crowd of mourners followed. It looked like something out of Sicily!

I walked into the center of the city, first taking a turn toward the bay itself, sitting for an espresso at a bayside bar.* I then turned back, taking the other lane which led into the shopping district, where the major bars, beautifully stocked groceries, wine stores, gift shops, clothing boutiques, and other more tourist-based activities existed. It was a very lovely town, ancient yet clearly modernized. Royal and larger palms dotted the city center, and if one turned from this street, as it ended, to the right, he arrived at a kind of esplanade that overlooked the ocean, at the end of which was a stark white church that appeared at first sight like something out of the American Southwest, as in New Mexico.

I sat for a while at Bar Maria with a lemon-lime juice trying to write. But I was so dripping with sweat that it fell even upon the pages, and I felt frustrated in the attempt. After I had caught my breath, I decided to buy a hat, an inexpensive white straw hat, just my size. Then I turned back to the hotel. I worried during the walk about my health, particularly since most of the return was an uphill struggle, the worst part being that last trek up the road to the hotel. But I survived— realizing that this is what is meant by exercise. Upon resting for a few moments in my room, I went for a swim. It took me nearly an hour to stop the racing of my heart—that was indeed a very good cardiovascular workout! I was sure that if I ate fish and drank as little as I had so far, I'd come home a bit thinner.

Marty and his students met from about 10:30 until

noon, and then again from 1:00 to about 3:00, discussing literature and their own writings. They'd been reading Dante when I arrived, but were talking about the Italian  poet Porta when I last listened in.

Rebecca was a true inspiration to all, getting Marty to the proper places and coordinating their travel plans with the hotel owner Maria, whom they call Mama, a friendly, scolding mother. Although breakfast was served until about 10:00, the next day Maria told the students that they must appear at around 8:30; they'd been missing breakfast, which wasn't good for them!

She insisted that when I swim I wear a cap! The filtration system, evidently, did not like hair—although the Germans were so covered with body hair I couldn't imagine that the hair on my head had any great effect. The next afternoon, however, I wore a hat!

Marty spoke Italian quite capably, trying out new verb tenses, etc. And the Germans, who often joined us at our table, were a quiet folk, very friendly, some of them having returned for over 10 to 20 years to this same spot.

On Wednesday we awoke to a completely clear

day, almost chilly, the wind tossing the waves against the cliff below. The sirocco had moved on, just as Maria had predicted. I walked into Forio again, this time taking photographs. I stayed at Bar Maria longer than previously, working on my Marinetti essay (writing on his novel *The Untameables*, a work located on some volcanic island with a beastly hot sun hammering the desert). But I still didn't stay too long in town since the hotel was even more pleasant, the views even better.

For dinner we had runner beans with Fusilli. At first, the combination sounded strange, but it tasted wonderful—remarkably fresh. Although they served swordfish, I chose grilled pollo, also flavorful, served with a beet salad. For lunch Marty, Rebecca and I had gone down the hill (in the opposite direction from Forio) to a small beach café directly on the water. It was absolutely cold there, with a strong wind. We met an acquaintance they had met the year before, a member, so they told me, of the Italian mafia—or the local Naples-based Camorra.

In the lobby I finished Rae Armantrout's new book of poetry, and returned to my room to type things up.

---

*Today, April 8, 2009, a small receipt suddenly floated out of my canvas tote bag, which I carry with me every day and clean out nearly every week. It was a receipt for 1.70 euros for "caffe" from the Bar La Lucciola on via Fillipo di Lustro in Forio D'Ischia from June 26, 2007, representing my first stop in Forio. How could it possibly have remained in that bag and why had it suddenly reappeared? Only two days earlier I had had lunch with Martin Nakell and Rebecca Goodman, during which we discussed at length how we might return to that Ischian paradise! Even stranger is the fact that I first posted that essay on my Green Integer Blog exactly one year from today.

ISCHIA, HOTEL CAPPIZZO, JUNE 28, 2007
Reprinted from *Green Integer Blog* (April 2008).

Five Tales from Ischia: The 3rd Tale (Lady Walton and the Croaking Frogs)

ON THE MORNING of June 28, 2007, on my fourth day on the island of Ischia, Marty Nakell, his wife Rebecca, two of his students (Daniel and Nidzára), and I left our hotel near Forio to visit the famed Castello Argonese on Ponte Ischia near the island's major city, Ischia Porto.

Built by the Syracusan Greek Gerone in 474 B.C., the castle served as a protective fortress for centuries while the surrounding countryside was plundered by various racial and tribal groups, including the Visogoths, Vandals, Ostrogoths, Arabs, Normans, Swabians, and Angevins. In 1301 it served as a refuge against the eruption of the local volcano, Mount Trippodi.

At its greatest "splendor," it hosted, in the 16th century, 1,892 families, a convent for Clarisse nuns, a Greek Basilian abbey, and a bishopric and seminary, as

well as the palace of the Prince along with his garrison. There were 13 churches, seven of which were independent parishes.

In 1809 the English attacked the castle, then owned by the French Aragons, nearly destroying it. In 1823 the King of Naples, Ferdinand I, used it as a political prison for people who opposed Bourbon Power.

The Italian patriot Guiseppe Garibaldi abolished the prison in 1860, joining the whole of Ischia to the Reign of Italy.

Since 1912 it has been owned by private individuals, which explains, perhaps, the existence, a few years ago, of a nightclub and today's rather swanky hotel—which Marty, Rebecca, and I visited. There is also a rather pleasant bar/café at its center, and the Ischia Film Festival is held in the castle's confines. The day we visited we saw an art show in the domed church.

But for all its heroic and near-mythical past, it is also a very eerie and somewhat frightening place, a seemingly haunted castle that made us all wonder

whether we'd be comfortable staying overnight in that small, elegant hotel.

From the very moment we entered, we encountered that sense of oddness of the place. Martin, who evidently suffers a bit from claustrophobia, determined that he would walk up the several stairs to the top, while Rebecca and I chose the elevator. Once we had entered I quickly pressed a button, realizing at that same moment that I had pressed one warning us not to touch. The door closed and we heard nothing nor felt any movement up, just the quietude of being encapsulated in such small quarters with strangers. After what seemed like a very long while, with an increasing sense of panic crossing Becky's face, the door opened, presenting us with the panorama of the top floor.

After meeting up again with Marty and taking a few pictures from this palisade of the picturesque city below, he and I checked out the cemetery of the Clarisse nuns, who also practiced, evidently, some very strange rites. In the so-called cemetery were numerous stone stools, upon which, so we were told, they sat their sisters after death, permitting their bodily contents to gradually decompose, their essences dripping into the hole below them while the living nuns daily prayed. One can only imagine the stench, to say nothing of the diseases, this awful worship of the dead begat.

After a short rest in the shady café while drinking Campari and orange, I checked out some of the higher passages of the castle, following my instinct until I had reached an odd room near the very top which appeared like a small prison, but from which one could glimpse a lovely view of the ocean and, in the far distance, Capri. After further exploration and meeting up with the rest of Marty's students, the three of us left the castle, eating a lunch of *pesce grilia* (calamari, octopus, white fish, with grilled onions, zucchinis, etc.) in a small restaurant at the base of Castello Argonese.

For a while I walked the streets of Ponte Ischia before meeting up again with the Nakells and the two students who had come with us, our group taking a small boat across the bay to Coco Beach, where Marty merrily swam and snorkeled out and around three large rocks jutting from the ocean floor. I managed a few side-strokes and dog-paddled close in where my feet could still touch bottom. But even here the sea floor was unpredictable, as I cut my thigh upon a rock—a long gash which the salty sea quickly healed.

Later in the afternoon we walked up to the tower above the beach which, I was told, had once served as Michelangelo's studio. There we met a taxi which whisked us back to our Forio-based hotel.

At nine that evening we met up with our hotelier, Maria, who had invited us and several of her favorite German regulars to the Botanical Gardens for a musical concert.

The gardens were stunningly beautiful, but the amphitheater lies far up the mountain, which requires trailing up hundreds of steps. I could hear a couple of elderly German ladies huffing and puffing behind us, we huffing and puffing ahead. Fortunately it was cool, and every once in a while, we briefly stopped to look at the evening lights of Forio spread out below. The city

lay behind the stage so that both "performances" were simultaneously visible.

The amphitheater was a gift of the wife of the late composer William Walton, Lady Susana Walton, who lives still in Ischia today. Playing that evening was a youth orchestra which, consequently, was required to perform at least one William Walton piece—in this case a truly miserable offering. The orchestra, filled with lovely young faces, also played three waltzes by Johann Strauss, a composer I cannot abide. Their performance of Gershwin's *American in Paris* was a valiant try, but they had difficulties with the constantly changing rhythms and did not seem to understand the jazz aesthetic. More successful was the overture to *Fidelio* and a charming Boccherini piece—all of these works accompanied by the madly croaking frogs of the nearby pond and the graceful antics of a small bat greedily snatching up insects in the space between audience and orchestra.

After the concert, I joined others waiting in line to greet Lady Walton. "Darling, it was so nice of you to have come," she took my hand. I invited her to my upcoming reading at a nearby winery. "Thank you so much, my dear," she replied. She was still beautiful with an elegant head of graying hair. "She must have married Will when she was ten," I conjectured (in fact, when they married in Buenos Aires, he was 24 years her senior).

On the way back, as we witnessed the youthful orchestra members carrying their instruments down the hundreds of winding stairs to the entrance of the park below, we wondered how they had gotten the ancient Lady Walton to the top. The Nakells had once seen her carried by hand in a kind of chaise through the waiting room of the nearby Naples airport. Had some servile men likewise carried her to the top of these gardens as well?

Down below the taxi drivers were furious over the crowded street and seemingly endless delays. As in Naples, they seem to have the ability to escape any *cul de sac*, and after much swearing and many shouts, we sped away to a Forio restaurant where we dined on a fish stew served with pasta, followed by the remainders of the bones which we each sucked dry.

FLORIO, ISCHIA, JULY 2, 2007
Reprinted from *Green Integer Blog* (February 2008).

Five Tales from Ischia: The 4th Tale (Cities of the Dead)

A FEW DAYS after my arrival on Ischia, Marty and Rebecca decided to travel during a holiday weekend to Pompeii and on to the Amalfi Coast, asking if I'd join them. Two Chapman University students, Daniel Fingerhut and Nidzára Pecenkovic, joined us. Daniel was a sensitive Jewish boy who kept kosher, Nidzára a beautiful Muslim girl with similar dietary restrictions (both nearly impossible on the Mediterranean diet). The other students in Marty's group had decided to spend the weekend in Rome.

We took the 9:00 a.m. ferry to Naples to pick up a car before setting out on our travels. To get to the car pick-up spot, we had to break up into two cabs. I, with the two students, had a driver who, when he overheard me say something about Norway, asked if I spoke *Norsk*. Suddenly we were talking Norwegian! He was Swedish. I remembered more of the language than I had for years, in part, I suspect, because speaking Norwegian was almost a refuge in the strange city of Naples, a city at once beautiful and absolutely ugly, poorer than nearly any European city in which I'd traveled—and more dangerous.

Our Swedish driver had obviously learned to drive like a Neapolitan, which means operating the vehicle almost as one might a Sherman tank, moving fearlessly in and out of traffic on both sides of the street, even onto the sidewalks if necessary. Since nearly all the other cars drove in a similar pattern, the driving experience was more like a bumper-car derby than anything else.

In any event, we eventually found the place, picked up our car, and inched ourselves into the same traffic. Marty, it turned out, had learned to fend for himself, darting into the oncoming lanes with the greatest of ease, even driving, at one point—when we had missed the turn-off for Pompeii—over a concrete medium, as others had done before us, to reach the coast highway. The authorities, in their inexplicable wisdom, had put the sign on the wrong side of the road.

We soon arrived in Pompeii and spent several hours walking through the vast ruins.

I hadn't imagined the enormity of the space. Pompeii was, after all, a city of about 30,000 people at the time of Vesuvius' eruption in 79 A.D. Although the city had already severely suffered from an earthquake in 62,

 some of Pompeii had been rebuilt before the volcano erupted.

As I entered the gate to the city, I overheard a young boy ask his mother how the city got destroyed by the volcano since clearly Vesuvius was too far away from the lava to pour out over it? She had no answer.

Hours later, after we had toured much of the space—one could spend days wandering down every street of the city—we stopped at a nearby pizzeria before continuing on our trip. I repeated the young boy's question, and suddenly we heard the voice of a middle-aged woman from the next table (there is always someone in my adventures waiting at the next table): "The child was right. The people of the city did not die from the lava but from the smoke and ash which fell over it a few days later. Actually, most of the population had evacuated the city by that time, and only 2,000 people actually died of the gasses and ash: those left behind, mostly servants and the children of the wealthy for whom they cared, along with pets." The woman was an American Latinist, visiting from upstate New York. For about half an hour she gave us an informative short lecture about Pompeii, Herculaneum (where the escapees were buried in caves into which they had retreated), and Paestum. She seemed apologetic for her erudite talk, but we were all transfixed by the information she  supplied—a performance far more entertaining than a standard Baedeker entry or conversation with a local tour guide.

A couple of days later, we visited Paestum, after a leisurely drive from Amalfi. I had long known of Marty's and Rebecca's tendency to wander, having previously traveled with them to Northern California, and, although I desperately tried to resist my instincts for organized and planned behavior, by this time I had begun to show some impatience with their sense of timelessness.

Although I had hoped to get an early start on our trip to Paestum, where we had decided to go before returning to Naples, I knew that Marty and Rebecca would never be able to rise at an early hour. So I slept it until 8:00. I was surprised when they telephoned me. They were having breakfast already! But it still took another three and a half hours to get through check out and to gather the students. It was 11:30 before we returned to the road—Rebecca (with the smallest

bladder on earth) had to pee, so a stop in Amalfi would be necessary.

Actually, we had all wanted to visit Amalfi during our stay on the coast, but when we finally reached the town, no matter where we looked, there was no parking. At the beach, Marty attempted to drive down into a lot that looked full to me, and then, because of traffic, he was unable to exit, and was forced to back up—while several shopkeepers along the way gave various and contradictory instructions—for what seemed like miles in a lane that was hardly wide enough to edge forward, let alone to speed away in reverse. Miraculously, he achieved our backward ascent, with a car driving toward us all the way up! But now, it was clear, Amalfi—which truly did look like a beautiful city—was out of the question.

We stopped instead in Maiori, where Becky and Daniel decided to get sandals made, while Marty got hungry and ordered a plate of mushrooms, cheeses, and olives. We weren't on the road again until 2:00. Then, just before Paestum, Marty had to stop for the famed local product of Campania, Mozzarella di Bufala (Buffalo milk Mozzarella). It was delicious, I admit, and well worth the further delay—although given the facts later revealed in the film *Gomorrah* of this region's pollution, we  now wonder how many years those delicate white bullets of cheese took from our lives.

We didn't reach Paestum, the 7th century B.C. Greek City lying in that countryside, until 5:00. And we had still to visit every tourist shop in Paestum, eat *gellati*, consume a few more drinks, and tour the ruins before we could even begin our return to Naples, which would require several further stops along the way. I pondered whether it would be possible to reach the last ferry in time. Oh well, I said to myself, if we miss the ferry, to quote both the Bourbons of Naples and James Bond, I'll "see Naples and die."

We had agreed to spend only an hour in Paestum, although I knew from the start that it would take longer for Marty, Rebecca, and the students to accomplish the task. I immediately bought my ticket and entered, and even as I moved toward the larger temples in the far distance, I knew I would already be finished touring the entire place before they even entered it. They could not

resist the many tourist shops gathered at the gate.

This fabulous Greek city on a flat dusty plain beside the ocean is an awe-inspiring sight. This is agricultural Italy, and corn and other crops grow up right to the fences that separate the ancient site from the farms hereabout.

There are three major temples: the Temples of Hera, Apollo, and Athena, all in quite good condition, along with the amphitheater.

I walked very slowly to the far end of the site, discovering a beautiful tree-covered *ristorante* with a bar at the far end, where I sat down and ordered a Campari and soda. After finishing it I returned to the park, having seen almost all of the major sites. I tried to dawdle, even loaf as best I could, wandering back toward the first gate, where the lovely white Temple of Athena stood. But all of this took only about 30 minutes. There—as I had predicted—came Marty and Rebecca, having finally entered the place.

I'm not complaining in reporting this; their sense of time was just different from mine, and as much as I tried to accommodate for the strolling-wandering life, I remained more clock oriented. I was impatient. But they so enjoyed their journeys, and the two of them were so similar in their patterns, that it was really quite lovely  to observe their peregrinations.

I left the park and sat at a café with another Campari. Fortunately, the drink is light and not terribly alcoholic (and relatively inexpensive—each about 4 euros). I waited 45 minutes longer for Marty, Rebecca, and the students to return. Then, as I had predicted, they had to have gellati, buy some water, and wander about the tourist shops a bit more! We left Paestum finally, at my urging, at 6:30 p.m.

Almost immediately we were in a long line of cars stalled bumper to bumper to Salerno and the entrance of the autostrasse. We thought perhaps it was the pay lines at the entrance that had so held back traffic, but after about an hour and a half, we saw that it was the autostrasse itself that was backed up! We entered the highway and sat in bumper to bumper autos for 5 ½ hours all the way to Naples (what might normally have been an hour trip)! Of course, we had to stop for the bathroom along the way, and everyone was hungry

again (except for me), and it was now clear that we probably would miss the midnight boat. There was nothing any of us could do but tell stories, sing, and laugh. Indeed, we had such a raucous time that Daniel suggested we meet again the next day in a car and "just hang out"! Our imitations of various family members might have made for a hit comic-skit.

Finally, we arrived in Naples, where all could observe that Marty was utterly exhausted as he seemed almost to change personalities, doggedly determined to get to the garage where we were to leave our car. The closer we had gotten to Naples, the more crazily he had begun to drive, and by the time we entered the city again he was a Neapolitan, speeding down streets on the left side of the road through red lights, traffic, and anything else that crossed our path as we made our way back to the garage. I suggested he should be awarded a medal for all the driving he had done.

At the garage, they called for a taxi, which soon arrived. If Marty had developed some Neapolitan techniques of driving, we suddenly realized that the taxi driver was the "real thing." Yet he was also used to tourists and respected their fears. He calmly drove a block as Marty explained that we were attempting to make the last ferry from Bevellaro. He turned back to the rest of us and beseechingly requested: "Permisso?"

The kids were confused, but I knew exactly what he meant. Marty and I nodded our heads in reply: "Yes, permisso." Suddenly we were tearing through the streets, jutting in and out of traffic, ignoring every red light, missing other cars by inches, jumping over medians, and generally creating havoc in space. Each time he broke through the traffic, Michali (taxi drivers each tell you their name, as if it were a personal relationship with them that you had established by entering their cab) shouted, "Permisso!" Laughing joyfully, like a terribly bad boy, he sped on. I believe we had clipped at least two cars along the way. We now realized that, although Marty had passed all the tests for Neapolitan driving, he was not yet a full-fledged citizen! The ride was breathtaking, as if we had gone into some amusement park—"the taxi ride"! Disneyland should add it to their park.

We arrived at Bellevaro just in time to get tickets to the last boat to Ischia—not to Forio, but to Ischia Porto. It didn't matter; we'd make it home that night.

The boat was a comfortable one, much nicer than the one I'd taken that first day, and roomier than the hydrofoil we'd taken across three days earlier. We also

stopped, as I had on that first day, in Procida, that beautiful little town. I tried to snap some photos with the night-vision setting, but the shutter took so long that any hand movement blurred the image.

When we finally arrived at Ischia Porto, the Nakells were determined to stop for pizza, but the students and I desperately needed a shower and bed. I was one of the first ones off, quickly capturing a taxi. The others were the last to leave the boat—indeed all passengers had departed about 15 minutes before these stragglers finally dragged themselves forward, nearly frozen in space once again!

As the three of us sped away to Forio, Marty and Rebecca, looking like exhausted refugees returning to their homeland, trudged down the street for their 2:00 a.m. snack! I think perhaps Marty just needed to decompress a while before entering another vehicle.

FORIO, ISCHIA, JULY 3, 2007
Reprinted from *Green Integer Blog* (April 2008).

City of the Living

MARY BEARD **THE FIRES OF VESUVIUS: POMPEII LOST AND FOUND** (CAMBRIDGE, MASSACHUSETTS: THE BELKNAP PRESS OF HARVARD UNIVERSITY PRESS, 2008)

WHAT I DESCRIBED as a dead city, Mary Beard, in her transformative study of Pompeii, *The Fires of Vesuvius,* reveals as a living—one might almost raucous—city of anywhere from 30,000 to 64,000 people. Beginning with the day of the eruption, August 25, 79 CE, Beard takes us back to the city's earliest known roots, which may have been Etruscan, through various sieges and political developments which ultimately brought it into the Roman Empire.

Early in the book Beard warns us of easy assumptions, forcing us to question even what visitors appear to witness on their pilgrimages to the city, reminding us that although the city was destroyed in 79 CE, there had long been warnings and smaller eruptions of the impending volcano, most of the citizens consequently

escaping, often with possessions in hand, long before August 25th. To date only around 1,100 bodies have been unearthed, and speculation is that, at most, 2000 people died in the August eruption. So what we see at Pompeii is not precisely a city with everything remaining frozen in time and space. In 62 CE, moreover, the city had been badly damaged in an earthquake, and as late as the Vesuvius eruption a great deal of repair work was still underway.

Although the world did not discover the wonders of Pompeii until the late 1700s, locals had known of the ruins for hundreds of years, over which time numerous digging looters had raided and destroyed several buildings. The original archeologists, moreover, were in some cases untrained and careless in their handling of artifacts. Even since its slow uncovering, the city has crumbled and faded in the Italian weather and sunlight. Bombings during World War II also damaged the city extensively. Five larger regions of the city remain unexcavated even today. In a sense, accordingly, what one witnesses in the vast array of buildings in Pompeii is a city often very different in appearance and quality from the Pompeii of 79 CE.

Step by step Beard takes us through the city through a series of lenses: general living, street life, house and home, painting and decoration, making a living, government, pleasure of the body, fun and games, and religion, all in a brilliant recreation of what it meant to be a Pompeiian citizen. The route, however, is not a easy one. Hundreds of standard assumptions are questioned, pet critical theories of scholars are challenged, and conflicting interpretations vetted. If there is one theme that the reader comes away with at the end of reading *The Fires of Vesuvius* it is that we know less about these subjects than we might presume.

Fascinating issues such as the filth of the streets (mixes of urine and dung [human and animal], garbage, and water)—which help explain several large stepping stones rising from the pavement—combined with night-time dangers of near-complete darkness,

make for a clear sense of danger for the average citizen. The small size of rooms for the average houseowner, combined with cohabitation of slaves and extended family, further adds to a modern reader's sense of discomfort. The noise, night and day, would seem to have been nearly unbearable, not to mention the proliferation of smells. Some of the most beautiful houses had to endure neighbors serving as fulleries (with its smells of hide and urine) or garum (fish oil) manufacturers. Homes and public buildings, inside and out, were apparently marked with graffiti.

Further, the myths we have of Roman dining— three to a couch while consuming a vast quantity of fish, fruit, and meats—seem to have had little reality in Pompeii. While some houses, such as The House of the Golden Bracelet, show evidence of elegant dining (in this case, surrounding a small pool within a garden), Beard argues that most individuals were forced to eat out, and even in wealthier homes eating shared more in common with fast-food dining in contemporary American households, as food was consumed in various places throughout the house.

It was also a society very much controlled by a few wealthy men. Women had little power (an exception may have been the wealthy benefactor and priestess Eumachia) and wives spent most of their lives raising the children and weaving. Men ruled the city, through *aediles* and *duoviri*, the latter of which were expected to pay for entertainments (public pantomimes or gladiator bouts) in return for their clout. The wealthy Pompeiian male found sexual pleasure in the bosom of his slaves (both male and female), while the poor sought sexual release in bars, some baths, or in the one likely brothel unearthed. Bathing, Beard explains, was a necessary social activity, but the pollution of the water was recognized to be a dangerous thing that could sometimes lead to infection, gangrene, even death.

Besides this more sordid information, the author also takes the reader on spellbinding trips through many of the homes, public buildings, and temples, pointing out their beautiful paintings and tiles, the arrangement of rooms, views, and other information, much of which is no longer visible. Beard explains to the lay-reader the centrality, yet cultural mix, of Roman religion. We begin to comprehend Pompeii's relationship to Rome itself. In short, by the time Beard completes these intellectual spins through the bustling, active city, we feel rather electrified by the exhausting trip. When the author returns us to the cities of the dead, the cemeteries just outside the city gates, we realize that Pompeii is something we might never before have imagined. Too bad I had not been able to read Beard's remarkable book before my own stumble through the ruins of that city in 2007.

LOS ANGELES, OCTOBER 22, 2009
Reprinted from *Green Integer Blog* (August 2009).

Roman Fantasies

POMPEII AND THE ROMAN VILLA: ART AND CULTURE AROUND THE BAY OF NAPLES, ON VIEW AT THE LOS ANGELES COUNTY MUSEUM OF ART FROM MAY 3–OCTOBER 4, 2009 / I SAW THE SHOW AT THE PRESS PREVIEW OF APRIL 29, 2009

GIVEN MY ISCHIAN isolation, my busy schedule, and the misgivings we all had that summer about Naples, I did not have the opportunity to visit the highly recommended National Archeological Museum of Naples and other major muse-  ums in Pompeii and the coastal villas. How wonderful, accordingly, that many of the treasures of those locations showed up this year—the year I had determined

 to publish my experiences in Ischia, Pompeii, Naples, and the Campania region— at the Los Angeles County Museum of Art, across the street from both my condominium and my office.

Unlike the previous show of some years earlier, which focused on Pompeii, this was centered on the Roman villas around Naples and the neighboring cities of Pompeii, Herculaneum, Stabiae (now Castellamare di Stabia), Surrentum (Sorrento), Capreae (Capri), Pausilypon (Posillipo), and Puteoli (Pozzuoli)—the last of which, as I describe above, was where my journey to Ischia began.

Selecting from the villas of the wealthy Romans, particularly the ruling families of the emperors Tiberius, Caligula, Claudius, and Nero, *Pompeii and the Roman Villa: Art and Culture Around the Bay of Naples* represents powerful sculptures, frescoes, interiors, courtyards, and gardens, as well as more modern representations of the great volcanic eruption of Vesuvius that ended this region's cultural dominance.

The model for these wealthy patrons was clearly

Greek, and many of the subjects and references of their art were to Greek figures of history, such as the beautiful sculpture of Homer of the 1st century, borrowed from the Museum of Fine Arts in Boston. Similarly, *Plato's Academy*, a mosaic from the Pompeian villa of T. Siminnius Stephanus, and the marble *Panel with a Dionysiac Procession* from Herculaneum, both also of the 1st century, attest to the Romans' commitment to Greek figures and themes.

Yet, it is through the detailed sculptures of the family members themselves that we come to recognize just how different these Greek-inspired works came to be in the Roman artists' depictions. The beautiful *Aphrodite/Venus*, discovered in Puteoli (Pozzouli), with its voluminous folds of dress and densely curled hair top-

ping the head, and
the striking head of
the dreaded emperor
Gaius (Caligula),
also from Pozzouli,
make clear that while
the models for these
works may have been

from the Hellenic culture, the Roman artists themselves found new expression in their renderings.

Perhaps some of the most spectacular work in this show is the recreation of a garden, including a magnificent fresco, *Garden Scene*, from Pompeii's House of the Golden Bracelet. At once the viewer feels as if he has entered the garden itself, and is awed by the theatrical-like settings.

A couple of the pieces, particularly the black basan-

ite sculpture of Livia (from the Paris Louvre museum), seem almost art deco in their modernity. The small paintings and frescoes of these villas themselves are worth the ticket of admission.

It is little wonder that when the excavations of Pompeii and Herculaneum were begun in the late 18th and 19th centuries,

the whole world became fascinated and enchanted by the vast numbers of antiquities unearthed, and artists began to reimagine the cities and villas caught in the unfortunate drama of nature.

None of these works, of course, can compare with the ancient art discovered in Naples and the surrounding region, but their dramatic expression of that violent end to these great cities and villas, such as Pierre-Henri de Valenciennes' 1813 canvas *Eruption of Vesuvius,* continues to awe us still today, creating myths larger than those even of the Italian citizens, great storytellers though they be, who continue to endure life in this region.

It is clear, after seeing this show and reading Shirley Hazzard's apologia for Naples, *Ancient Shore* (a review of which follows), that I shall have to return to the city, if for no other reason than to pay homage to such a splendorous past.

LOS ANGELES, MAY 17, 2009
Reprinted from *Green Integer Blog* (May 2009) and *Art Là-bas*
    (October 2014).

Pilgrimage to Napoli

SHIRLEY HAZZARD AND FRANCIS STEEGMULLER
ANCIENT SHORE: DISPATCHES FROM NAPLES (CHI-
CAGO: UNIVERSITY OF CHICAGO PRESS, 2008)

IN HER BEAUTIFULLY written apologia for Naples and
the Campania region, author Shirley Hazzard begins
her "dispatches" with a differentiation between traveling to a country, merely living in another country, and
a stay of pilgrimage. The first, no matter how rich the
experience may be for the traveler, is usually defined by
a brief stay in a place, with little deep knowledge of, or
appreciation for, its history or culture; tourists generally travel through a country without having the time
or ability to take in its rich heritage. Certainly Hazzard
and her husband Frances Steegmuller (a well-known
editor, translator, critic, and literary biographer) could
be described as a couple living in another country—
Hazzard's father's career as a diplomat forced the family
to move several times in her early life, from Australia to

Japan, Hong Kong, England, and New Zealand, before she ended up in New York City and, some time later, worked for the United Nations in Italy—but their experience is quite different from those individuals living in another place who continue to define their lives by their ultimate return to their homeland. For Hazzard, her journeys, particularly her move to Naples and Campania, are of another kind, what she calls a "pilgrimage," resulting in experiences that appear as "an elixir, a talisman: a spell cast by what has long and greatly been, over what briefly and simply is." The difference, she argues, is that the pilgrim traveler becomes temporarily one with the place, "learning to match its moods with one's own," combining "human expectation" with "an exquisite blend of receptivity and detachment."

Hazzard, accordingly, takes the reader through her Italy—the headland of Posillipo, Vesuvius and Pompeii, Capri, the Sorrentine peninsula, and through the streets of Naples itself. She shows us its museums and treasures—the ancient villas of the Romans, the churches, the fishermen returning with their catches, and the Spaccanapoli, the sequence of streets (Via Benedetto Croce, Via San Biagio dei Librai, and Via Vicaria Vecchia) that cuts through the heart of the Naples' historical center.

In a particularly riveting chapter, "In the Shadow of Vesuvius," Hazzard describes not only the great volcano that buried Pompeii and Herculaneum, but other eruptions and earthquakes since—detecting, in the continual destruction and rebuilding right up to the lip of the volcano, the Neapolitan sense of time and the inevitable. As the author repeats, "Naples requires time," like the city itself with its ancient layers of reality; the experience of the city must be something encountered over long stretches if it is to reveal itself. In dazzlingly beautiful sentences, Hazzard indeed allows the reader to intellectually wander the city along with her, characterizing it as a "city of secrets and surprises":

Persisting, you will soon discover the opera house,

the spacious galleria, and the huge Castel Nuovo that dominates the port. Even so, the city eludes the search for its center. The truth is that there are many centers at Naples, each vital to its own city quarter. And Naples is rifest perhaps at its oldest point, the district of Spaccanapoli, where the city splits along its Greco-Roman decumanus.

Hazzard's writing, accordingly, is an often brilliant travelogue in which the reader is made to recognize what he or she may have missed in the elusive city. But there is occasionally a sense in her homage to Neapolitan wonders that seems almost forced, as if she were somehow in league with the city's tourist industry. Indeed, so in love with Naples is Hazzard that she only once mentions the notorious Camorra mob—an obvious danger for those living in the entire region—and she appears never to have experienced the heaps of garbage I encountered there in 2007, a perfect invitation to a blight of rats and disease. Although she and her husband describe riding through the city in taxis, neither seems to have witnessed the complete abandonment by the Neapolitan drivers of the rules of the road. While admitting that, "Unlike Florence or Venice, Naples long allowed her great monuments to languish in disorder," she argues that they should remain in their authentic context, and that "Private acts of faith and rescue have

not been lacking in recent years." Although she advises several times that visitors should never carry a purse or bag, she hardly hints at the violence that might occur if one were to ignore her suggestions.

The longest chapter in this book, however—a piece titled "The Incident at Naples," penned by Steegmuller—describes just such an event. Carrying an empty bag, and forgetting for an instant to roll it up or put it in his pocket, Steegmuller, dangling it by the handles, is suddenly attacked by two young men on a motorcycle, and, in the usual pattern, is dragged along the street until the bag becomes loosened from his arm. In this case, the victim is quite seriously hurt, with severe lacerations to his nose, hands, and legs. But even in this one instance of described violence, Steegmuller finds the decaying hospitals to be filled with kindly doctors who, because of the nationalized health system, do not even bill him. Returning to the US, he misses the kindnesses of the Neapolitan doctors and the immediate assistance of close Italian friends. The clean white clinics of New York seem less interested in him as a human being than did the decaying facilities of Naples, and he returns to

Italy, after healing, to thank the several individuals who helped him get through the affair—one of whom tells the author that the robbers might have killed his son had he not removed the baby from its stroller at the moment of attack.

I have no doubt, given my own personal experiences with Neapolitans, that he received such a genuinely personal response, and one applauds both Hazzard's and Steegmuller's praise of these interpersonal relationships that continue to exist throughout the region. Nonetheless, it often appears that the Naples and Campania of *The Ancient Shore* is a world more of the past and shadow than of the piercing glare of contemporary Southern Italian daylight.

LOS ANGELES, MAY 23, 2009
Reprinted from *Rain Taxi* [online edition] (Summer 2009)

Cemetery of Garbage

MAURIZIO BRAUCCI, UGO CHITI, GIANNI DI GRE-
GORIO, MATTEO GARRONE, MASSIMO GAUDIOSO, AND
ROBERT SAVIANO (SCREENPLAY, BASED ON THE BOOK
BY ROBERTO SAVIANO), MATTEO GARRONE (DIRECTOR)
GOMORRAH / 2008, RELEASED IN THE US IN 2009

GIVEN THE RHYMING name of the Neapolitan crime
group Camorra, *Gomorrah* is a rambling narrative of
five different sets of characters in and about Naples, all
of whom can be tied to the notorious gangs of that region, and all of whom are destined to kill or be killed
themselves.

The film centers—if there can be said to be a central focus—on a young boy, Totò (played by Salvatore
Abruzzese), a wide-eyed urchin living in the vast apartment compound Vele di Sampi where most of the film's
action takes place. Totò's mother survives by running a
small grocery; and as a delivery boy for her, Totò visits various units of the apartment complex, getting a

close-up view of more
violence and suffering
than any child should
have to endure. Like
other, slightly old-
er children of this
world, he clearly sees
the violence around him as a natural phenomenon.

Two other boys, Ciro and Marco, soon to be young adults, play a kind of theatrical game of imitation, miming scenes and imaginatively recreating the events of the American gang movie *Scarface*. When these boys later discover a cache of guns and other weaponry hidden by the Camorra at a nearby farm, they turn their games into deadly action, shooting up the empty backwaters of their neighborhood. Garrone's film relies more on memorable images than upon a coherent story, and one of the best of these is a scene in which the two boys, stripped to their underwear, meaninglessly shoot off their Uzis in mad imagination of the day when they will overtake the local Don—a wretched, unshaven, and (so the boys claim) unclean thug whom it is not hard to imagine is as vulnerable as anyone else in this hellish spot.

Garrone refuses to glamorize any part of the Camorra. Hardly anyone, not even the wealthy gang leaders, lives better lives than anyone else. And most characters are trapped in the confines of small, dark rooms, allowed to continue living by small financial handouts provided by the Camorra, some of which are put right back into the Camorra economy through the purchase of coke and heroin or a trip to the local sex club—the only pleasures this world seems to offer.

One of the major figures we fellow, in fact, is the money runner, Don Circo (Gianfelice Imparato), who, like Totò, is privy to each household as he delivers mob money to those deemed worthy of support. His job may seem, at first, to offer some sense of purpose or even power, but we soon discover, like everyone else, he too is forced to live life at the edge with the possibility of being killed by rival ("secessionist") gangs and being hated by those to whom he delivers the money for the mob's penurious offerings. As one recipient shouts each week, how do they expect me to live on this? Don Circo's attempt to leave the mob ends in another round of murders.

Even the local haute couture designer, given a contract to produce several gowns—including one, we discover later, that will grace the body of actress Scarlett Johannson on Oscar night—lives in near-destitution and all-night working sessions. His top dressmaker lives so poorly that he is willing to sell his knowledge, night by night, to the owner of a local Chinese dress factory, who sneaks him in and out of the shop in the trunk of his car. As a so-called "traitor," he too is nearly killed, and escapes with his life only by leaving his previous occupation behind, becoming a truck driver.

Perhaps the only man who seems to live life a little better than the others is Franco, who, with his new assistant Roberto, plans to turn an empty quarry into a dumping ground for garbage that will cover over a bed of dangerously toxic containers of chemicals. When one of the truck drivers delivering the barrels has a mishap, bleeding and fearful of the chemicals' effects, Franco unflappably orders the regular drivers out of the trucks, temporarily leaving the scene to bring back young street boys who are more than happy to drive these mammoth machines down to the pit where the garbage will be dumped. When a local farmer, who has previously sold Franco land, offers him pears, Franco kindly accepts them, but once on the road demands Roberto dump them: they are polluted like all the land of Campania thereabouts. Roberto (perhaps a stand-in for the author Roberto Saviano), refusing to rejoin Franco in his determined destruction of the region, is perhaps the only individual in the film who escapes unscathed—although in real life Saviano must live in hiding, fearful of the mob's wrath.

It is inevitable, accordingly, that the young, innocent Totò must ultimately be entombed in the Camorra's codes of behavior. He is recruited by a secession-

ist group, a younger fringe of the Camorra followers determined to kill the mother of a rebel. As a delivery boy, Totò is the only one for whom she will open her door. Desperately trying to remain uninvolved in these treacherous acts, Totò will not answer their query: "Are you with us or not?" But as he knows, there is no ground in between, and he has no choice but to call the woman out to her murder.

So are Ciro and Marco lured to a country spot and shot, their bodies loaded into a forklift of a giant caterpillar truck and dumped, perhaps in the very cemetery of garbage created by Franco and his kind.

Dramatically speaking, *Gomorrah* is nothing but a mish-mash of different stories weaving in and out of each other, much like the unfocused images of Garrone's background figures throughout the film. Yet the implications of these characters' purposeless acts, where human life has no more or less value than a bottle fly buzzing around a room, are absolutely mesmerizing and memorable. The only time death means anything for the figures of this film is when the gun is aimed at their own heads. But, like members of such self-destructive cultures everywhere, the moment they survive the heat, they seem utterly to forget— just like the boys who are told they have been transformed into men by letting a mob henchman shoot

them, a bullet-proof vest pulled over them for probable protection, directly in the chest; the force of the bullet momentarily flattens them upon their backs, but eventually they stand up again to blindly face the bullets of another day. Let us hope that readers of Saviano's book and movie will remember, and help to put a halt to these internationally destructive acts.

LOS ANGELES, FEBRUARY 19, 2009
Reprinted from *N^{th} Position* [England] (March 2009).

Five Tales from Ischia: The 5th Tale (The Trip to Amalfi)

FROM POMPEII, Marty, Rebecca, the two students, and I had planned to travel up the Amalfi coast to the small town of Praiano, where Rebecca had found a hotel in which we would stay the night. Somehow, however, we missed the coastal road, and Marty decided to take the mountain route, coming in from Ravello and driving down to Praiano.

For what seemed like forever, he darted down side streets in the town near Pompeii, but we soon lost any signs that might indicate the direction of the road we were seeking. Indeed, there seemed to be no other path, and we repeated it several times before pulling into a small gas station. Suddenly two beefy men, covered with grease, came forward as Marty, speaking in Italian, attempted to get directions. The bovine mechanics looked us quickly over, as one leaned into the car on Rebecca's side where a map sat on her lap. He began to speak and soon after reached in and pointed on a spot on the map. The other quickly followed his lead, furtively placing his hand on the map as well. All of us looked on in consternation as they joyfully punched at the map, pleasuring themselves, evidently, by touching the paper that separated them from Rebecca's crotch. We quickly pulled away, realizing that we would never receive any cogent information from them.

Soon after we pulled down a side street, stopping in front of an old man who stood on the sidewalk. Marty called out to him, again explaining what we sought. Suddenly the man beamed a huge smile, as if absolutely delighted with the question, almost as if he had been waiting his entire life for just this moment. He moved a bit forward and began to talk:

> Abon me uh da umm bunbun ju jee gon abonma
> fe quo ja ja,

he mumbled, continuing for a long while in a private language of babble of which none of us could discern a single recognizable word.

> Me a mo abon jug on de de mmmmm aaaabbbbb
> jjjjjjooooooo,

he continued, smiling beneficently. Daniel and Nidzára

had slipped to the floor of the back seat in uncontrolled giggles, as the remaining three of us sat erect, pretending a friendly comprehension of everything the old geezer said. I waved to the students, hand out of sight, to pipe down, but they simply could no longer hold it in as we continued the charade.

Grazie, said Marty as he began to drive away. We had moved only a few feet when Marty stopped the car and we all exploded into gales of laughter.

Another circle around the area brought us to a gellati truck, where this time Rebecca asked for directions in Italian. The gellati workers said they would be happy to give directions—if we would all buy ice cream from them. Rejecting that idea, we drove away, one of them jumping onto a motorcycle that began to follow us, finally speeding away in a whoop of derision.

The only thing we could imagine now was to turn around and take the same route in the other direction. Sure enough, a large sign proclaimed the way to the road we had sought!

Soon we were approaching Sorrento, thereafter climbing into the mountains on roads so narrow that, when a bus approached, we had to pull over as close as we could to the treacherous lip of the highway just to let it pass. The drive continued in an excruciatingly terrifying manner that, from time to time, triggered my sense of vertigo, forcing me to simply close my eyes.

But when I did open them, briefly, I witnessed beautiful sites.

After winding up and down the mountain trail, we reached Ravello, where we stopped, grabbing up the only parking space that seemed to remain, to tour that small, lovely city, celebrating its annual music festival. The square at Ravello looks out over the mountains on one side, and is flanked by two large cafes, at the center of which sits a lovely, white, stucco church. The light was absolutely luminous, reflecting, so it seemed, the colors of the large stanchions of flowers that stood about the place.

Ravello is also the center of a region famous for its tiles and mosaics, and several of the shops were devoted to that craft. A gallery, showing work by Yoko Ono

and other performance artists, was of particular interest to our small group. We also attempted to enter the church where many of the festival's concerts were

held, but it was, at the moment, closed. We walked about the town for an hour before returning once again to the road.

We passed the town of Amalfi, reaching our destination, the hotel Smeraldo in Praiano. I don't know how Rebecca had discovered this gem of a small hotel. A recent check of hotels in Praiano on the internet showed 10 hotels, without listing our choice. Once we had reached our rooms, we had all fallen in love with the place.

What a surprise to find these exceptionally beautiful accommodations—Marty and I stayed in the hotel proper, while the students slept at a hotel apartment (three bedrooms, a kitchen, and a bath) across the street—all for a nightly rate of 140 euros.

My space had its own entry room off the street (a stairway with what seemed three million steps to the sea—Marty later reported that he'd been told it was actually 400 steps!). That room, like the bedroom, was completely tiled in red, containing two stylish chairs, paintings, a large mirror, and a window that opened up to view those never-ending steps. A sizable bathroom stood off to the side.

The bedroom it-self was designed in a style that I might have described as "sheik monk," with crosses hanging over the large double bed and an-other single bed (for  any altar boy I might meet, I guess). The room, even by American standards, was gigantic, with a full desk and a huge dressing cabinet.

On the balcony was a round, stylish, metal table appointed with two Mediterranean-style chairs. In both corners of the balcony sat marine-blue lounging chairs. The view from the balcony, both from the front and the side, was spectacular—the sea below and the coastline, with a view of the entire city of Positano. For the first night a large yacht lay moored beneath my win-dow. Marty and Becky had a Jacuzzi on their balcony, a couch in their room. But I liked my room better.

We had a pleasant dinner at the hotel restaurant, homemade, thick, flat noodles for primi and grilled fishes (swordfish and large prawns) for the secondi. We ordered a bottle of white wine and Daniel had brought a gift of a very good red wine.

After dinner (11:30), all came to my balcony to the watch the holiday fireworks in the ocean below. Tentatively the Nakells and the students wondered what I might feel about staying on for a second day. "Oh, we must!" I readily concurred. "We're in heaven."

The next morning we all got up rather late for breakfast. Marty was especially exhausted from all the driving. As in Ischia breakfast consisted of beautiful rolls, breads, jellies, fresh fruits, and meats—prosciutto, Genoa salami, etc. We drank juices and thick muddy coffee served with hot milk.

I toured the small city after, walking down some of the 400 steps and back, visiting the lovely church of S. Gennaro, and stopping by the local fruit stand to buy some water and a peach. Marty and Rebecca were obviously off on their daily wander, and the students (we discovered later) were walking almost to Amalfi, running up and down the 400 steps, and doing various other endless activities.

I determined to return to my beautiful balcony to finish my essay on Marinetti. The writing moved quite slowly, but I plodded through into early afternoon and finally completed it. I briefly napped and then begin reading *IT*, an exceptional book of poetry by the Danish poet Inger Christensen. It was truly pleasant in the blue lounging chair. What bliss!

The Nakells briefly stopped by before retiring to their room next door. We decided to dine at a restaurant at the bottom of the 400 steps at 7:30.

I retreated to a nearby bar, sipping on a Campari, nibbling on prosciutto, crustini, and green olives while reading my book.

At 7:00 we met for the long descent. Marty, Rebecca, and the students all chose one of the daily fish, while I selected a local squid, cut differently than calimari, into long strips, and served with fried potato rounds. It was excellent, and I far preferred my choice to theirs. They all had marzipan fruits stuffed with gellati, I a slice of lemon cake for dessert.

It was now quite late, and we knew we could never again climb the steps. So we took the advice of the waiter and took a water taxi over to the neighboring city, Positano, planning to return by land taxi to Praiano. There's something truly exciting about being in a small boat in the ocean in the middle of the night!

Positano at midnight was a madhouse of celebration, filled with young and middle-aged, rich, loud frat-boy and sorority-girl types, and women dressed up in bizarre fashions that made them look more like call girls than the attractive, wealthy women we knew them to be. It was the first time I had heard so much English since I arrived. The whole city seemed to be par-

 tying, hopping with drunken whoops of noise. I didn't like it, and, like some Puritan elder, led the way through the narrow streets up and up where we might find a taxi, the others trailing in their obvious desire just to wander about. When I arrived at the point where I recognized that a taxi might appear, I could see the Nakells conferring with the students, and soon Becky came forward to announce that they wanted to stay on in Positano for a while. Fine with me, I responded, but I was taking a taxi back. I was tired. It was now 1:00 a.m. I told them to go on and enjoy themselves, but as they often do, they stood frozen in place, and when the taxi finally appeared, Daniel suddenly decided to join me. He had seemed to be in a kind a funk all day. And the next morning he explained that he had run out of his thyroid medicine, which had drained him of energy. By that time, his whole personality had returned to normal.

Marty and Rebecca, so I later found out, had sat with Nidzára in a bar for a while, before wandering on, until someone poured a bucket of water upon Rebecca from a window overhead. By 1:30 I was safely snuggled up in bed.

The morning after we had returned to Ischia, I taught Marty's class, discussing my publishing activities and attempting to explain what publishing was in relationship to being a writer. Then I turned to my own poetry, *Bow Down*, a book in both English and Italian which they had previously read. It went nicely, although they had only a few questions.

I then walked into Forio again, forgetting it was a holiday. The town was dead, with no shops open except for the bars. I sat at my favorite, Bar Maria, for a single Campari, where I caught up on my daily journal and attempted to make some notes on Paul Auster's novel, *Oracle Night*, which I'd finished reading on the plane.

The next day I returned to Forio, where I had a lemon-lime soda at Bar Maria, writing letters and updating my journal. I returned to the hotel, read some, and wrote a little before dressing for my scheduled poetry reading at a nearby vineyard.

We took a taxi to the vineyard up the hill from the hotel. It was a lovely spot, under a pergola of grapes where visitors come to taste the wine. The vineyard also served dinners (everything grown fresh, fish caught in the sea below, and rabbits trapped in the hills about), and the Nakells and I decided to return for dinner two days later as my going away celebration. Since everything was cooked to order, we were asked to decide on

our dinner choices ahead of time. I ordered the rabbit. But Marty and Becky couldn't escape the vision they'd had of a man with a bag of rabbits they'd encountered in Ischia Porto a few days earlier. Obviously he was on his way to slit their little throats!

The reading was attended by the students and two British women doctors (M.D.'s) who had happened to visit the vineyard from their hotel in Ischia Porto. It went very nicely, with the handsome Jean-Luc (the manager-owner of this small winery) reading three of the poems in Italian. He was an excellent reader, who told me he'd performed all the Goldoni plays in high school.

We then returned to the hotel for a dinner of pasta and fresh pesce, retiring to the terrace to sip a dessert wine Marty had purchased at the vineyard. It had four fruits—apricot, cherry, and two others—consisting of

45% alcohol content! Our waiter, Augusto, served it up as if it were wine (the bottle might have lasted for many months), and Marty and I had no choice but to drink up the brew right there and then! I woke up the next morning slow and achy, not quite awake.

Rebecca reminded us why we were feeling so groggy!

I had slept well again, however, listening to the ocean waves all night.

The following day, July 4th, Marty took the students on a boat trip around the island of Ischia. Already filled with good memories and needing to get some time to write, I stayed behind to work on my essay on Auster. I read, and caught up with my cleaning. Despite all the shirts I'd brought, I didn't have enough clothing for all the heat and perspiration I had endured.

The meal the next evening at the winery was excellent, a perfect balance of each course and pre-selected wines—but it was so filling I was almost ill. Besides, I was now quite depressed. In another day I would have to leave Ischia, when I felt my time on the island had just begun. By now, however, most of the Germans had left, and the Neapolitans—not at all appreciated by the local Ischians—were soon to arrive.

At a birthday party for one of the students, Wesley Frazee, I sadly said goodbye to the hotel staff and students. The next morning Marty and Rebecca went with me by taxi to the ferry for my last trip across the bay. "I can't leave yet," I protested. "We never did get to see Amalfi!" By midnight I had flown back to Dublin, leaving for Los Angeles again early the next morning.

LOS ANGELES, JULY 9, 2007
Reprinted from *Green Integer Blog* (April 2008).

Facing the Cold

LUIGI ILLICA AND GIUSEPPE GIACOSA (LIBRETTO,
BASED ON *SCÉNES DE LA VIE DE BOHÈME* BY HENRI
MURGER), GIACOMO PUCCINI (MUSIC) **LA BOHÈME**
ROBERT DORNHELM (DIRECTOR) **LA BOHÈME** [A
FILM] / 2008

ON SUNDAY, September 27, 2009, Howard and I attended a movie presentation of the opera *La Bohème* at the Music Hall theater in Beverly Hills.

Although my intention in this short piece is not particularly to evaluate the film or opera itself, I should mention that I found a great many of the filmic details to be quite annoying. Dornhelm's aerial flights between scenes gave the "realist" drama a fairy-tale-like quality, as if God-in-all-his-wisdom were looking down on these poor folks, which was further enhanced by a presentation of the Latin Quarter—which in this version looked more like some Alpine village—in black and white before fading into color.

Continuity throughout the film was poor, with obviously false snowflakes alternating between a blizzard and gentle snowfall in a matter of seconds. Mimi's eyes in some scenes looked less like those of a victim of consumption than of a prize-fight boxer who'd been terribly roughed up; yet a few seconds later her make-up lightened and she was relatively pale.

Dornhelm also presented some of the operatic duets as internal dialogues rather than sung recitatives, giving the characters a strangely mute appearance, often at the most lyrical moments of the music.

For the most part, the singing was admirable, with beautiful performances by Rolando Villazón as Rodolfo, Anna Netrebko as Mimi, and Nicole Cabell as Musetta. But why Dornhelm could not find two Baritones, Marcello and Schaunard, who could both act and sing (George von Bergen's and Adrian Eröd's performances were sung by Boaz Daniel and Stephane Degout) is beyond me. I thought every young Baritone cut his teeth on these roles. I found the lip-synching distracting.

For all that the opera was as joyful and emotionally wrenching as any *La Bohème*, and most of the rather geriatric audience could be observed weeping at opera's end.

Normally, I might not have even written on such a well-known chestnut, presuming there is little more to be said. Yet, given this year's selected "topic," "Facing the Heat," I could not but observe that the major tropes of this work are related; throughout the opera, the characters seek, other than food and money, primarily only three things: heat, light, and love. Of course, love can also provide some spiritual heat and light and light, in turn, often results in heat and, particularly in the spring, emanations of love.

The problem for these bohemians, however, one they daily face, is that they have little of the first two. Luigi Illica's and Giuseppe Giacosa's Paris has always seemed to me to be more like a Siberian settlement than the City of Light. Yes, we know it snows in Paris, and the temperature can be frigid: in January of this year, thousands of travelers were stranded at Charles DeGaulle International Airport, the Eiffel Tower was closed, and temperatures for several weeks plunged to 10° Celsius. But most would tell you that, while it snows in Paris, it is not a common event. Yet the world of *La Bohème* is a particularly dark one, in which, so it seems, every day is a frigid challenge.

Roldolfo and his friends begin the opera singing of their cold bodies, determining to burn either the room's only chair or Marcello's new painting; Rodolfo offers up the pages of a new play, which "perform" very badly. The "play," so they jest, is not one that will last. Schaunard arrives just in time, food and wood for the fireplace in hand; he has been paid for playing the piano to a parrot.

Soon after, with Rodolfo alone in the room, Mimi knocks, claiming her candle has gone out, and much of the rest of the scene is spent with the two of them crawling about in the dark as they look for her lost key and fall madly in love. Rodolfo's first touch of her shivering hand reveals what will remain the theme throughout the opera, how to keep Mimi warm. As their candles both dwindle, they sing of their dreams, their love of the spring and light, Mimi explaining her pleasure of roses.

One of the first of Rodolfo's acts after meeting Mimi is to buy her a bonnet, his attempt, symbolically, to warm her. The Second Act continues the warming theme with food, drink, and the emotionally-wrought and comic song of Musetta, aimed primarily at her former lover, Marcello. Sparks fly. All in all, this is the most well-lit and warm scene in the entire production.

Act Three, performed entirely in the cold winter air and, symbolically, at the very gate of the city, is the coldest of the opera. The characters remain not only outside of society and at the very edge of the city, but literally outside on the street. It is here, after suffering the symbolic heat of her lover's jealousy and fury, that Mimi tells Marcello of Rodolfo's  behavior and determines to leave him. But, as we know, she does not return home, staying to overhear Rodolfo's woeful tale of her tuberculosis and her certain death, all made worse by the fact that he has no way of altering their fate. His own poverty provides no warmth for the frozen woman, no light, and, in this context, no proper expression of his love. In this regard Puccini and his librettists create a "frieze," placing their characters costumed, in this movie version, in dark coats and dresses against the white frozen world in which they are attempting to survive. As if Rodolfo's sorrow and Mimi's shocking discovery of her own condition were not enough, Marcello and Musetta also begin to fight, the terrified foursome revealing even further that love is nearly impossible in the world they inhabit.

Rodolfo and Mimi are too deeply in love, however, to separate in this frozen landscape; they can only wait until April, when, at least, light returns with its flowers, and the warmth of spring and summer.

The end of this constant struggle, the necessity of

having to continually face the cold, is played out in the last act, inevitably, with Mimi's death. It's no surprise that, as they try to symbolically warm her, Musetta and Marcello running out to buy Mimi a muff, there is little warmth and even less light. Even trying to warm Mimi's medicine is an effort, as the flame threatens to go out. Singing to his coat—the only thing he has to keep the cold away from his flesh—Colline prepares to pawn it, and share the money with his fellow sufferers. Love, it is clear, has survived in all of these good people, but without heat or light their love cannot heal or salve the living.

LOS ANGELES, SEPTEMBER 28, 2009
Reprinted from *Green Integer Blog* (September 2009).

Tosca's Kisses

LUIGI ILLICA AND GIUSEPPE CIACOSA (LIBRETTO, BASED ON A PLAY BY VICTORIEN SARDOU), GIACOMO PUCCINI (MUSIC) **TOSCA** / PREMIERE AT TEATRO COSTANZI, ROME, JANUARY 14, 1900 / THE PRODUCTION I SAW WAS FROM THE METROPOLITAN OPERA'S HD PRODUCTION OF OCTOBER 10, 2009 (THE ENCORE PRODUCTION I WITNESSED WAS ON OCTOBER 29, 2009)

BY COINCIDENCE, soon after seeing a filmed version of Puccini's *La Bohème*, Howard and I attended the high-definition film production of The Metropolitan Opera's October 10, 2009 performance of Puccini's *Tosca*.

Both Howard and I had watched *Tosca* on film and, together, witnessed the Berlin Opera's production at the Kennedy Center in 1975-1976. Howard saw the same production in Berlin the next year.

Accordingly, we felt we knew the opera quite well, and perhaps I do not need to repeat the entire plot for most readers, although it is easily summarized.

The painter, Mario Cavaradossi (brilliantly sung by Marcelo Álvarez), is at work on a painting of the Madonna in the Church of Sant'Andrea della Valle in Rome when he discovers a friend, Cesare Angelotti (former Consul of the Roman Republic), hiding in a family crypt nearby. Angelotti has just escaped from prison, and Cavaradossi offers him a hiding place in his nearby villa.

Enter the noted opera singer Floria Tosca (Karita Matilla), Cavaradossi's lover, who immediately becomes suspicious that her beloved is seeing another woman, having overheard Cavaradossi whispering to someone. He assures her that he is in love with only her, but when she notices the painting on which he has been working, she recognizes the face of the Marchesa Attavanti (Angelotti's sister), who Cavaradossi has observed praying at the church. Her jealousy returns, as she demands Cavaradossi change the blue eyes of the painting to her own darkly-colored eyes.

A cannon is shot from the prison; they have detected the escape of Angelotti, and Cavaradossi promises his help to his friend. Enter the Chief of Police, the evil Baron Scarpia (George Gagnidze), who, upon discovering the Marchesa's fan in the crypt, successfully stirs up Tosca's jealousy once again. He himself would like to become Tosca's lover, and, as he sings of his evil machinations, the priests, chorus boys, and attending

parishioners march forward in the *Te Deum*, which, in total hypocrisy, he finally joins.

Later that night, Scarpia awaits Tosca in his home in the Farnese Palace. His henchman have discovered and arrested Cavaradossi in his home, suspecting him of having hidden Angelotti. As Tosca arrives, Scarpia orders Cavaradossi to be tortured in the next room. He demands Tosca tell him what she knows about Angelotti, but she claims to have no knowledge and refuses his demands. As the torture continues, however, she wavers, and finally unable to bear her lover's cries, confesses that Angelotti is hiding in a well near Cavaradossi's hut. The artist is released, taken off to prison to be hung.

Tosca now pleads with Scarpia to save Cavaradossi, but he is unwilling to do anything unless she gives herself over to his sexual desires. In what is perhaps the most dramatic scene of the opera, Tosca hatefully gives herself up, but only if Cavaradossi's life is spared and they, together, are given a letter of free passage out of the country. Scarpia orders his henchmen to perform a mock-shooting of the artist and writes out the letter. As he moves to Tosca for his reward, she stabs him in the stomach, proclaiming the knife to be "Tosca's kiss."

The final act is a short one, as Cavaradossi waits to be killed. Tosca arrives, quietly telling him the news that she has killed Scarpia and the artist's life has been spared. All he has to do is dramatically fall as the soldiers pretend to shoot, and when they leave she will tell him when it is permissible to "return to life." Liberty is at hand!

But even in death Scarpia has extended his control over them. The guns are filled with real ammunition and Cavaradossi is murdered. The dark irony of their love is dramatized by Tosca's continued warnings to the artist to wait just a little longer, just a little longer, as the soldiers march away; finally, she commands him to stand, but as she rushes over to help him, she discovers the reality that he is dead. As the policemen arrive, having discovered Scarpia's corpse, she rushes to the parapets of the fortress, screaming, "O Scarpia, we shall

meet before God!" before jumping to her death.

There have been numerous books and hundreds of essays written about this popular opera, and I have little of great originality that I could add. I would just reiterate the fact that, although this opera seems, in Puccini's hands, to be centered upon emotional issues of love and passion, jealousy and hate, it is just as significantly motivated by the politics of the moment. The opera is set on a single day, June 17, 1800, a day in which, after having crossed the Alps with his army, Napoleon Bonaparte met in the Battle of Marengo with the Austrians, led by General Mélas. The events of the play follow the historical reality. Early in the play we hear that Napoleon amazingly has been defeated by the

Austrians, and Tosca's evening performance is given, in part, in celebration for that event. Later in the day, however, the truth is revealed: new troops joining Napoleon's army have helped reverse the situation, and by evening, just as Tosca is performing in celebration for the French defeat, Napoleon's army crushes the Austrian forces. When the news reaches Scarpia's rooms, we observe Cavaradossi celebrating the fact before he is taken away to be tortured.

A little back history may explain the situation. Just two years earlier, in February 1798, French troops, headed by Napoleon's general Louis Alexandre Berthier, occupied the Vatican State, proclaiming the establishment of the Roman Republic. The Pope, Pius VI, was forced to flee to Tuscany, and, ultimately, to France where he died. Cavaradossi's friend, Angelotti, was one of the Republican leaders, a consul.

The Bourbon king Ferdinando IV, King of Naples, attempted to rescue the Pope and restore the Vatican but was defeated. For a brief time in 1799, the Roman Republic was incorporated into the Napoleon-supported Parthenopean Republic, which included Naples; but by April of that year General Suvorov, heading the Austrian-Russian army, crossed into northern Italy and defeated the French Republicans. Soon after, the Bourbons were returned to power, which, under the orders of Maria Carolina of Austria, wife of Ferdinando

IV, began a "cleansing" of former Republicans, liberals, artists, scientists, and others who had supported or been sympathetic to French rule. Both Angelotti and Cavaradossi, accordingly, were in danger, Angelotti imprisoned for his political position and Cavaradossi under suspicion for his artistic avocation. Thousands of men and women were killed under the eye of the newly appointed Baron Scarpia (upon whom Scarpia is said to based).

In reverse of Napoleon's battle, what seems to have saved the day in Cavaradossi's and Angelotti's lives ends in death.

Tosca's political position in this time of general turmoil is quite vague. She comes from northern Italy, which clearly is attempting to defend itself from Napoleon's advance, and her intense religiosity seems to suggest, as does her participation in the celebration of Napoleon's supposed defeat, that she has aligned herself, despite her lover's sympathies, with the Bourbons.*

In any event, we can observe in the very political context of these momentous times that all the characters of this opera are, as one observer has suggested, not what they seem to be. The artist is also a revolutionary, the diva and sexually attractive lover is also religiously devout, the outwardly devout chief of police is a lustful lecher and liar. Even Angelotti is ready to don a woman's dress to escape. If for no other reason, the shifting realities of these figures might justify director Luc Bondy's decision to remove the brilliant colors of Franco Zeffirelli's previous Metropolitan production, leaving the viewer with vast abstract spaces murkily lit. It may be justified, but, in my estimation—and apparently in those of many other opera-goers, who loudly booed the opening night production—it was not successful. At times it was simply difficult to "see" these brilliant singers, and one missed the elaborately artificial trappings in which they might have further hidden their identities.

My point in all this historicity (other than my feeling that, in part, it is the very basis of the *My Year* volumes, in which I am attempting to remember what is so easily forgotten) is that, politically speaking, the characters are at "war" with one another even before the curtain has been raised.

Floria Tosca is not only emotionally at war with both Cavaradossi and Scarpia because of her love and jealousies, but is spiritually at war with them, more pious than Cavaradossi's all too human depiction of the Madonna and Scarpia's hypocritical worship of the symbols of the church. She is, as Cavaradossi warns early in the opera, a natural confessor, telling her own priest "everything." It is strange, accordingly, that he allows her to discover the circumstances surrounding Angelotti, for, inevitably, even if it is presumably to save

Cavaradossi's life, she betrays the cause.

Tosca's kisses, accordingly, are all inevitably lethal, not only to Scarpia, whom she kisses metaphorically with the knife, but to Cavaradossi, whom she kisses passionately, only to condemn him, unintentionally, to death. In such a world, in short, no one is to be trusted, for it is a world in utter chaos, official rule changing nearly instant by instant. The Battle of Marengo allowed Napoleon easier access to Italy, and Rome would soon fall to his forces. His son was given by birth the title "His Majesty the King of Rome."

---

*In Shirley Hazzard's 2008 book, *Ancient Shore* (see my essay above), she describes a 20th century dinner conversation with friends, a couple fiercely debating still about the Bourbon reign of Italy. Apparently, Italians are still divided on these issues.

LOS ANGELES, OCTOBER 30, 2009
Reprinted from *Green Integer Blog* (October 2009).

Imitations of Art

ELEANOR GRIFFIN AND ALLAN SCOTT (SCREENPLAY, BASED ON A NOVEL BY FANNIE HURST), DOUGLAS SIRK (DIRECTOR) **IMITATION OF LIFE** / 1959

PHILLIP YORDAN, BEN MADDOW, AND NICHOLAS RAY (SCREENPLAY, BASED ON A NOVEL BY ROY CHANSLOR), NICHOLAS RAY (DIRECTOR) **JOHNNY GUITAR** / 1954

and suddenly I saw a headline
LANA TURNER HAS COLLAPSED!
there is no snow in Hollywood
there is no rain in California
I have been to lots of parties
and acted perfectly disgraceful
but I never actually collapsed
oh Lana Turner we love you get up

—Frank O'Hara

ON AUGUST 21ST of this year, I attended the 50th

anniversary showing of Douglas Sirk's *Imitation of Life*. At the Samuel Goldwyn Theater of The Academy of Motion Picture Arts and Sciences in Beverly Hills,  the audience was also treated to a special interview with the remaining living major cast members, Juanita Moore (who plays Annie Johnson) and Susan Kohner (who played Annie's daughter, Sarah Jane), by Susan Kohner's son Paul Weitz and film critic Stephen Farber.

Although I had previously seen the film several times on television, I'd never before seen it on a large screen, which is truly necessary for this highly color-saturated and artificed film.

Behind my interest in seeing this movie were several pieces written in 2008 and 2009 by then-16-year-old Felix Bernstein on various aspects of artifice in film and theater and, in particular, a brief discussion of the camp elements in Sirk's works. Just a few weeks earlier, I had also caught a television showing of the 2002 film *Far from Heaven*, a film (on which I write in *My Year 2002*) that is an homage to many of Sirk's films and cinematography. In the end, I realized that all of these coincidences had led up to a necessity to write on this movie and its effects.

Certainly, as many have, one could begin by describing Sirk's *Imitation of Life* as a soap-opera, or—with another kind of backhand dismissal of the work—as a "woman's picture." In introducing the film to the audience of 1,000 viewers, Farber himself, while clearly an admirer of the film, admitted to some terribly clichéd moments of the work, particularly in Sirk's montage of the passing years of Lora Meredith's (Lana Turner) career.

To my way of thinking, however, to use these adjectives is to miss the point. For the film is not simply a tearjerker or even a slightly over-the-top portrait of a woman determined to have a career, but is an intentional—if artful—presentation of the American Dream as kitsch.

I have never been able to comprehend the great attraction of so many directors to the vague acting skills of Lana Turner, but Sirk knows a woman determined to be a star when he sees her, and uses Turner's exaggerated posturings to their best effect. In the interview after this film's showing, Juanita Moore revealed that Lana spent much of every morning with her discussing the events of Turner's 14-year old daughter's murder of Johnny Stompanato, Turner's lover, the actress often breaking down in tears. It is clear that Sirk could not have found a more vulnerable and over-wrought figure for his purposes.

Lora Meredith is a woman with a young daughter, surviving on the pittance she makes from labeling envelopes, who by accident meets Annie Jackson (a woman Moore herself described as little more than a black mammy) with Jackson's daughter in tow at Coney Island. Even worse off than Meredith and her daughter, Jackson and Sarah Jane have come to the end of their resources, without even a place to sleep. Jackson craftily negotiates a bed in the Meredith flat in return for all the services of a maid, and, in the process, quickly insinuates herself and daughter into their household.

Meanwhile, would-be photographer Steve Archer (John Gavin), who Meredith also meets at Coney Island, has fallen in love with the Turner character: "My camera could easily have a love affair with you." Archer is even willing to go to work at an advertising company to support Meredith. But she, we quickly discover, is utterly determined to become an actress, despite the fact she is no ingénue. At the very moment that Archer attempts to propose, Meredith receives a telephone call, promising her a career. In response to his demands that she return to reality, Meredith summarizes her position and the film's often absurd dialogue: "Well, I'm going up and up and up—and nobody's going to pull me down!"

Indeed, like some rising balloon, Meredith quickly

floats away from her moorings, and, as any reader of popular fiction might predict, ultimately loses touch with her daughter Susie (Sandra Dee) and her servant-confidante-friend Jackson. Time and again Archer is sent away—indeed the platinum-haired Meredith appears to have become a celibate devoted only to stage and film—and Susie is given "things" instead of love.

If the movie stopped here we might easily describe it simply as a soap-opera. But although Sirk pretends to center the work on the achievements of his star and on the success of those for whom the American Dream might be possible, his camera and the script focus instead on the "backstory" of the black mother and daughter living in her house. Although Annie Jackson has long acclimated herself to a menial and forbearing life, her light-skinned daughter is as determined as Meredith to achieve the American Dream, even if it means giving up her own identity and becoming white. While the white figures in the film seem almost oblivious to the problems faced by Jackson and Sarah Jane, Annie herself knows them all too well. In response to Meredith's dismissal of Sarah Jane's attitude, Annie replies: "Miss Lora, you don't know what it means to be... different...." At another point she summarizes: "How do you tell a child that she was born to be hurt?" That "hurt" is witnessed time and time again in this film, as Sarah Jane is beaten by her racist boyfriend (played by Troy Donahue) and turned away from all her jobs the moment she is discovered to have black blood.

While Meredith accumulates, Annie, it is apparent, becomes more and more giving until she has little left to give except her own life. In those humane actions she becomes the only *real* figure in the film. The title may have you believe that the characters are "imitating life," but their true actions are even more perverted, as one by one they attempt to imitate "art." Just as the film intentionally pushes the limits of its own credibility, so do they seek out worlds that cannot and do not exist. Lora may have become a "star," but we recognize, precisely in Sirk's montage of stage titles, that her string of hits has all the craft of the mediocre plays of Margo in *All About Eve* or of Auntie Mame's *Midsummer Madness*. Archer seeks to become a great photographer, but

 ends up as an advertising executive. Sarah Jane finds a career as a cheap singer and dancer in dives and supper clubs. Susie imagines herself having a relationship with a man twice her age (Archer). Through his use of popular clichés Sirk reveals that the dreams of this all-white world are also outrageously kitschy. When art becomes a kind of commodity, a symbol of a desirable something missing in life, there is little chance of normality.

The movie ends with another vision of art, with Jackson's theatrical funeral, attended by the numerous friends and admirers who Meredith could not even imagine existed. Decked out with a great singer (Mahalia Jackson), a band, and a hearse pulled by four white horses, Annie's funeral—an event created by Annie herself—is a fuller artistic realization than any of the performances or activities of the other characters. And that creation points not to art, but to another kind of eternal life.

LOS ANGELES, AUGUST 22, 2009

417

A FEW DAYS after seeing *Imitation of Life*, I happened upon a television broadcast of *Johnny Guitar*, a movie I'd seen once or twice previously, which I suddenly saw in a new way within the context of Sirk's movie. Like Sirk, Nicholas Ray has often been praised (and criticized) for locating his films in the context of popular genres (in Ray's case, most often in teenage melodramas such as his *Rebel without a Cause*) and for his oversaturated color prints. In this work of 1954 Ray attempts a western—if you can call it that. For Ray's "western," as François Truffaut has described it, is "phony"; or, if it is a western, it's "the *Beauty and the Beast* of westerns, a

Western dream."

As most commentators have noted, in *Johnny Guitar* the standard gender roles are reversed: the two major male figures, Johnny Guitar (played by a laid-back Sterling Hayden) and the Dancing Kid (Scott Brady), are in thrall to the powerful saloon-keeper Vienna (Joan Crawford). Guitar, her first love, does not even wear guns, having put them aside in an attempt to alter his life. Vienna's current lover, the Dancing Kid, spends most of his time with his all-male gang, only occasionally returning to Vienna's isolated saloon for entertainment. Brooding over her male customers is the simmering, glowering, wise-cracking Crawford, wearing various colors of blouses and pants, generally topped with a bright red scarf tied round her neck. Her lips are the reddest lips in the world.

A savvy business woman, Vienna has purchased her saloon on land that is destined to become part of the railroad, and she plans to sell it and her property as a railroad stop for a hefty price. The problem is that the bar lies in the territory of local ranchers who want no railroad junction in their open lands, no new development that might bring settlement fences with it. Led by an equally powerful woman, Emma Small (Mercedes McCambridge), the ranchers are determined to rid their territory of the Dancing Kid and his followers, along with Vienna. As the movie opens, robbers have hit a stage coach, killing Emma's brother; Emma and the ranchers arrive at Vienna's saloon to arrest her and the gang.

The heart of this battle, however, is not really financial, but psycho-sexual, for the Dancing Kid has also caught Emma's eye, teasing her with his nightly dances and sexual energy. Emma, dressed almost throughout the film in black, is a closet Puritan, longing for his company while, out of guilt, seeking his punishment through his death.

In this very first scene, Ray lays out the entire story: Emma and her men will ultimately kill Vienna, unless Vienna kills her first.

The power of the film lies in its dialogue: witty, fast-paced, rarely allowing for a sentimental moment. Hayden and Crawford, in part because of their absolutely opposing temperaments, are near perfect in their dueling tangle of words. In the following dialogue, it is useful to note how Hayden speaks the lines which in most movies a woman might speak, Crawford responding more like a stereotypical male:

> JOHNNY: How many men have you forgotten?
> VIENNA: As many women as you've remembered.
> JOHNNY: Don't go away.
> VIENNA: I haven't moved.
> JOHNNY: Tell me something nice.

VIENNA: Sure, what do you want to hear?

JOHNNY: Lie to me. Tell me all these years you've waited. Tell me.

VIENNA: [*without feeling*] All those years I've waited.

JOHNNY: Tell me you'd a-died if I hadn't come back.

VIENNA: [*without feeling*] I woulda died if you hadn't come back.

JOHNNY: Tell me you still love me like I love you.

VIENNA: [*without feeling*] I still love you like you love me.

JOHNNY: [*bitterly*] Thanks. Thanks a lot.

In truth, Vienna has sent for Johnny Guitar to help her in her fight against the ranchers. She seems so self-sufficient, however, so able to keep the ranchers and sheriff at bay, that both her male suitors are almost insignificant. As she puts it to those who would take her off to jail, standing, as she does for much of the early parts of the movie, at the top of a staircase: "Down there I sell whiskey and cards. Up here all you can get is a bullet in your head."

Ray's male characters, like most of Sirk's figures, are ghostly beings in the real world, living as dreamers determined to mold their realities around an imitation of art: music in Johnny Guitar's case and dance for the Dancing Kid. Consequently, their inner beings are as dimensional as the names they have created for themselves. As the plot meanders toward its expected conclusion, contrarily we suddenly see a different side of Vienna, a woman still very much in love with Johnny and a figure terrified by the difficulties she must face. She is the only one with any depth.

With their mine panned out, little money left, and accused of committing a robbery and murder of which they are innocent, the Dancing Kid and his gang determine to rob the small-town bank at the very moment that Vienna has decided to withdraw her money. The coincidence makes it seem as if she has been involved, particularly since the Dancing Kid kisses her as he rides off with Emma's and the ranchers' savings.

Facing the inevitable, Vienna awaits the posse—quickly rounded up while still in funeral garb for the burial of Emma's brother—dressed in a full-cut white dress, revealing an entirely different possibility in her life. The scenes which follow, the vengeful burning of her "estate" by the now near-mad Emma, Vienna's near death by hanging, and her nighttime run, are made even more strange and absurd by her costume. Dressed as she is, there is no way to hide, let alone escape.

Quickly changing back into blouse and pants, she leads Johnny into an underground passage that takes the two to their destiny: the hideout of the Dancing Kid's gang and the long-expected duel between the two

women.

Determined to settle the battle, Emma fires up the ranchers with hateful statements similar in style to those made by the right-wing during the House Un-American Activities Committee trials, a parallel recognized by many critics and admitted by Ray. Yet even here, the film does not rest in its Freudian implications, as the posse, sickening of the violence, leaves Emma to herself. She kills the Dancing Kid, the only man she has apparently loved, before turning the gun on Vienna (the name, one might note, of Freud's home city). Vienna shoots Emma dead. Love and life win out over hate and Emma's cult of death.

LOS ANGELES, AUGUST 25, 2009
Both parts reprinted in *World Cinema Review* (August 2009).
Reprinted from *Reading Films: My International Cinema* (Los Angeles: Green Integer, 2012).

Pictures Resembling Creatures

INGER CHRISTENSEN **AZORNO**, TRANSLATED FROM
THE DANISH BY DENISE NEWMAN (NEW YORK: NEW
DIRECTIONS, 2009)

AS ARE MOST of her writings, Inger Christensen's 1967
fiction *Azorno* is a highly structured work. In this case,
seven characters—Randi, Katarina, Louise, Xenia,
Bathsheba (Bet), Sampel, and Azorno—each of them
pregnant, are in the process of writing fictions. Each of
their narratives—although one would be hard pressed
to describe any of them as having a plot—contains similar actions, phrases, and events.

Various of these figures write on pages topped by
the address Rome, Via Napoli 3, and the telephone
number 484.409-471.565. Several of the characters
travel through Alpine passes: Oberalppass 2044, Passo
S. Gottardo 2109, Disentis/Mustér 1133, Passo del
Lucomagno 1917, and Biasca 2931 before approaching via Lugano 334 "in the hot, crisp, spicy landscape

around the border at Chiasso and Como 201," singing
with the car window open. Other figures wake each
morning to watch the person across the way dress, then
go to a small cafe where, to free the locals from feeling
observed, they stare at a rag, a sandstone sculpture, and
a little greenish mannequin. Or they go out at other
times, sitting in the Piazza della Repubblica, without a
hat or gloves, observing the man (or woman) across the
way. They return to write on papers headed with their
name and address, kept, while they are traveling, at the
bottom of a suitcase full of "a multicolored heap of
extra bras, girdles, panties, stockings, sandals, scarves,
gloves, creams, cosmetics, and a white hat, all rolled up
in a glossy transparent plastic tube with a handle made

of twisted gold thread.

Indeed lists dominate the structures Christensen employs to help this work to cohere. At several points characters visit a beautiful lake home, approachable only by boat, where Sampel has created a rose garden with special breeds of roses: "Rosa rugosa, Rosa rubignosa, Rosa pimpinellifolia, cream-colored Rosa 'Nevada,' yellow Rosa hugonis, and deep scarlet Rosa moyesii."

Several of the women of this fiction write one another, perceived by other figures as liars or exaggerators of the truth. Bet Sampel, Sampel's wife, at one point invites all the other women to join her in the lake house, whereupon they discover that each of them is pregnant and, together, upon the arrival of Sampel, proceed to claw him to death. The dog in that house is called Goethe. A small fountain that does not imitate the sound of rain sits on a terrace.

At other times, several figures gain comfort from staring at a picture which they call "the composer," who seems to be staring at a small cigarette burn or a black dot. Some of the women go to Tivoli in Copenhagen or other parks where they order two Dubonnets, and/ or two martinis, quickly drinking them and paying, after pulling the table close to them. Most of these figures speak of two ways of destroying life: with poison or freedom:

Both equally gently. Every confinement can be terminated from within: e.g., by giving the tree poison and quickly paralyzing the tissues in their multiple functions. When everything stands still this way, a mute block, all movement begins to go downward: flowers disintegrate, leaves curl up, rustle, are carried away, twigs on branches dry up, break, and the trunk cracks, caves in. Slowly consumed by everything. Or the confinement can end from without: e.g., by giving the tree freedom, an excess of space, light, air, water, nourishment, by which it's made to unfold in a series of ecstatic flowerings, abruptly followed by exhaustion, withering. At last the tree dries up, a mute block that is slowly consumed by itself. By everything.

In many respects one might say that the two methods of death described above are at the center of this "story." In several instances the women seem trapped, metaphorically poisoned by the relationships or lack of relationships they must suffer; one sits in a dark room where outside it perpetually rains. Another is locked away in an institution. Another is trapped in Sampel's bedroom at the beautiful lake house. Others move, like Beckettian figures, "in" and "out" in seeming freedom, but with nowhere to go, they wander the streets, sit at tables to drink, or cross the various Alpine passes by car.

We soon realize that these figures are all, in some way, creations of the artist Azorno, who, when he sits at Via Napoli 3 to write, admits to using the pseudonym Sampel. In their imagination, in the telling of the various sets of scenarios, each is indeed made pregnant by the author, and each rearranges these series of events like the bouquet of various-colored tulips that is described in many scenes.

Christensen asks again, but in a highly original manner, what is reality, who of us is real? Several of her figures often have the feeling that somewhere there is a person who exactly at the present makes the same notes to be woven into a novel about him or herself.

It is only in the final section of this lyrical work that we sense we may have broken through to a seeming "reality." In that section, Azorno and Bathsheba are in Paris (not Rome) where he is writing and she, accompanying him, shops and walks the streets. Here too are many of the elements we have seen at work throughout the book: he loves listing the roses from his garden as if even saying it were a charm. The suitcase is packed with the several tablets and toiletries as described elsewhere. Just as another character cuts through a withered plant to reach its thorns, Azorno destroys such a plant in the Luxembourg Gardens. Yet here Goethe, the dog, has been transformed into a small porcelain figure set atop the wardrobe in their room. And while Azorno attempts to write his story, Bathsheba (no longer called Bet) ponders, since she has been told she will be in his novel, whether she should consider herself as "simply a human being" or "as a human-made being." As elsewhere in the book, she carries an umbrella, meets a man (Azorno), and joins him at a table she draws close to herself as she orders two Dubonnets.

Yet this time, she challenges her husband, who claims to have had a vision of her, to tell her what she is wearing. As in another scene in the fiction, he responds that she wearing a white coat, white hat, and white gloves, and when the wind blows the coat open, underneath is a large-flowered dress. In fact, when she opens her coat, she is wearing "an orange sleeveless dress made of a thin fabric that hung loosely on her and moved with every little puff of wind," something outside of the repeated elements of the work. In short, we now understand that she is an image to him, not a reality. She, as are all people in a world in which we create realities for them, is "a human-made being."

Christensen does not leave the story there, but finally takes it into a possible reality, as Bathsheba announces she is going to have a baby. The couple put their arms around each other and kiss, yet, as the author describes the event, it is still a symbolic act: "It was a question of gentleness."

At that same moment, however, Azorno seems to suddenly come alive, realizing for the first time that the woman "With the dark orange dress against her dark skin against the dark evening" is something separate from himself, that the mass of people around him are not the same as his creations, that he is living not *a* life but his life, his *only* life. He realizes that he is "A person. Maybe more. Who just now thought exactly this." The revelation changes everything as the author, mimetically, becomes one of us, living human flesh:

> When the gardens were about to close and the water jets sank down so that the water's surface became calm, there was a moment of soundlessness, everything was silent, though certainly never completely silent, since there was the sound of many people's movements quickly increasing, as the sound of all that I have written was quickly increasing and limiting my freedom to experience, but it was in this moment of soundlessness that we got up, and the whole time I heard Bathsheba breathing, and I kissed her, it was in that moment that we kissed each other, that for the first time in our lives we experienced the mild even air. And sang.

And with that song the "pictures resembling creatures," of which Søren Kierkegaard writes in Christensen's epilogue, are transformed into the creatures themselves.

The death of Inger Christensen in January of this year has left us without one of our greatest celebrants of life.

LOS ANGELES, SEPTEMBER 27, 2009
Reprinted from *Green Integer Blog* (September 2009) and *PIP (Project for Innovative Poetry)* (October 2009).

Creatures Afire

JACK SMITH **FLAMING CREATURES** / 1963 / THE
SCREENING I SAW WAS PRESENTED WITH A TALK BY J.
HOBERMAN AT REDCAT (ROY AND EDNA DISNEY/CA-
LARTS THEATER) AT THE WALT DISNEY CONCERT HALL
ON NOVEMBER 9, 2009

FOR YEARS I'd been hearing about the sensational film
Flaming Creatures which influenced filmmakers and
dramatists from Andy Warhol, John Waters, and Fed-
erico Fellini to Cindy Sherman and Richard Foreman.

From the beginning, after its New Bowery Theater
showing in 1964, screenings were rare, and in the late
1960s Smith took the film out of circulation. For all
these years, accordingly, I had been seeking an opportunity to attend a rare showing, and despite the fact
that I was scheduled to teach a literature course on November 9th, I arranged from the first day of class that we
would skip the week in question.

Listening to J. Hoberman's historical recounting of

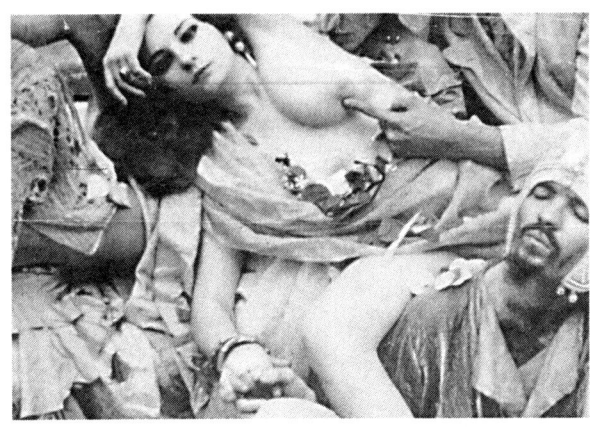

the film, which was deemed pornographic on its release and was denounced in the media and even in the halls of Congress (one congressman being outraged that it was not even *good pornography*, suggesting he couldn't get an erection), it is difficult not to let out a hoot of laughter.

Indeed, in today's world, Smith's orgiastic figures of mostly gays and transvestites seem almost innocent. Yes, from time to time, one or another shakes a flaccid penis in the camera's face, but, for the most part, the figures of this pastiche of scenes and music, reminiscing from Maria Montez to Josef Von Sternberg's films and numerous other popular cultural references, seem utterly childlike. Hoberman himself describes the film in those terms:

> *Flaming Creatures'* forty-five washed out, dated
> minutes depict a place where a cast of tacky trans-
> vestites and other terminal types (some costumed
> as recognizable genre faves—a Spanish dancer, a
> vampire, an exotic temptress), accompanied by re-
> cordings of popular music, shrieks, and snatches of
> Hollywood soundtracks ("Ali Baba is coming! Ali
> Baba is coming!") dance, grope, stare, posture, and
> wave their penises with childlike joy. The marriage
> of Heaven and Hell presented with playful deprav-
> ity.

The creatures in Smith's film are aflame with buried
desires—blindingly bright passions to show off, to love,
to dance, to cry out, perhaps even to die—burning up
before our eyes. What makes this film so troubling to
some I believe is that it is almost a screed simultaneously to life and to extinction, a kind of mad portrayal
of Heaven and Hell: not St. Peter's heaven paved with
good acts nor Lucifer's burning inferno but the internal
heavens and hells within each of us, often so potent that
coherent language and expression cannot be reached.
Smith himself described the work as "a comedy set in
a haunted movie studio," which at first, given the very
ludicrousness of the actors' portrayals, I dismissed.

Clearly, however, there is something comical about

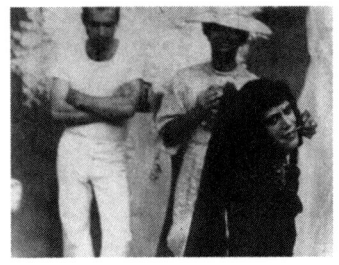

the full-throttle simmering of the heap of human flesh at the center of this short film. And yet, it is a haunted, ghostly world, left behind by the cheap and gaudy reality that Hollywood directors have presented us with as alternative spaces in which to exist. And in that sense *Flaming Creatures* is an inevitable product of filmmaking itself. In a strange way this silly, tawdry, outrageous depiction of a hopped-up bacchanalia is no more or less unbelievable than hundreds of scenes from Cecil B. DeMille epics such as his 1949 *Samson and Delilah*, Bible-tales turned into fantasylands for a world of displaced souls.

LOS ANGELES, NOVEMBER 13, 2009
Reprinted from *World Cinema Review* (November 2009).
Reprinted from *Reading Films: My International Cinema* (Los Angeles: Green Integer, 2012).

Forces of Gravity

GIOVANNI FRANCESCO BUSENELLO (LIBRETTO, AD-
DITIONAL TEXT FROM *TERRORE NELLO SPAZIO, PLANET
OF THE VAMPIRES*, A FILM BY MARIO BAVA, 1965, AND
QUEEN OF OUTER SPACE, A FILM BY EDWARD BERNDS,
1958), FRANCESCO CAVALLI (MUSIC), **LA DIDONE** /
REDCAT (ROY AND EDNA DISNEY/CALARTS THEATER),
LOS ANGELES / THE PERFORMANCE I SAW WAS ON JUNE
14, 2009

KNOWN FOR ITS innovative retellings of major dramas
and events (*Hamlet, The Hairy Ape, The Emperor Jones*,
etc.), The Wooster Group has moved into even more
challenging territory with their newest extravaganza,
La Didone, a retelling, in operatic form, of Francesco
Cavalli's 1641 opera of the Carthagian Queen Dido
and her new lover, Aeneas.

Not only has director Elizabeth LeCompte taken
on the challenges of opera in this work, but she has
overlaid the Cavalli work (unknown to most opera-
goers) with a grade-B science-fiction, directed by the

Italian filmmaker Mario Bava, *Terrore nello spazio*, known in this country as *Planet of the Vampires*. The film has its fans, Ridley Scott among them, whose film *Alien* was obviously influenced by this campy movie.

On some levels it seems quite justifiable—and may have appeared to be absolutely "brilliant" in the early inception of the work—to bring the two (what used to be called "high culture" and "low culture") together, allowing them to comment on each other and to elucidate related themes. Both worlds, Dido's Carthage and the planet Aura, are visited by outsiders: Aeneas, prince of Troy, washes up on the shores of Africa after the a deadly sea storm; the spaceships Argos and Galliot, investigating mysterious signals coming from Aura, are caught in a force of gravity and plummet quickly to the new planet's surface, the Galliot destroyed in the process.

That same kind of gravitational pull seems to happen to Aeneas, as Cupid (disguised as Aeneas' son Ascanius) plunges an arrow into Dido's breast. Having remained true to her the memory of her dead husband, she suddenly finds herself madly in love with the visiting stranger.

The worlds for both sets of explorers suddenly shifts, as the remaining members of the Argos crew sense strange beings around them who they cannot see, and Aeneas is drawn into a boar hunt—presented almost as a frenzied sexual prelude—during which he and Dido retire into a cave to make love.

The inhabitants of the planet Aura, it turns out, are invisible beings whose sun is dying, and who can survive only by taking over the bodies of their visitors. As in *Invasion of the Body Snatchers*, these beings *become* the people whose bodies they invade; and, as the now-repaired Argos takes off into space, there appears to be only one "real" survivor left, the others having been transformed into Aurans.

Similarly, Dido hopes by conquering the heart of Aeneas to lure him into Carthage society. But the gods call him back to Italy, and Dido is left alone with a broken heart. In the *Aeneid* she commits suicide, but in Cavalli's version, she regains her sanity, marrying the nearby King Jarbas, who has long been in love with her.

The Argonauts, in a Rod Serling-like plot development, realizing they do not have the energy to return home, choose a planet on which to settle: the third planet from the sun. We realize that either we are already the ancestors of these alien zombies or are about to be invaded.

As always, The Wooster Group performs all of

this lunacy with great seriousness, and that, in turn, saves most of this work from simply becoming camp. The singing, particularly Hai-Ting Chinn's Dido, John Young's Aeneas, and Andrew Nolen's Jarbas, was excellent and enticed one to see the complete Cavalli opera (the original lasts four to five hours, while this production ran for about an hour and a half). Yet for all of the bravado and talent of the company, there remained something about the production that left one feeling that the connections were frail and facile.

Certainly, it challenged its audience. Just the attempt to keep two simultaneous stories straight—one in Italian, the other in a quietly-spoken film jargon, both of whose words often scrolled quickly forward at the same moment that computer screens delivered up various images—was, as *Los Angeles Times* theater critic Charles McNulty described it, "an exhausting cerebral spin." Experienced often enough, such intellectual activity could possibly save one from early dementia.

Yet, at heart, I felt this work was intellectually empty, and spiritually had no real soul. The laughter it evoked was from the bland sci-fi jargon ("How do we repair the meteor rejector, Mark?"), while the delight it offered was only of the musical sort. Between the two lay a hollow art.

LOS ANGELES, JUNE 18, 2009
Reprinted from *USTheater, Opera, and Performance* (June 2009).

I saw one other production of The Wooster Group, L.S.D., at the Los Angeles Festival of Arts in September of 1987. I remember little about it at this point in time. Despite my feelings about La Didone, *however, I hope to see other Wooster Group productions in the future.*

How to Save the World

EDMUND H. NORTH (SCREENPLAY, BASED ON A STORY BY HARRY BATES), ROBERT WISE (DIRECTOR) **THE DAY THE EARTH STOOD STILL** / 1951

BARRÉ LYNDON (SCREENPLAY, BASED ON THE NOVEL BY H. G. WELLS), BYRON HASKIN (DIRECTOR) **WAR OF THE WORLDS** / 1953

DANIEL MAINWARING AND RICHARD COLLINS (SCREENPLAY, BASED ON A STORY BY JACK FINNEY), DON SIEGEL (DIRECTOR) **INVASION OF THE BODY SNATCHERS** / 1956

STIRLING SILLIPHANT, WOLF RILLA, AND RONALD KINNOCH (AS GEORGE BARCLAY) (SCREENPLAY, BASED ON A NOVEL BY JOHN WYNDHAM), WOLF RILLA (DIRECTOR) **VILLAGE OF THE DAMNED** / 1960

IRWIN ALLEN AND CHARLES BENNETT (SCREENPLAY, BASED ON A STORY BY IRWIN ALLEN), IRWIN ALLEN (DIRECTOR) **VOYAGE TO THE BOTTOM OF THE SEA** / 1961

WALTER BERNSTEIN (SCREENPLAY, BASED ON A NOVEL BY EUGENE BURDICK AND HARVEY WHEELER), SIDNEY LUMET (DIRECTOR) **FAIL-SAFE** / 1964

STANLEY KUBRICK, TERRY SOUTHERN, AND PETER GEORGE (SCREENPLAY), STANLEY KUBRICK (DIRECTOR) **DR. STRANGELOVE OR: HOW I LEARNED TO STOP WORRYING AND LOVE THE BOMB** / 1964

NELSON GIDDING (SCREENPLAY, BASED ON A NOVEL BY MICHAEL CRICHTON), ROBERT WISE (DIRECTOR) **THE ANDROMEDA STRAIN** / 1971

STEVE DE JARNATT (SCREENPLAY AND DIRECTOR) **MIRACLE MILE** / 1988

DEAN DEVLIN AND ROLAND EMMERICH (SCREENPLAY), ROLAND EMMERICH (DIRECTOR) **INDEPENDENCE DAY** / 1996

ANYONE WHO IS at all knowledgeable about film history knows that there are numerous movies devoted to the subject of the world's destruction. And recent examples such as *Independence Day, Armageddon, Deep Impact, The Core*, and the remake of *War of the Worlds* have been enormously successful with younger audiences.

I have chosen to focus, however, on a few films, primarily from the 1950s through the early 1980s, in an attempt to discern the varying views of how our earth might be destroyed and what our possible solutions are in those scenarios. I am sure some of this has been discussed before—perhaps in greater depth—but my current focus on these films is to explore if there are any coherent answers for our own time.

Given my smaller selection of choices, moreover, there is a kind of strange chronology concerning the possibilities of salvation available to mankind. In the 1951 classic, *The Day the Earth Stood Still*, for example, there is actually no immediate fear that the planet we live on will be destroyed. Klaatu (in the form of British actor Michael Rennie), along with fearsome doomsday machine Gort, descend to earth simply to warn us that if we continue on our ways we are doomed to destruction. The masses are always dangerous in these films of possible annihilation, and the Americans of *The Day the Earth Stood Still* are no exception, individuals, along with soldiers and police, gathering in violent groups around the spacecraft, while authorities try to capture and kill the peaceful messenger. Helen Benson (Patricia Neal) and her son are among the few examples of human kindness in this picture, but even her boyfriend, Tom Stevens, is determined to turn in the alien and perhaps get rich in the process.

Klaatu quickly realizes that he cannot trust the "people," and turns instead to the help of world scientists—who today, in the frictional world of various oppositions to scientific experimentation (activists against the use of animals in experiments and Christian fundamentalists who outrightly oppose and disbelieve in the science itself), might more likely be represented as the least worthy of trust—who find it difficult even to come together in Washington to hear out Klaatu's warnings. But Professor Jacob Barnhardt (played by Sam Jaffe as a kind of Einsteinian mathematical genius) at least reassures us that, if only the authorities will listen before shooting, there may be a hope for our survival.

By 1953, however, the filming of H. G. Wells' *War of the Worlds* offers no such way out. Here the aliens attack and win, implanting their colonies filled with their oddly tentacled bodies across the globe. While science again tries to win the war, frenzied mobs erupt in the streets, destroying everything in their path, including the vital findings of the scientists at work on the aliens' destruction. While the masses huddle against the Hol-

lywood Hills, the world's destruction appears imminent, without a hope in sight.

My companion Howard, having witnessed this movie as a child, recounts his utter horror at such a breakdown in global authority, and as he walked home from the showing, his imagination conjured up a spacecraft in the skies. He was unable to sleep for nights. In the film, however, we are saved, as suddenly the alien ships, one by one, begin to fall from the skies. If *scientists* cannot save us, science itself, as represented by our natural world, does; oxygen is fatal to these celestial intruders.

Once again in *Invasion of the Body Snatchers*, we witness an outside force, this time in the form of an alien bacteria that grows into giant pods ready to take over and imitate the very form of man himself, successfully overcoming a population, if only the people of a small region of California.

I have already written on some of this film's implications in *My Year 2004*, so I will not repeat the underlying hysterias of the time that energize Siegel's fascinating work. What is important for my purposes here is that only a triumvirate of medical doctors, the military, and the police working together can save the day, one presumes, by destroying the seemingly normal but inwardly empty people of Santa Mira and the surrounding villages.

Once again the masses have to be stayed before order can be restored, but in this 1956 fantasy, the destructive military is turned against its own citizens, and there is the uneasy feeling that somehow the salvation of the world may be botched. Certainly that was conveyed in Phillip Kaufman's 1978 remake. If in the original Dr. Matthew Bennell stays awake long enough to make a run for it, convincing the outside world of the dangers ahead, in Donald Sutherland's portrayal, years later, he himself screams out as an alien against a surviving human friend. In Kaufman's version it is apparent that the world may be taken over after all.

Similar, in some respects, to *Invasion of the Body Snatchers* are the strange births of blond-haired, blue-eyed children in the village of Midwich, England in the 1960 film *Village of the Damned*. It is not apparent whether these gifted monsters intend to take over the world or not, but it is clear that their supernatural powers have made it nearly impossible for them to be normal citizens of Midwich, and in their stolid attempts at education these children clearly have grander plans. Like the scientists and doctors of the previous movies, Gordon Zellaby (George Sanders) at first attempts to investigate these incidents within a rational context, but it quickly becomes apparent, given the young terrorists' ability to read minds, that the only way to destroy them is to give up rationality and blow them (and himself) up.

The masses are at it again in Irwin Allen's *Voyage to the Bottom of the Sea* (1961), where in the person of Admiral Harriman Nelson we have both a military man *and* a scientist at the helm in his attempt to save the world from the Van Allen radiation belt, which has caught fire and is quickly scorching and torching the planet. Nelson (Walter Pidgeon) and his able assistant (the oddly cast Peter Lorre) are convinced that the only way to save the planet is to blow up the belt near Mauritius island on an specific day and time. Despite the continued destruction of earth, numerous other scientists, joined by the masses, disagree and plan to scuttle the attempts of Nelson's nuclear submarine. Eventually, he is almost brought down by the machinations of his  own medical doctor, Susan Hiller (Joan Fontaine), with her psychological aspersions, directed to Captain Lee Crane (Robert Sterling), against the Admiral. The imperiled world is saved, once again, by a kind of violence, an explosion that jettisons the radiation belt into outer space. How that might affect our continued survival is never revealed.

By 1964 the military increasingly becomes the enemy itself. That year's *Fail Safe* and the darkly comic *Dr. Strangelove, or How I Learned to Stop Worrying and Love the Bomb* both feature a military world out of control and ready to release nuclear weaponry upon the enemy, resulting obviously in the total world destruction of which *The Day the Earth Stood Still*'s Klaatu had warned. The plot to bomb Russia by military higher-ups in *Fail Safe* is foiled by a saner head, in the form of the President (Henry Fonda), who, however, must allow millions of New Yorkers (including his own wife) to be killed in retaliation for the destruction of Moscow. The

 earth is saved in *Fail Safe*, but at what expense?

Kubrick's *Dr. Strangelove* took that world destruction to its obvious conclusion. In this mad world of both military and political leadership, there is no "fail-safe," and the planet, quite obviously, is up for a totally dark comic annihilation. I have never been a fan of Kubrick's work, perhaps because it allows for no possible solution.

The 1971 motion picture *The Andromeda Strain* continues to explore the madness of the military, but also points its fingers at the scientific world. Discovering a small desert town completely destroyed (except for two seemingly unconnected individuals, a crying baby and an alcoholic addicted to antifreeze), even the plane flying over the site is downed, its pilots' blood turned to dust. Obviously, a massive bio-chemical accident has occurred. The always malicious military suggests bombing the site to smithereens, but scientists warn that will only spread it across the area. Meanwhile, the dangerous chemicals may be caught up in the winds, killing millions, if an antidote cannot quickly be discovered. Noted scientists, already slated for this job, are

449

gathered in a forbid-
ding, chemically im-
penetrable bunker to
seek an answer. For 96
critical hours in man's
history (so claims the

film's tagline) these specialists struggle to analyze the
dangerous bio-chemical. They nearly fail, but as in *War
of the Worlds* they ultimately discover that the natural
world may provide the salvation, that heavy doses of
oxygen will ultimately destroy the new virus. In their
explorations, however, they also reveal the cozy—and
dangerous—interplay of politics and science of which
most of these films have previously hinted.

Finally, in Steve De Jarnatt's 1988 offbeat *Miracle
Mile*, filmed almost entirely in my own neighborhood
and including images of my office and home, mass hysteria is all we have left. Neither the military nor scientists appear on the horizon. We never, in fact, discover
the reason for the impending nuclear bombing of Los
Angeles; indeed, it is only by a fluke—a wrong number
to a public phone picked up by an unsuspecting visi-
tor—that forecasts what will surely result in the end of
the world. Escape to an isolated spot (as in the 1959
film *On the Beach*) is only a temporary salvation. And
the "hero" falls, just before the bombs, into the La Brea
Tarpits to be embalmed in water and tar like the mam-

moths of ancient days.

Most of the contemporary "end of the world" films are not as bleak. The 1996 film *Independence Day*, for example, returns to a triumvirate of the President, military, and scientists to save the day. But there is a strong feeling, particularly in more dystopian works such as the *Mad Max* movies (1979 and 1981), the Japanese animated film *Akira* (1988), and Ridley Scott's brilliant 1982 film *Blade Runner*, that the government, the military, and science will only make matters worse.

If in 1951, we might have been able to hope our scientists, if only left alone, could save us, over the next few decades it became clearer that we the people, the military, the political forces we elect, as well as the scientific world would be in collusion to fail in the fight against any real global threat to our existence—a skepticism, I suggest, that is a horrific specter of what might happen in any natural or terrorist threat we may soon face.

At first I thought someone must take leadership since—along with most of the films I have discussed and, I might add, our founding fathers—I am somewhat doubtful that answers to any global threat will come from the "common folk." The events of 9/11 demonstrated, however, that it was the everyday fast-responding firefighters and fellow workers who saved the most lives. Scientists would only show up at the

World Trade Towers in retrospect. The President remained protected in a Florida classroom and aboard Air Force One. Even New York mayor Rudy Giuliani could do little but declare his good intentions after the fact. And that event, we must remember, threatened only a few New York City blocks, not an entire planet.

And it was "common folk," after all, who prevented United Airlines Flight 93 from crashing into the US Capitol or White House.

Accordingly, I might now argue that the struggle to save the world depends upon every one of us—not in the way the New Jersey Transit suggests, urging us to "Report any suspicious acts," but by becoming involved in the world around us and acknowledging our lives as being linked to global events.

LOS ANGELES, JULY 12, 2009
Reprinted from *World Cinema Review* (July 2009).

Returning to the Closet

RAYMOND FEDERMAN **SMILES ON WASHINGTON SQUARE** (LOS ANGELES: SUN & MOON PRESS, 1995)

RAYMOND FEDERMAN **THE TWOFOLD VIBRATION** (LOS ANGELES: GREEN INTEGER, 2000)

RAYMOND FEDERMAN "REFLECTIONS ON WAYS TO IMPROVE DEATH"

ON TUESDAY, October 6, 2009, Raymond Federman died in his San Diego home at the age of 81.

I published—or more correctly, I *re*published—two books by Ray, *The Twofold Vibration* in 2000, a fiction first published in 1982 by Indiana University Press, and *Smiles on Washington Square*, first published by Thunder's Mouth Press in 1985.

I seem to have known Ray (who preferred to be called Raymond, but who I knew as Ray) forever. Long before I met him, I had read his criticism, *Surfiction: Fiction Now and Tomorrow*, and referred to it extensively in my PhD dissertation of 1979. Ray seemed to me

one of the few critics of the time who had attempted to do what I myself was trying to accomplish, to define the differences between modernist and non-modernist (narrowly referred to as postmodern) fiction. Like Ray, I saw its roots from the beginning of the 20th century, from Gertrude Stein on, and I wanted to create a kind of handbook which would help people see its different approaches to voice, character, place, theme, and, most of all, form.

I think I must have first met him in the flesh—and the words "in the flesh" are important when describing Ray because he is so very much larger than life—in the early 1980s, when I began distributing Fiction Collective and other small presses along with my own Sun &

Moon Press. I had found a small band of independent sales representatives to sell these and my own books across the country, and each season I would meet with them, describing the new titles, in New York.

Ray, whose important fiction *Take It or Leave It* was published by the Fiction Collective, was a member of that group, and he and others wanted to meet with my representatives to sell their own titles. The art of describing new works to sales people who have hundreds of books to represent each season is a difficult one, which I felt I had mastered. Accordingly, I tried to dissuade the Fiction Collective authors from coming to speak with my representatives, but they were insistent. Ray, along with Russell Banks and Jonathan Baumbach (yes, the father of Noah Baumbach, played by Jeff Daniels in the film *The Squid and the Whale*)—all sublime egoists, each capable of dominating any conversation—showed up late to the meeting and took so much time describing their three new titles that my reps insisted that they would never see them again! I was, accordingly, put in the difficult position of scolding the three, but two of them, at least Ray and Russell, remained lifetime friends.

That is not to say that I wasn't a bit taken aback by Ray's dynamic personality. Indeed, in his unpredictable enthusiasms, directed mostly toward his own writing projects and, later, his understandable delight with the French and German attention to his writing, along with his winking sexual innuendos about women, he sometimes irritated me and even, on occasion, scared me a little. I liked him enormously, but on occasion he was not where you thought he was. As one of his own characters describes "the old man" in *The Twofold Vibration* (clearly a mirror image of the narrator, Federman):

> yes, that's how our old man was, so unpredictable, so changeable, and so careless with his own life, despondent one day, hopeful the next, always more interested in the process than finalities...not an easy man to deal with

And then there was his voice, with a French accent, of course, but seemingly also from another time and place. As French fiction writer Jean Frémon once told me, "When I met Raymond Federman I could not believe what I was hearing. It was a voice from another time. Only a small neighborhood in Paris spoke French that way, the way Maurice Chevalier had spoken and sung, and it has long disappeared. I asked him, my God, where did you get that accent? He told me his story, how as young boy he was hidden away from the Nazis in a closet. And when he finally came out, that was the way he would remain the rest of his life, since by the end of the War he had escaped to the US, joining the Army."

Federman's family—his mother, father, and sisters—were sent to Auschwitz, where they died.

When I visited SUNY-Buffalo several years later, on tour with fellow poet Rae Armantrout, we dined with Susan Howe, Charles Bernstein, and the Federmans, Ray and his wife Erica, at a very pleasant Italian restaurant. On our way home, after having left the Federmans and Susan, Rae and I chuckled to ourselves about Ray's grandiose manner, I adding my reservations about the man. Charles quickly interrupted, "How else might you expect him to be, given the life he has led, his childhood, the condition of creating several new beings? He had no choice but to become a series of alternating voices."

I was embarrassed, and realized the truth of what Charles had said. To be fair, moroever, Ray has never denied the forcefulness and energy of his own being. In fact, he celebrates it, just as he celebrates a world in which all the action is placed on something in process without ever coming to fruition. He writes what he calls "pre-texts," texts that exist before any happening; and, in that respect, his work is about potentiality more than plotted events, the writing existing as a potential for changes not only in the future but the past.

Smiles on Washington Square, for example, is the

story of a chance meeting between a poor, immigrant American, Moinous (one of Federman's regular stand-ins for himself), and a New England-born, slightly older sophisticate, Sucette (who shares some of Erica's qualities). The two meet, but say nothing, only smiling at one another. The rest of the tale is a series of possibilities for their future encounter(s) and relationship, all of which entail a great deal of patient waiting and outright frustration for Moinous. Their relationship, in this non-existent reality (which is, at its heart, what all fiction is about), is a touching, even romantic tale, as these two opposites gradually reveal themselves before the inevitable breakup.

This work is perhaps Federman's closest in tone to his friend Samuel Beckett. For here, the major character, like many of Beckett's tragic clowns, is an insecure, lonely, and despairing figure who bluffs his way through life. Like Federman, he has lived in the protective closet before sneaking out to enter—barefoot, armored only by an outsized overcoat—a world of excitement and danger. He is a tyrannical innocent ("A typical bull with his feet on the ground and his head in the clouds who struggles constantly to conquer vanity and indolence") in a world he can never completely comprehend.

In Federman's futurist fiction, *The Twofold Vibration*, his friends Moinous and Namredef (Federman spelled backwards) attempt to discover what "the old man" has done to be sent to the space colonies along with other undesirables on the eve of the new millennium. To Federman, the writer, they tell the story of their friendship and as much as they know about "the old man's life," but have no clue, in this comic Kafkaesque tale, what his criminal acts have consisted of.

Like Ray, "the old man" has been hidden in a closet, and to this part of his own story he adds other tales, such as how he was later arrested and sent to the camps, escaping from his railway car at the stop to eat potatoes in another train car that had paused alongside them. More stories emerge: a brief involvement in radical politics, a short affair with a Jane Fonda-like movie star, and travels across the US and Europe, including a visit to a concentration camp, encompassing excesses and suffering, boisterous outbursts of philosophical thoughts, and deep retreats into fear and doubt. His famed "Voice in the Closet" screed was to have been at the center of this work, but was rejected by Indiana University Press' editors.

Through it all, Federman is represented to his reading audience as outsized, as being at once affable and slightly embarrassing. Yet his friends—and that might include any sympathetic reader—can find nothing in his past so terrible that it might result in his being sent into outer space for what, most believe, is certain death.

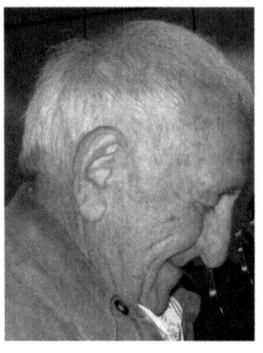 The search for his unknown crime is played out almost like a mystery tale, but, as usual in Federman's works, no ending seems appropriate. When the thousands of soon-to-be expelled individuals are gathered in a large room, Moinous and Namredef are there to see their friend off. "The old man" appears reposed, even resigned, finally ready for his fate. One by one the names are called, the prisoners taken on board and their families sent off, until only "the old man" remains. The shuttle is about to be sent into space without him! What has happened? his colleagues wonder. "BUT WHAT ABOUT ME, WHAT ABOUT ME?" the old man cries out, striking his chest with his hand. He has been put back into the closet a second time. The snake has swallowed its own tail; the past has become the future, a twofold vibration. The survivor without a clue how to survive is left to start his struggle all over again.

Now, finally, Ray has been removed from that closet, that coffin-like precursor of death, forever. He has joined the dead by giving up his voice. For us still here, still trapped in each of our personal closets, so to speak, we can only, like "the old man," become lonely and forlorn. We miss that larger-than-life wise fool so very desperately. And we need to speak of our great emptiness, to share it with others. As Ray himself wrote some time before his death, however, in the humorous and profound short essay, "Reflections on Ways to Improve Death":

> The fact is that Federman cannot say I am dead. The fact of being unable to speak one's death is the supreme category which abolishes all the others. It is the ultimate category, the category of the unspeakability of death. Whether one dies in bed, dies in one's books, dies with one's boots on, dies on the vine, dies in harness, dies prematurely or in one's sleep, dies in a gas chamber, dies while making love to one's lover, when all is done and said, that is the category of death that has reached total improvement because it can no longer be spoken.

> Language vanishes into death, and death vanishes into silence. Or is it, death vanishes into language, and language into silence?

LOS ANGELES, JANUARY 9, 2010
Reprinted from *Sibila* [Brazil] (February 2010).
Forthcoming in a festschrift for Raymond Federman, projected for publication in 2016.

Index